# Third Edition

# Solutions

## Advanced

### Workbook

Tim Falla    Paul A Davies

Jane Hudson   with Alex Raynham

OXFORD
UNIVERSITY PRESS

Great Clarendon Street, Oxford, OX2 6DP, United Kingdom

Oxford University Press is a department of the University of Oxford.
It furthers the University's objective of excellence in research, scholarship,
and education by publishing worldwide. Oxford is a registered trade
mark of Oxford University Press in the UK and in certain other countries

ACKNOWLEDGEMENTS

*The authors and publisher are grateful to those who have given permission to reproduce
the following extracts and adaptations of copyright material*: p.28 Adapted
from 'How the invention of paper changed the world' by Tim Harford,
www.bbc.co.uk/news, 13 March 2017. Reproduced by permission. p.51
Adapted from 'Aral Sea', https://en.wikipedia.org/wiki/Aral_Sea. The material
is licensed under the Creative Commons licence https://creativecommons.
org/licenses/by-sa/3.0/. p.72 Adapted from 'These brothers built a mine-
sweeping drone' by Coby McDonald, Popular Science, www.popsci.com. Used
with permission of Popular Science Copyright © 2017. All rights reserved.
p.94 Extract from 'Highest Migrant' from www.guinnessworldrecords.com/
world-records/highest-migrant. Reproduced by permission of Guinness
World Records. p.101 Adapted from 'Why can't people write good endings
any more?' by Allen Palmer, 10 March 2010. Reproduced by permission.
p.106 Adapted from 'The oldest living thing on Earth' by Marnie Chesterton,
www.bbc.co.uk/news, 12 June 2017. Reproduced by permission.

*Sources*: www.bbc.com/news, www.bbc.com/earth, www.economist.com,
http://economictimes.indiatimes.com, http://metro.co.uk, http://news.
nationalgeographic.com, www.newscientist.com, www.theguardian.com,
www.theringer.com

Although every effort has been made to trace and contact copyright holders
before publication, this has not been possible in some cases. We apologize for
any apparent infringement of copyright and if notified, the publisher will be
pleased to rectify any errors or omissions at the earliest opportunity.

*Cover image by*: Shutterstock (mosaic background design/Hakki Arslan).
*Back cover photograph*: Oxford University Press building/David Fisher.
*Illustrations by*: Phil Burrows pp.6, 22, 74 (motorway); Lorenzo Sabbatini/The
Organisation pp.21, 23.

*The publisher would like to thank the following for their permission to reproduce
photographs*: 123RF pp.5 (market/Chee-Onn Long); 8 (woman/Fred Goldstein),
(cake/Alejandro Miranda), 31 (friends/Ian Allenden), (dog/Cathy Yeulet),
76 (Dunguaire castle/matthi), 77 (Mozart/Antonio Abrignani), 85 (Alcatraz/Jan
Hanus), 86 (man with glasses and woman/ammentorp), 87 (money/Scott Betts),
88 (hacker/scyther5), 97 (cake/zerbor), 101 (cinema/Denis Raev), 112 (angry
man/Antonio Guillem), (Tokyo/Sean Pavone), 113 (Shanghai/Liu Fuyu);
Alamy Stock Photo pp.7 (Amsterdam/Chris Harris), 20 (paparazzi/Stephen
Bisgrove), 24 (friends with tablet/Barry Diomede), (street survey/Janine
Wiedel Photolibrary), 25 (cast from *Stranger Things*/Xinhua), 30 (*Help* poster/
AF Archive), (*The Shawshank Redemption* poster/Moviestore Collection Ltd),
(*Fried Green Tomatoes at the Whistle Stop Café* poster), (*Thelma and Louise* poster/
AF Archive), 41 (eco housing/John Peter Photography), 57 (balloon/Chronicle),
58 (man crossing road/Alex Segre), (beach trader/Roger Cracknell 15/South
East Asia), 75 (Bali/Hemis), 78 (Henry Brown/Everett Collection), 86 (couple
arguing/Antonio Guillem Fernández), 89 (coffee/Folio Images), 99 (Cornish
flag/Anthony Pilling), 100 (crowd/Anna Omelchenko), 108 (artist/RossHelen
editorial), 110 (bookshop/Andrew Beattie), (e-reader/Mk_Malin), (theatre
tickets/Paul Greaves), 115 (Bryce Canyon/Timothy Mulholland); Arnos Design
Ltd p.13 (bookshelf/David Oakley); Joseph V. Brown p.56 (Rod Coronado);
DARPA p.113 (robot); Getty Images pp.4 (girl at desk/David Schaffer),
10 (clones/DaveLongMedia), 11 (hugging/Paul Mansfield photography),
20 (author/Roslan Rahman), 24 (business meeting/Chris Ryan), (begging/Matjaz
Slanic), 44 (Montgomery/Ullstein Bild), 52 (soldiers/STR), 53 (climbing wall/
STR), 54 (couple chatting/hoozone), 58 (woman on building site/Tom Stewart),
(woman speaking/Tetra Images), 62 (Laura Dekker/Marcus Brandt), 63 (Jerome
Jarre/Marc Piasecki), 64 (Fanni Bullock Workman/APIC), 77 (Amundsen/
Illustrated London News), 84 (Jeffrey Wigand/J. p. Aussenard), 96 (aliens/
Matjaz Slanic), 108 (woman on guitar/Tim Roberts), 109 (wrestling/Ramzi
Haidar), 111 (book fair/Deshakalyan Chowdhury), 114 (Naica mine/Carsten
Peter/Speleoresearch & Films); Istockphoto pp.9 (crowd/simonkr), 102 (woman
at interview/sturti); Oxford University Press DAM pp.8 (child under tree/
FamVeld/Shutterstock), 34 (bat/Kirsanov Valeriy Vladimirovich/Shutterstock),
42 (houses of parliament/r.nagy); Rat Race Adventure Sports p.55; REX/
Shutterstock pp.13 (still from E.T./Universal Kobal), 19 (still from
Sir Tim Berners-Lee/Nils Jorgensen), 20 (still from *Donnie Brasco*/Mandalay Baltimore/Kobal), 30 (*Lord
of the Rings* poster), 116 (*The Day After Tomorrow* poster/20th Century Fox/Kobal),
117 (*Deep Impact* poster); Riken p.46 (Robear robot); Science Photo Library
p.79 (clock/Carol and Mike Werner); Shutterstock pp.12 (yoga/Rawpixel.com),
13 (abstract background/vs148), 32 (shaking hands/Stephen Coburn), 34 (baby/
Voronin 76), (feather/Ilya Akinshin), (glove/Aleksandr Belugin), (horse/pirita),
(grey mouse/Sascha Burkard), 36 (friends/Ann Haritonenko), 40 (lightning/
Vasin Lee), 41 (UN flag/Yuriy Boyko), 43 (walking/Jacek Chabraszewski),
65 (Crystal Palace/Hein Nouwens), 66 (angry woman/pixelrain), 67 (pencil/
Lightspring), 68 (child in toy plane/Vasilyev Alexandr), 80 (windsurfing/
waldru), 98 (Angkor Wat temple/Waj), 99 (St Ives/mubus7), 101 (film reel/
Vectomart), 116 (dog statue/Tony Worrall Photography/FLICKR); Topfoto
p.110 (Dian Fossey).

 # Introduction

## A Past simple and present perfect

*I can use the past simple and present perfect tenses.*

**1** Complete the sentences. Use the past simple or present perfect simple of the verbs below. Sometimes you need a passive verb.

be  be  change  come  invent  live  prove  rule  see  start  tell

1 Come quickly! The film _____!
2 She _____ a lot since I last _____ her. I hardly recognised her.
3 '_____ paper _____ by the Chinese or the Egyptians?'
'By the Chinese.'
4 Queen Victoria _____ for 63 years, until her death in 1901.
5 Tom _____ very busy this week.
6 As a child I _____ in Oxford for a number of years.
7 'When _____ you first _____ to the UK?'
'In 2012, so I _____ here for about five years.'
8 Ever since he was little he _____ that he wasn't very bright. Now he _____ them wrong!

**2** Choose the correct tense. Sometimes both answers are possible.

1 'What's **happened / been happening**?'
'I've **cut / been cutting** my finger.'
2 How long have you **known / been knowing** Jason?
3 Haven't you **finished / been finishing** your essay yet? You've **worked / been working** on it for days!
4 I wonder why we haven't **heard / been hearing** from Kate. I've **expected / been expecting** her to phone for a while now.
5 How long have you **lived / been living** in France?
6 Who's **used / been using** my phone? The battery's dead.

**3** Write suitable responses. Use the present perfect simple or present perfect continuous.

1 Your hands are covered in mud!
*Yes, I've been working in the garden.*
2 I wonder why Ben hasn't been at school lately.
I guess _____.
3 The floor in the kitchen is slippery.
That's because Dad _____.
4 Harry and Jess aren't speaking to each other.
I know. _____.
5 You're looking very slim!
Thanks. _____.
6 Why aren't you going to the football match.
Didn't you know? It _____.
7 Why are you so tired?
_____.
8 Look outside. The road is all wet.
Yes, _____.

**4** Complete the email with the verbs in brackets. Use the past simple, present perfect simple and present perfect continuous.

To: sally@email.com

Hi Sally,

I'm so sorry I ¹_____ (not be) in touch for a while. I ²_____ (try) phoning you a couple of times last week but you ³_____ (not pick up). Anyway, I ⁴_____ (hardly / have) a moment to myself these past few weeks – I ⁵_____ (revise) for my exams, which ⁶_____ (start) on Monday. I ⁷_____ (have) three already: French, maths and history. Maths and history ⁸_____ (be) awful, but French ⁹_____ (go) well, which was a bit of a surprise as I ¹⁰_____ (only / learn) it for two years.

As soon as I ¹¹_____ (finish) my exams I plan to go to France. I ¹²_____ (apply) for quite a few jobs and I ¹³_____ (receive) a couple of offers. But I ¹⁴_____ (not hear) back yet from the one I really want – working as an au pair in Bordeaux.

Anyway, give me a ring when you have a spare moment.

Love, Hannah

# Past tenses

*I can use different past tenses correctly.*

**1 Complete the sentences with the verbs below. Use the past simple or the past continuous.**

argue  borrow  get  not listen  not seem  revise  spend  think

1 Jake didn't want to come to the park with me because he _____ for his exam.

2 I noticed the sad look in Lucy's eyes and knew she _____ about her grandfather.

3 After retiring, our neighbour _____ two years travelling around the world.

4 As the teacher gave the instructions, she could tell some of the students _____.

5 Outside, it was a miserable day: the sky was grey and the rain _____ heavier.

6 My cousin _____ my bike a year ago and has never returned it.

7 Kelsie woke up suddenly; in the street outside, two men _____ loudly.

8 Even though their holiday was about to start, the children _____ excited.

**2 Tick (✓) the correct verb form to complete the sentences. Tick (✓) both if both are correct.**

1 By the age of eighteen, Ben _____ his university degree.
   **a** had completed   **b** had been completing

2 Her face was pale, as though she _____ a ghost.
   **a** had seen   **b** saw

3 As we _____ in Spain for several years, we all spoke good Spanish.
   **a** had lived   **b** had been living

4 Lucy wasn't at home when I called for her; she _____ into town.
   **a** had gone   **b** went

5 He _____ a shower when we arrived, so he hadn't heard us knock at the door.
   **a** had had   **b** had been having

6 I wish I _____ more attention when we studied this grammar point in class.
   **a** had paid   **b** had been paying

7 His eyes were red, as though he _____.
   **a** had cried   **b** had been crying

8 As soon as _____ his dinner, he went out.
   **a** he'd finished   **b** he finished

**3 Look at the timeline. Then write sentences using the prompts and the correct past tense.**

## TOM WOODWARD

▼ **1984** – born in Liverpool
▼ **1991** – moves to London, changes school
▼ **1993** – moves to Bristol, changes school again
▼ **1995** – starts secondary school in Bristol
▼ **2001** – leaves school but is unable to find work
▼ **2003** – gets a job in London, moves there
▼ **Today** – continues in the same job and home

1 in 1986 – live in Liverpool
   *In 1986, Tom was living in Liverpool.*

2 by 1992 – move to London
   _____

3 in 1994 – live in Bristol
   _____

4 by 1997 – go to secondary school – two years
   _____

5 between 2001 and 2003 – not have a job
   _____

6 by 2013 – work in London – ten years
   _____

**4 Complete the blog post using the correct past tense of the verbs in brackets.**

Two years ago, I ¹_____ (decide) to move to Japan for six months. I ²_____ (always / want) to learn Japanese and I ³_____ (even / try) a few online lessons, but without much success. The only answer, in my opinion, ⁴_____ (be) to live there for a while. During the the eight years since leaving university, I ⁵_____ (work) non-stop in a well-paid job, so taking six months off ⁶_____ (seem) financially possible. Three months after making the decision, I ⁷_____ (sit) on a flight to Tokyo! Finally, my dream ⁸_____ (become) a reality. Before leaving the UK, I ⁹_____ (find) an apartment to rent in a quiet part of the city. I remember waking up on my first morning there and thinking how beautiful everything looked. The sun ¹⁰_____ (shine) and the birds ¹¹_____ (sing) in the trees. I ¹²_____ (go) out to buy some food from the nearest shop – and that's when my problems ¹³_____ (begin).

# Articles

*I can use articles correctly.*

**1** Choose the correct articles to complete the text.

Cockneys are ¹– / **the** working-class Londoners, especially those born in ²**an** / **the** East End of ³– / **the** city. Cockneys have ⁴**a** / **the** distinctive accent when they speak, and they also use ⁵– / **a** particular kind of slang. ⁶**An** / **The** accent includes dropping the 'h' sound from ⁷– / **the** start of words like 'have' and 'house' and replacing ⁸**a** / **the** sound 'th' with 'f' or 'v'. So 'I think his brother has a house in Hampstead,' would become, 'I fink 'is bruvver 'as an 'ouse in 'amstead.' The slang traditionally associated with Cockneys is ⁹– / **an** unusual form of rhyming slang in which the rhyming word itself is usually omitted. 'Apples' is ¹⁰– / **the** term for 'stairs' (apples and pears) while 'china' refers to ¹¹**a** / **the** friend or 'mate' (china plate). ¹²**A** / **The** reason for omitting ¹³**a** / **the** key word is not certain, but perhaps ¹⁴– / **the** original intention was to make it more difficult for other people to understand – for example, if ¹⁵– / **the** criminals wanted to confuse ¹⁶– / **the** police.

**2** Add definite articles to the sentences which are not generalisations. Tick (✓) the other sentences.

**1** The river is so polluted that _____ fish have died.

**2** Antarctica is so cold that _____ trees and _____ plants cannot grow there.

**3** We love skiing in the Alps because _____ scenery is beautiful there.

**4** Bengal tigers live in _____ rainforests of south-east Asia.

**5** I like _____ holidays in the countryside, but I find _____ beaches boring.

**6** This resort is very popular with tourists, and _____ beaches are often crowded.

**3** Complete the sentences with *a, an, the* or nothing – (no article).

**1** _____ Red Crescent is _____ international organisation that provides _____ disaster relief in _____ Muslim countries such as _____ Afghanistan, _____ Iraq and _____ United Arab Emirates.

**2** _____ Mount Everest is _____ world's highest mountain, but _____ tallest is _____ Mauna Kea in _____ Hawaii, although half of it is submerged beneath _____ Pacific Ocean.

**3** _____ largest freshwater lake in the world is _____ Lake Baikal in _____ Russia, which contains about _____ fifth of the world's fresh water – more than _____ Great Lakes of _____ North America combined.

**4** In London, _____ Ritz Hotel is considered to be _____ place to have _____ afternoon tea, _____ traditional English meal which includes _____ sandwiches and _____ cakes.

**5** In 1957, six countries in _____ Europe, including _____ Germany and _____ Netherlands, formed _____ union for economic co-operation, which _____ United Kingdom, _____ Denmark and _____ Ireland joined in 1973.

**6** _____ Nile flows across _____ Sahara desert (which is almost the size of _____ USA) and into _____ Mediterranean sea.

**4** Each sentence contains one mistake with articles. Find the mistakes and write the sentences correctly.

**1** During his twenties, he moved from a job to another, trying to find a career that interested him.

_____

**2** I only listen to radio when I want to hear the news.

_____

**3** A Mr Ellis phoned; he says he's journalist.

_____

**4** We arrived at the airport in the morning and spent one hour or two shopping.

_____

**5** She earns €500 the week as a plumber.

_____

**6** We're planning to go camping a weekend in July.

_____

**7** She spent a week in the Lake District, staying in a hotel near the Lake Windermere.

_____

# Talking about the future

*I can talk about predictions, plans, offers, routines.*

**1** Complete the sentences with the verbs below. Use *will* or *going to*.

apply   carry   come out   have   lend   love   travel   vomit

1 Did you know that Joseph _____ for a place at Oxford University?

2 I _____ my car serviced next week. It's booked in for Tuesday.

3 I _____ one of your suitcases, if you like.

4 I feel terrible. I think I _____.

5 Look! The clouds are beginning to break up. The sun _____.

6 'What are your plans for when you leave school?'
'I _____ around Asia for a year.'

7 _____ you still _____ me in ten years' time?

8 'Oh dear. I've forgotten to bring any money.'
'Don't worry. I _____ you some.'

**2** Choose the correct future forms. Sometimes more than one answer is possible.

1 There's the doorbell. I**'ll answer / 'm answering** it.

2 I promise I**'ll text / text** you as soon as I **get / 'll get** to the music festival.

3 Chelsea **will / are going to** beat Manchester United in the final, for sure.

4 Phone me tomorrow. I**'ll be / 'm / 'm going to be** at home.

5 We**'ll probably go / probably go / 're probably going to go** to Italy next August. We usually go there in the summer.

6 My sister isn't sure what she**'ll do / 's going to do / does / 's doing** when she graduates from university.

7 The bus **leaves / will leave** Manchester at seven, and as long as there **are no / 'll be no / aren't going to be any** delays, it**'ll arrive / arrives** in London at ten.

8 I **visit / 'm visiting / 'm going to visit / 'll visit** my grandparents on Saturday.

**3** Four of these sentences would be better expressed with a different future form. Identify and rewrite them.

1 Have you heard? Liam and Sarah will have a baby.
_____
_____

2 'When is the next episode of that drama on?'
'On Monday evening at nine.'
_____
_____

3 If you don't work harder, you're certainly failing your exams.
_____
_____

4 Watch out! That ladder will fall!
_____
_____

5 You definitely aren't going to be able to use a calculator in your maths exam.
_____
_____

6 'What are your plans for when you leave school.'
'I'm going to take a gap year.'
_____
_____

**4** Complete the conversation. Use *will*, *going to*, the present continuous and the present simple.

Henry   ¹_____ you _____ (go) to Jake's party on Friday?

Martha   No, I ²_____. I ³_____ (go) away this weekend with my mum and dad. We ⁴_____ (head off) to Amsterdam. We ⁵_____ (visit) the Van Gogh museum and the Rijksmuseum.

Henry   Oh, that ⁶_____ (be) interesting.

Martha   Yes, I ⁷_____ (look) forward to it.

Henry   What time ⁸_____ (be) your flight?

Martha   It ⁹_____ (leave) at six from Heathrow, so we ¹⁰_____ (be) in Amsterdam by eight.

Henry   Well, have a good time. I ¹¹_____ (see) you some time next week.

Martha   Thanks. I ¹²_____ (phone) you when I ¹³_____ (get back).

 # Beginnings

## A Memories
*I can describe childhood memories.*

**1** Circle the words which mean 'remember'.

blot out   call to mind   evoke   recall   recollect   remind

**2** Choose the correct words to complete the text. If both are possible, choose both.

In general, people have surprisingly few ¹_____ from their early childhood. They may be able to call to ²_____ a small number of vivid scenes, but most of what they experienced during those formative years can never be ³_____. However, for a handful of individuals in the world, it is very different. For the fifty or so people in the world who have a condition called hyperthymesia, every single day is ⁴_____.

Not only can these people ⁵_____ everything that has happened to them; they can also pinpoint the exact date. Interestingly, their amazing memory only applies to details about their own life. They are no better than average at ⁶_____ other information. While there are benefits to having hyperthymesia, there are also disadvantages. For example, people with the condition are unable to ⁷_____ unhappy or embarrassing memories. Many people probably look back on their childhood with a sense of ⁸_____ precisely because they have conveniently forgotten some of the bad bits!

| | | |
|---|---|---|
| 1 **a** memories _____ | **b** recollections _____ | |
| 2 **a** brain _____ | **b** mind _____ | |
| 3 **a** recalled _____ | **b** reminded _____ | |
| 4 **a** lasting _____ | **b** unforgettable _____ | |
| 5 **a** recollect _____ | **b** reminisce _____ | |
| 6 **a** recalling _____ | **b** remembering _____ | |
| 7 **a** blot out _____ | **b** suppress _____ | |
| 8 **a** nostalgia _____ | **b** recollections _____ | |

**3** 🎧 **1.02** Complete the questions about speakers 1–5 with the words below. Use each word once. Then listen and choose the correct answer (a–c).

evocative   lasting   recalling   reminding   reminiscing

1 What made a _____ impression on Speaker 1?
   **a** A friend's act of kindness.
   **b** The unpleasantness of a house full of pets.
   **c** The feeling of walking to school alone.

2 Why did Speaker 2's mother find their trip to Paris very _____?
   **a** It brought back memories of a holiday with her husband.
   **b** It reminded her of a visit to Paris with her own father.
   **c** It took her back to her days at university.

3 What do Speaker 3's father and uncle spend hours _____ about?
   **a** The farm where they grew up.
   **b** Family get-togethers when they were young.
   **c** The adventures they had by the sea.

4 What keeps _____ Speaker 4 about an embarrassing event?
   **a** A particular food at her work canteen.
   **b** Meeting the teachers from her primary school.
   **c** Eating in a restaurant.

5 Which part of his childhood does Speaker 5 spend little time _____?
   **a** The time he spent living in Italy.
   **b** The first few months after returning to the UK.
   **c** The time he spent as part of a football team.

**4** Complete the idioms with the words below. Then match them with the correct endings (a–f).

bell   brains   heart   lane   memory   sieve

1 I've been racking my _____ but ... _____
2 Your name rings a _____ but ... _____
3 It was a trip down memory _____ when ... _____
4 You jogged my _____ when ... _____
5 I've got a memory like a _____, so ... _____
6 I know my aunt's address by _____, so ... _____

**a** we visited my old primary school.
**b** I'm always missing meetings and appointments.
**c** I can't remember the name of my first teacher.
**d** I don't need to look it up on my phone.
**e** we've never met before.
**f** you mentioned it was Frazer's birthday.

# Question forms

*I can use a variety of high-level question forms correctly.*

**1 Read the sentences. Then write questions for the answers.**

1 Kylie ordered pasta for lunch.

_____?

Pasta.

2 Jake ordered a sandwich.

_____?

Jake.

3 Max's mother studied engineering at university.

_____?

Engineering.

4 A candle caused the fire alarm to go off at school.

_____?

A candle.

5 The police hadn't noticed the broken window.

_____?

The broken window.

6 Izzy wants Ryan to be team captain.

_____?

Izzy.

**2 Identify the three subject questions in exercise 1. Rewrite them in a more emphatic way using an auxiliary verb (*does*, *did*, etc).**

1 _____

2 _____

3 _____

**3 Write reply questions for these sentences.**

1 My brother spends two hours a day practising the piano.
*Does he?*

2 When I arrived, they'd already finished lunch.

_____

3 It's snowing harder now than it was before.

_____

4 Everybody knows at least one poem by heart.

_____

5 Nothing interesting ever happens here.

_____

6 My friends would never lie about me.

_____

**4 Write negative questions asking for confirmation that:**

1 the next basketball match is on Friday.
*Isn't the next basketball match on Friday?*

2 Jack's brother used to live in China.

_____

3 the school fees have to be paid online.

_____

4 the exams start next month.

_____

5 Maria's been late every day this week.

_____

6 it's time we tackled global warming.

_____

7 Pierre and Marie Curie discovered Radium.

_____

**5 Put the words in order to make questions. Then add them to the correct sentence below.**

a not / why / go / eat / we / out / before / ?

b ~~why / so / bother / ?~~

c complain / why / but / ?

d all / why / fuss / the / ?

e not / of / why / them / both / invite / ?

f take / a / but / chance / why / ?

1 If I told him the truth, he wouldn't believe me. *So why bother?*

2 _____ They only asked you to work one extra hour!

3 'Anna says she can't come to the party because she's arranged to see Fiona.'

'_____'

4 We've probably got enough petrol to get there. _____
Let's stop at the next service station.

5 The restaurants in town are so expensive. _____

6 It wasn't a great concert. _____ I got a free ticket!

## Listening
# Designer babies
*I can understand a debate about gene editing.*

**Revision:** Student's Book page 11

**Listening Strategy**

When you listen, you may need to distinguish facts from opinions and speculation. Listen out for phrases that indicate when somebody is voicing an opinion (e.g. '*The way I look at it ...*') or speculating (e.g. '*The likelihood is ...*').

1 Read the Listening Strategy. Then complete the phrases to introduce opinions and speculation using the words below.

are as for my no say

a as far _____ I'm concerned ...

b the chances _____ ...

c to _____ mind ...

d I dare _____ ...

e _____ doubt ...

f _____ me ...

2 🎧 1.03 Listen to ten short extracts. For each speaker, decide whether they have stated a fact or expressed an opinion / speculation.

1 Speaker 1 fact _____ opinion / speculation _____

2 Speaker 2 fact _____ opinion / speculation _____

3 Speaker 3 fact _____ opinion / speculation _____

4 Speaker 4 fact _____ opinion / speculation _____

5 Speaker 5 fact _____ opinion / speculation _____

6 Speaker 6 fact _____ opinion / speculation _____

7 Speaker 7 fact _____ opinion / speculation _____

8 Speaker 8 fact _____ opinion / speculation _____

9 Speaker 9 fact _____ opinion / speculation _____

10 Speaker 10 fact _____ opinion / speculation _____

3 🎧 1.03 Listen again. Which speakers express these opinions? Which phrase (a–f) from exercise 1 do they use?

A '_____, cloning should be banned; it may have consequences beyond our control.' Speaker _____

B '_____, scientists should not interfere at all with human genetics.' Speaker _____

C '_____, the important thing is to welcome scientific progress, not fear it.' Speaker _____

D 'If the technology exists to clone humans, _____ criminals will misuse it.' Speaker _____

E '_____ scientists will one day use cloning to grow new organs, so they can cure diseases.' Speaker _____

F '_____ the super-rich will try to clone themselves so they can live forever.' Speaker _____

4 🎧 1.04 Listen to a man and woman discussing cloning. Who is in favour of it?

The _____ is more in favour of cloning.

5 🎧 1.04 Listen again. For each question, choose the best answer: a, b, c or d.

1 The man and woman agree that the radio programme was

a a little confusing.

b not reassuring.

c very interesting.

d difficult to believe.

2 Which one of these points is stated as a fact rather than an opinion or speculation?

a There are regulations to control human cloning.

b There are more GM crops than there used to be.

c GM ingredients are in the food we eat but we don't realise it.

d One day soon, all our crops will be GM.

3 The man and woman agree that the super-rich are likely to

a achieve immortality by cloning themselves.

b use cloning to replace certain parts of their bodies.

c use their money to make cloning available for everyone.

d pay for further research into cloning.

4 The woman is unhappy about therapeutic cloning because she

a thinks it is unlikely to work.

b believes the body should be left to heal itself.

c thinks it would only work for less serious diseases.

d does not trust the scientists to stay within limits.

5 In the man's opinion, the woman's worries about cloning are

a based on good evidence.

b not necessarily justified.

c the result of inadequate regulations.

d influenced by science fiction.

# Habitual actions

*I can talk about habitual actions in the past and present.*

**1** Read sentences 1–6 and circle the word *would* where it is used incorrectly.

1 My grandma would live in France as a child.
2 Every summer, our family would go camping for a month in the mountains.
3 When I was at primary school, the school bus was unreliable and would often arrive late.
4 Before becoming a teacher five years ago, my uncle would have a job in a factory.
5 Before the age of five, I wouldn't be keen on swimming.
6 When I was in my first year at school, my favourite subject would be music.

**2** Rewrite the sentences from exercise 1 which use *would* incorrectly. Use *used to* instead.

_____
_____
_____
_____
_____
_____

**3** Rewrite the sentences using the present or past continuous with *always*, *constantly* or *forever*.

1 I hate playing my brother at chess because he will cheat!

_____
_____

2 Kyle is a good friend, but he will message me in the middle of the night!

_____
_____

3 I liked my primary-school teachers, but they would make us sing in the morning.

_____
_____

4 My dad will embarrass me in front of my friends.

_____
_____

5 When our dog was a puppy, he would chew my trainers.

_____
_____

6 My mum will wake me up early for no reason at weekends.

_____
_____

**4** **USE OF ENGLISH** Choose the correct words (a–d) to complete the text.

When I was a kid, I $^1$____ use to spend much time with my brother. Being eight years older than me, he $^2$____ to go out with his friends rather than stay at home with his baby brother. I $^3$____ asking him to play with me but usually he'd say no! He $^4$____ never unkind to me; but the age gap was too wide. When I was ten, he went off to university and I only $^5$____ to see him during the holidays. I had a $^6$____ to follow him around all the time – perhaps because I'd missed him – and he was $^7$____ to get annoyed with me. Now we're both adults, the age gap seems less important. We get on well and $^8$____ often meet for a quick coffee in town.

1 **a** didn't **b** wouldn't **c** won't **d** wasn't
2 **a** kept **b** use **c** would **d** tended
3 **a** tended **b** was **c** would **d** kept
4 **a** used **b** was **c** kept **d** tended
5 **a** used **b** would **c** wouldn't **d** was
6 **a** habit **b** tendency **c** prone **d** use
7 **a** apt **b** used **c** tendency **d** habit
8 **a** tend **b** will **c** keep **d** forever

**5** Complete these sentences about things you regularly do now and things you often did in the past.

1 At weekends, I'll _____
_____

2 I have a tendency to _____
_____

3 I keep _____
_____

4 I tend to _____
_____

5 As I child, I'd _____
_____

6 I often used to _____
_____

7 I was always _____
_____

8 I had a habit of _____
_____

# Phrasal verbs (1)

*I can recognise and use phrasal verbs correctly.*

**1** Complete the text with the correct form of the verbs below.

blend  carry  come  go  make  stand  turn

There can be many different reasons for changing your name. Singers and actors sometimes [1]_____ up a 'stage name' because they don't think their real name is suitable. For Peter Gene Hernandez, changing his name to Bruno Mars certainly [2]_____ out to be a good decision. Sometimes people with unusual names decide that they would prefer to [3]_____ in more. When these people change their name, they usually [4]_____ for something very normal, like John Smith. Others take the opposite approach: they change their names because they want to [5]_____ out more – like the British teenager who changed his name to Facebookdotcom Forwardslash-MountaindewUK after the company who make Mountain Dew drinks offered a cash prize for their biggest 'super fan'. Some women who get married choose to [6]_____ on the tradition of taking their husband's surname. But these days, you also [7]_____ across couples who combine their surnames to create a new name. For example, when Mr Pugh married Miss Griffin in 2012, they became Mr and Mrs Puffin.

**2** Complete the second sentence so that it means the same as the first. Include a phrasal verb from below in the correct form.

account for  bring about  get away with  go down  look into  put up with

**1** Police are investigating the cause of the fire.
Police _____ the cause of the fire.

**2** The crime rate has fallen since January.
The crime rate has _____ since January.

**3** Car crime represents half of all crime in this area.
Car crime _____ half of all crime in this area.

**4** New street lights have caused a fall in crime.
New street lights _____ a fall in crime.

**5** Most cybercriminals are not caught.
Most cybercriminals _____ it.

**6** People will not tolerate an increase in traffic noise.
People _____ an increase in traffic noise.

**3** Complete the sentences by writing a suitable pronoun in ONE of the gaps.

**1** Her company offered her a promotion, but she turned _____ down _____.

**2** She inherited some paintings from her father, and later passed _____ on _____ to her daughter.

**3** I was disappointed to fail my Spanish exam, but my maths result made _____ up _____ for _____.

**4** A year after Kirstie and her husband moved to New York, she walked _____ out _____ on _____.

**5** She sometimes made fun of her brothers, but she always stood _____ up _____ for _____ too.

**VOCAB BOOST!**

When you come across new phrasal verbs, use a dictionary to find out not only their meaning but also whether they are separable or inseparable. If you record them in a vocabulary book, include an object (sth / sb) where appropriate, and add arrows if the position can change. For example:

*to look down on sb* = to believe sb is inferior to you

*to give sth ↔ up* = to stop doing a particular activity or eating a particular food

**4** Read the *Vocab Boost!* box. Then find a phrasal verb in each sentence and record it using 'sth' or 'sb' and arrows if appropriate. Add a definition.

**1** We signed up for after-school yoga classes.
_____
_____

**2** I haven't seen this film. Don't give the ending away!
_____
_____

**3** She dropped out of university in her second year.
_____
_____

# Bad beginnings

*I can understand a text about overcoming obstacles.*

**Revision:** Student's Book page 14

**Reading Strategy**

When you are looking for information in a text with several sections:

1 skim read the whole text quickly to get an overall sense of the information it contains.
2 go through the questions one by one. For each question, use your knowledge of the text to locate where the information you need is.
3 scan the relevant part of the text for the information you need. If it is not there, scan other parts of the text until you find it.

1 Read point 1 of the Reading Strategy. Then skim read the text and answer the questions.

1 Which person left their home and later returned?

_____

2 Which person thought they had succeeded but soon faced disappointment?

_____

3 Which two people have helped to create successful films?

_____

2 Read points 2 and 3 of the Reading Strategy. Then match people A–D with questions 1–10. Each person can be matched with more than one question.

Which person ...

1 founded two companies? _____
2 temporarily gave up? _____
3 left education before reaching university age? _____
4 was badly affected by a natural disaster? _____
5 helped a family member with their business? _____
6 was persuaded by a family member to try again? _____
7 was prepared to work for no pay? _____
8 did not achieve success under their real name? _____
9 was rejected because of their appearance? _____
10 did not get a place at their first-choice university? _____

# If at first you don't succeed ...

### A Stephen King

Stephen King's novels have sold more than 350 million copies and many have been made into films, including *The Shining* and *Pet Cemetery*. But his career had a difficult beginning. Having graduated from the University of Maine, King worked as a teacher while also writing his first novel. At one point, he became so frustrated that he threw the manuscript in the bin. His wife, Tabitha, found it, read it and convinced her husband that it was worth finishing. Eventually, he sent the completed work to a publisher and they agreed to publish it. The novel, which was called *Carrie*, went on to become a best-seller and was made into a successful film of the same name.

### B Lady Gaga

At the age of nineteen, Stefani Germanotta dropped out of stage school to focus on her music career, but record label after record label rejected her. Some said she did not look right; others told her that the songs she'd written would never be hits. Finally, one company, Island Def Jam records, offered her a recording contract under her new name, Lady Gaga. She was thrilled. But only three months later, her joy turned to despair when the company dropped her. It took her two years to secure another deal, but when her first album, *The Fame*, was released in 2008, it was a huge hit.

### C Steven Spielberg

As a director, Spielberg's box-office hits include *E.T. The Extra-Terrestrial*, *Jurassic Park*, *Jaws* and the Indiana Jones movies. But when, as a teenager, Spielberg left high school and applied to the University of Southern California's film school, they rejected him because his grades were not high enough. He eventually found a place at a different university and, more importantly, took an unpaid job at Universal Studios. This eventually led to a contract there, at which point Spielberg dropped out of university and began his career as a film-maker.

### D Soichiro Honda

Soichiro Honda, born in a small village in Japan in 1906, learned about mechanics as a child by helping his father with his bicycle-repair business. Having dropped out of school at fifteen with no qualifications, Honda moved to Tokyo to work as a mechanic before returning to his home region and starting his own business. But luck was not on his side. His factory was destroyed by bombs during World War II, and again by a huge earthquake in 1945. Honda sold the remains of his business to Toyota and started again. His new company, which initially made motorised bicycles, eventually grew into one of the world's largest car and motorbike manufacturers.

# 1G Speaking
# Interview
*I can talk about myself and my opinions in an interview.*

> **Speaking Strategy**
> Avoid speaking in short, simple sentences. Try to use complex sentences and include explanations and examples. Use a variety of conjuctions and other expressions for extending your sentences.

**1 Read the Speaking Strategy. Then match the two halves of the sentences. Pay attention to the highlighted phrases.**

1 It's been a very busy summer, what with ... _____
2 During my gap year, I'll need to work, seeing as ... _____
3 Our team had quite a good season, bearing in mind ... _____
4 He decided not to study medicine, owing to ... _____
5 Expecting everyone to cycle to work is unrealistic, given that ... _____
6 I've decided not to spend long in Central Africa, in view of ... _____

a two of our best players had left.
b many people have to commute long distances.
c moving house and organising a family party.
d the dangers of travelling alone in that region.
e I'll have to pay rent at university.
f disappointing results in his science exams.

**2 Choose the correct ending (a or b) for these sentences. Pay attention to the highlighted conjunctions.**

1 I was happy at my primary school, even though
  a I had few friends.
  b the teachers were kind.
2 I'd like to spend a year in France whether or not
  a I study French at university.
  b I spend it in Spain instead.
3 Running is my favourite way to relax, unless
  a I can listen to music while I run.
  b the weather is very bad.
4 I usually choose the vegetarian option when I eat out, provided that
  a I occasionally allow myself to eat bacon.
  b it is not too spicy.
5 I think of myself as a confident person, whereas
  a most of my friends are quite shy.
  b I'm happy to chat to people I've only just met.

**3 🎧 1.05 Listen to a student answering questions. Which four questions does she answer, and in what order? Number them.**

A How would you describe your diet? _____
B What is the best film you've ever seen? _____
C What are the best and worst things about your own personality? _____
D What sports or activities do you most enjoy? _____
E Can you tell me about a friend you've known for a long time? _____
F What do you plan to do after you finish your education at school? _____

**4 🎧 1.05 Listen again. Complete the missing words in these extracts.**

1 _____ employment, I really don't have much idea ...
2 _____ snacks _____, I try to go for healthy things ...
3 _____ negative qualities, I can be impatient ...
4 _____ sports, I'm not very good at ...

**5 Read the examiner's questions and make notes. Think about which ideas could be joined together into complex sentences.**

1 Where in the world would you most like to live?
_____
_____
2 How important is it to be physically active?
_____
_____
3 What are the best and worst things about smartphones?
_____
_____
4 Do you need to do well at school in order to be successful in life?
_____
_____
5 Who do you argue with most often and why?
_____
_____

**6 Now answer the questions from exercise 5. Use highlighted words and phrases from exercise 1 and 2 to join your ideas.**

## Writing
# Opinion essay
*I can write an opinion essay.*

**1** Complete the personality adjectives with the words below.

effacing minded narrow self skinned tempered

**1** self-_____
**4** _____-assured
**2** _____-minded
**5** broad-_____
**3** thick-_____
**6** quick-_____

**2** Complete the definitions with the personality adjectives below.

gullible placid punctual reserved shrewd spontaneous

**1** A _____ person is always on time.
**2** A _____ person is clever and perceptive.
**3** A _____ person remains calm.
**4** A _____ person does not show their feelings.
**5** A _____ person believes anything you tell them.
**6** A _____ person acts on impulse and shows their feelings.

> **Writing Strategy**
> When you write an opinion essay, remember to:
> - avoid informal words and expressions.
> - link your ideas together in a logical way using appropriate adverbs and conjunctions.
> - divide your essay into clear paragraphs.
> - state your conclusion in the final paragraph.

**3** Read the Writing Strategy. Then read the essay and answer the questions.

**1** Which word or phrase in paragraph 1 is too informal? What should replace it?

_____

**2** Which of these linking adverbs best fits the gap in paragraph 2? _____

however indeed instead nonetheless

**4** Paragraph 3 should be two paragraphs. Where should the final paragraph begin? Write the first four words.

_____

Do role models help to shape your personality as you grow up?

**5** Read the task and think about your opinions. Plan an essay with these four paragraphs:

**1** introduction
**2** points relating to one side of the argument
**3** points relating to the other side of the argument
**4** conclusion, including your overall opinion

### Can a difficult childhood sometimes have a positive effect on your personality?

Although some aspects of your personality are present from birth, the things you experience during childhood undoubtedly have an effect on your character. So if you have loads of bad experiences, what effect does that have?

Sometimes, having to face problems when you are young can make you more thick-skinned. _____, children who never encounter any difficulties or challenges cannot develop the strength of character they will need as adults. In other words, you only become self-assured by discovering that you can cope when things go wrong. If nothing ever goes wrong, how can you become self-confident?

However, while certain challenges in your childhood may help to build a strong character, very traumatic or upsetting events may cause lasting damage. For example, a child who suffers violence at the hands of adults may grow up to distrust everyone. Consequently, they might be unable to form normal relationships or lead a happy life. For people like this, a difficult childhood would certainly not have a positive effect on their personality. So to sum up, I believe that a certain amount of difficulty during childhood can have a positive effect on your personality by making you more confident and determined. However, a traumatic childhood would probably cause damage to your personality and make it difficult to become a happy, well-balanced adult.

**6** Write your essay (220–260 words) using your notes from exercise 5.

> **CHECK YOUR WORK**
> **Have you ...**
> - ☐ used appropriate language in your essay?
> - ☐ checked your spelling and grammar?
> - ☐ included conjunctions and linking adverbs to connect your ideas in a logical way?

# 1 Review Unit 1

## Vocabulary

**1 Complete the text with the correct form of the words below.**

blot  evoke  lasting  mind  nostalgia  recall  recollection  remind

Have you ever smelt something and suddenly [1]_____ a particular moment in your past? You're not alone: many people report that some smells [2]_____ strong [3]_____ of the past – sometimes even of memories that our [4]_____ has tried to [5]_____ out. Humans process smells in an organ called the olfactory bulb, which is very close to two parts of the brain involved in memory formation. It's therefore not surprising that certain smells can become linked to particular moments in our lives – [6]_____ us of when we smelled them and creating [7]_____ memories of the event and the smell. This creates feelings ranging from [8]_____ to discomfort decades after the association was formed.

Mark: ___ / 8

**2 Choose the correct words to complete the sentences.**

1 Returning to my old college so many years later was a real **jog / trip** down memory lane.

2 The girl in that photo **rings a bell / comes flooding back**, but I can't quite remember who she is.

3 I know that poem by **rack / heart**. Should I recite it?

4 This used to be one of my favourite songs. Hearing it again really **racks my brains / takes me back**.

5 Joshua had **pleasant / bitter** memories of wonderful summers spent by the beach when he was a boy.

6 My memory of that day is so **vivid / vague** that it feels like it all happened yesterday.

7 The mind can suppress **fond / traumatic** memories so that they don't cause us too much pain.

Mark: ___ / 7

## Word skills

**3 Complete the sentences using the correct form of the verbs below and one or two prepositions.**

account  bring  come  fit  get  put  sign  turn

1 I don't want to _____ you _____ entering the competition, but I don't think you'll win.

2 I _____ some old photos when I was tidying the house. Looking at them really took me back.

3 Are you going to _____ the trip?

4 Kelly applied for a scholarship, but they _____ her _____.

5 Ryan was often bullied about her name. That probably _____ her tough personality.

6 You'll never _____ lying to the teacher. She can easily tell when we're lying.

7 I don't really _____ well in my summer school because everyone in the class is older than me.

8 The protestors are hoping to _____ a change in the law.

Mark: ___ / 8

**4 Match the metaphors below to the definitions.**

a cloud hanging over (sb's) future    a kick in the teeth
follow a different path    go off the rails
set sb on the right track

1 a sudden problem which affects you badly

2 to suddenly start behaving unacceptably or criminally

3 to help a person to improve their life

4 something which threatens to stop someone from achieving what they could

5 to aim for different goals from other people

Mark: ___ / 5

**5 Write 1–2 suitable words to complete the phrases to introduce reasons and explanations.**

1 In _____ of the fact that you've been ill, I'll give you more time to do your essay.

2 _____ as the weather isn't very good, I think we should change our plans for the weekend.

3 It's been a really busy week, _____ with revising for exams and my family moving house.

4 _____ that you usually get good marks, I don't understand why you failed this test.

5 There are long delays on the motorway today, _____ to construction work.

6 _____ mind how young your baby sister is, she's very well behaved.

Mark: ___ / 6

**6 Match the quotes to the personality adjectives below.**

broad-minded  gullible  introvert  self-effacing  shrewd  spontaneous  trustworthy

1 'You didn't really believe that story about a ghost in our cellar, did you? We were only joking.'

2 'Let's pack a bag, then go to the airport with our passports and get the first cheap ticket we find – to anywhere!'

3 'I really didn't do anything very brave. In fact, I don't know why they gave me a bravery award.'

4 'OK, I'll help you to finish your essay. But what will you do for me in return?'

5 'All people are equally important. It doesn't matter who they are, what they believe or where they are from.'

6 'Thanks for inviting me but I'm not really very good at parties. I'd rather stay at home with a good book.'

7 'Samuel would never tell anyone your secret. You can rely on him.'

Mark: ___ / 7

## Grammar

**7** Match the statements 1–8 and replies a–h and complete the replies with the words below.

Did she   Then who did   Wasn't it   Well who has
Were you   Why do that   Why go   Why not

1 I don't like this film. _____
2 It was Carrie's birthday last Saturday. _____
3 I've given up my summer job. _____
4 Suzie split up with Andrew last weekend. _____
5 Penny didn't spread the gossip about you and Ruth. _____
6 Of course I was at your band's concert on Friday. _____
7 I haven't got your tablet. _____
8 I had to carry the heavy box home from the shop. _____

a _____? That's a big surprise! I thought they were made for each other.
b _____? Only a few people knew about us going out.
c _____? Someone must have taken it.
d _____? The acting is pretty good, and the special effects are brilliant.
e _____? Mike said you didn't come.
f _____ to all that trouble when you could have ordered it online?
g _____? You enjoyed doing it, and you were saving up to buy a new laptop.
h _____ the week before? She posted her party photos on Facebook.

Mark: ____ / 8

**8** Tick (✓) the correct sentences and rewrite the others, correcting 1–2 words.

1 When I was a child, my parents forever took me to the zoo.
_____
2 My dog wouldn't hurt anyone, but he would bark.
_____
3 Dan's always arrive late when we agree to meet.
_____
4 You've become very rude. You used not be like this.
_____
5 People will gossip – it's human nature.
_____
6 We used live there. I wonder who lives there now.
_____
7 Ana would always borrowing my things when we were kids.
_____
8 Helen is reminding continually people that I used to fancy Josh. It's really embarrassing.
_____

Mark: ____ / 8

## Use of English

**9** Complete the second sentence so that it has a similar meaning to the first. Use 3–6 words, including the word in brackets.

1 Ian and Fran are good friends, despite being very different. (although)
Ian and Fran are good friends _____ very different.
2 Rachel is often late for class. (tendency)
Rachel _____ late for class.
3 I think gene editing is wrong. (concerned)
_____, gene editing is wrong.
4 How about coming to London with me? (why)
_____ to London with me?
5 Mandy always gossips about people. (keep)
Mandy _____ about people.
6 Josh often gets into trouble. (continually)
Josh _____ into trouble.
7 We'll come to your party unless we have an exam the next day. (provided)
We'll come to your party _____ have an exam the next day.
8 Going on the course will be a good experience even if I don't need the qualification. (whether)
Going on the course will be a good experience _____ need the qualification.

Mark: ____ / 8

Total: ____ / 65

## I can ...

Read the statements. Think about your progress and tick (✓) one of the boxes.

★ = I need more practice.          ★★★ = No problem!
★★ = I sometimes find this difficult.

| | ★ | ★★ | ★★★ |
|---|---|---|---|
| I can describe childhood memories. | | | |
| I can use high-level question forms correctly. | | | |
| I can understand a debate about gene editing. | | | |
| I can talk about habitual actions in the past and present. | | | |
| I can recognise and use phrasal verbs correctly. | | | |
| I can understand a text about overcoming obstacles. | | | |
| I can discuss myself and my opinions in an interview. | | | |
| I can write an opinion essay. | | | |

 # Stories

## A Talking about stories
*I can talk about books and stories.*

**1 Complete the email with the words below. There are two extra words.**

believable  dialogue  evocative  happy  humour  identify
intriguing  love  mystery  pace

To: casey@email.com

Hi Casey,

Thanks for the book. I like novels with a fast ¹_____ and
an ²_____ plot, and that novel had both. And even though
I don't usually like a ³_____ ending, it wasn't sentimental
at all. There was a lot of ⁴_____ in it too – I laughed out
loud several times!

Anyway, it's my turn and I'm sending you *Parallel*, by Lauren Miller.
It's about a girl who wakes up one day in a different life and then
has to solve the ⁵_____ of how she got there. The
character of the girl (Rory) is very ⁶_____, and you can
easily ⁷_____ with her. Her ⁸_____ interest is
a handsome but slightly annoying boy called North. I really hope you
enjoy it – I'm putting it in the post today.

Happy reading!

Katerina

**2 Choose the correct words to complete the book review.**

# GERMINAL

Émile Zola's masterpiece
*Germinal* is ¹**set / written**
in the poor French mining
village of Montsou in the
mid-1800s. The novel
²**hinges / opens** as a young
man, Étienne Lantier,
arrives one cold March
day. He stays, and soon
feels outrage at the poor
villagers' desperate lives. As the story ³**unfolds / is
written**, Étienne leads a miners' strike, which is brutally
repressed. ⁴**Central / Drawn** to the plot is the theme
of how the poor are exploited by the powerful, but the
novel has many interesting ⁵**points of view / twists and
turns**, and the characters are beautifully ⁶**set / drawn**.
Although the ⁷**action / narrative** is written in the third
person, Zola's ⁸**portrayal / point of view** of Étienne is
vivid and memorable.

**3 Match the adjectives below with the words and phrases. There are two extra words.**

chilling  compelling  evocative  humorous  predictable
slow-moving  thought-provoking  unconvincing

1 'Nasty and frightening.' _____
2 'Unbelievable.' _____
3 'Unsurprising.' _____
4 'Amusing.' _____
5 'Addictive reading.' _____
6 'It really makes you think.' _____

**4 Complete the idioms and set phrases.**

1 The illustration on the front is awful, but don't judge a
book _____.
2 It's a real page-_____. I couldn't put it down.
3 The book is at first heavy _____, but it speeds up
later.
4 Jack's a real _____ – he spends all his money in
bookshops.
5 It isn't good _____ because it's scary and
it'll keep you awake.
6 He doesn't say he hates the government, but you
understand that if you read _____.

**5 🎧 1.06 Listen to four people talking about books. Which
literary form does each speaker talk about?**

1 _____
2 _____
3 _____
4 _____

**6 🎧 1.06 Listen again. Match the descriptions A–E with the
speakers 1–4. There is one extra sentence.**

This speaker …
A says that the book has both humorous and macabre
moments. _____
B thinks the work is unconvincing in places but has good
descriptions. _____
C says that the story has a lot of suspense and likes the way
the plot contains some red herrings. _____
D says that the work is light-hearted but not shallow. _____
E finds the story very touching and compares it to another
type of literature. _____

**1 Choose the correct words to complete the sentences.**

1 I would have slept much better last night if you **hadn't told / didn't tell** me that horror story.

2 If Jack had found out about the party, he **would / will** be here.

3 If you **had read / read** this book, you'd really like it.

4 We **would have enjoyed / would enjoy** the film more if the characters had been more believable.

5 We**'d have / 'll have** nicer costumes for the play if we'd spent a little more money on them.

6 The novel would be too sentimental if it **would have / had** a happier ending.

**2 Write sentences using mixed conditionals.**

1 we / have / an easier time in Paris last month if we / speak / French

_____

_____

2 I / not have to / fix your computer all the time if you / buy / an anti-virus programme

_____

_____

3 if people / not invent / cars, trains / still be / the main form of transport

_____

_____

4 if Toby / apologise / for what he said, I / not be / so angry with him

_____

_____

5 if you / check / Facebook more often, you / know / about the Literature Festival

_____

_____

**3 Tick (✓) the correct sentences and rewrite the incorrect ones.**

1 Should Claire phone I'd tell her that you're busy.

_____

_____

2 You'd do well, were it not for your lazy attitude.

_____

_____

3 Had you not come, I wouldn't know anyone here.

_____

_____

4 Was I more confident, I'd ask Darren out.

_____

_____

5 Had you have asked me, I would have helped you.

_____

_____

**4 Match the parts of the sentences and complete them with the words below. Use the words more than once.**

in case   provided   supposing   unless

1 Take some money with you ...

2 _____ they ask me why I want the job, ...

3 _____ you need to contact me, ...

4 Max will come to the cinema with us, ...

5 I won't forgive you _____ ...

a _____ that he doesn't have to work late.

b here's my email address.

c what shall I say?

d _____ they don't accept credit cards.

e you apologise for what you said.

**5 Choose the correct words to complete the text.**

## A world without the internet

Tim Berners-Lee is usually credited with inventing the world wide web in the 1980s, but ¹_____ for many other people, today's internet would not exist. If computer technology ²_____ advanced rapidly after World War II, we wouldn't have had the infrastructure needed to build the internet. The computer revolution ³_____ taken place without the work of Alan Turing, who built the first modern computer in the 1940s. And ⁴_____ people hadn't used binary code for centuries in smoke signals, Morse code and textile machines – would we have thought of using it to write computer programmes?

It's difficult to imagine what the world would be like today if we ⁵_____ the internet, because the technology is so interwoven with our daily lives. But ⁶_____ the internet suddenly stopped working? Some scientists think this ⁷_____ one day – if the energy from a big solar storm hits Earth, it ⁸_____ electronic devices worldwide. ⁹_____ we protect computer networks better, we ¹⁰_____ one day be in big trouble!

| | | | |
|---|---|---|---|
| 1 | a wouldn't it | b had it not been | c were it |
| 2 | a wouldn't | b hadn't | c didn't |
| 3 | a hadn't had | b didn't have | c wouldn't have |
| 4 | a provided | b in case | c supposing |
| 5 | a hadn't invented | b wouldn't invent | c won't invent |
| 6 | a as long as | b provided that | c what if |
| 7 | a would happen | b happens | c could happen |
| 8 | a disabled | b disables | c may disable |
| 9 | a As long as | b Unless | c Supposing |
| 10 | a may | b would | c can |

# Investigative journalism
*I can predict the kind of information I need to listen for.*

**Revision:** Student's Book page 23

**1 Complete the text with the words below.**

dig around  ethics  gruesome  gutsy  infiltrate
revelations  scandal  tip-off

In 2014, Singaporean investigative journalist Zaihan Mohamed Yusof published a book called *Foul!* It contained startling ¹_____ about how criminals were paying footballers to 'fix' matches by playing badly. This helped the criminals to win money by betting on the other side. The book caused a big ²_____ in Singapore when it came out, and it called into question the ³_____ of the billion-dollar sports betting industry.

It all started when Zaihan received a ⁴_____ about the problem and decided to ⁵_____ for more information. In the end, he managed to ⁶_____ a Singaporean criminal network that was fixing matches in places as far away as South Africa. Zaihan's car was vandalised twice by criminals during his investigation, and he also received ⁷_____ death threats – but he's a ⁸_____ individual, and the threats didn't deter him from investigating. His book and newspaper articles have lead to many arrests, but sadly the problem of match fixing continues.

**Listening Strategy**
Read the task carefully and try to predict the type of information you need to listen for. This is especially important in sentence-completion tasks.

**2 Read the Listening Strategy. Then look at sentences 1–4. What kind of information do you think you will need to complete them?**

**Investigative reporters and the paparazzi**

1 Famous people expect to be photographed occasionally, but would like part of their lives to remain _____.
2 Some celebrities use _____ to ruin paparazzi photos.
3 A photographer says that having good _____ is more important than waiting for people for hours.
4 Photographers couldn't sell photos of Daniel Radcliffe because of his _____.

**3** 🎧 **1.07 Listen to four people talking about celebrity photographers. Complete the sentences in exercise 2 with a word or short phrase.**

**4 You are going to listen to a person talking about an undercover FBI agent. Read sentences 1–8 and think about what kind of information you need to listen for.**

**The Real Donnie Brasco**

1 When Pistone joined the FBI, most agents relied on _____ to do their job.
2 He invented a _____ for himself when he was undercover.
3 Pistone became friends with a criminal called Benjamin Ruggiero, and Ruggiero _____ him.
4 Ruggiero gave the FBI a lot of _____, but he didn't know it.
5 Nobody _____ Pistone's identity because he looked and acted like a member of the Mafia.
6 Eventually the Mafia wanted Pistone to _____ for them.
7 Some people are worried about the _____ of an agent working with criminals for so long.
8 Because of Pistone, New Yorkers learned about _____ who took money from the Mafia.

**5** 🎧 **1.08 Listen to the recording and complete each sentence in exercise 4 with a word or short phrase.**

## Grammar
# Inversion of subject and verb
*I can use adverbials at the start of the sentence.*

**1 Choose the correct words to complete the sentences.**

1 **No longer / Not since** the summer after leaving school had we all met.

2 **Only if / So** you train really hard will you be ready for the competition.

3 **Such / So** surprised were we to meet by chance after all these years that we couldn't quite believe it.

4 **Never / No longer** were they married, but they remained good friends.

5 **Had / Would** I known you were in town last week, I would have invited you to dinner.

6 **There / Had** we sat on the summit of the mountain, tired but happy.

**2 Complete the sentences. Use the cues below.**

crash / go    hardly / the prime minister / arrive
in no way / should / you    little / we / know
never / I / witness    seldom / he / state his opinion    up / go

1 _____ such a terrible sight as those poor, hungry people.

2 _____ feel responsible – it wasn't your fault.

3 _____ when reporters wanted to speak to him.

4 _____ how meeting Jess would change our lives on the day when she appeared at our door.

5 _____ the red flag, and we were given a penalty.

6 _____ but this time he told us exactly what he felt.

7 _____ the vase as it hit the floor and broke.

**3 Correct the sentences.**

1 Nowhere we could see Kelly.

_____

2 No sooner we saw Jake's face than we realised that something was wrong.

_____

_____

3 Not until I knew I was safe I stopped running.

_____

4 Under no circumstances you should touch that cable.

_____

5 Not for one second we didn't believe Sue was guilty.

_____

6 Not only he was rude when we arrived after our journey, but he didn't offer us anything to eat.

_____

_____

**4 USE OF ENGLISH Rewrite the sentences using the words in brackets so that the meaning stays the same.**

1 There are some DVDs in the cupboard if you get bored. (should)

_____, there are some DVDs in the cupboard.

2 I sat down, and the phone rang. (hardly)

_____ when the phone rang.

3 It's forbidden for you to enter the building. (circumstances)

Under _____ enter the building.

4 You aren't ready to take the exam. (way)

In _____ ready for the exam.

5 We never believed Mike's story. (moment)

Not _____ we believe Mike's story.

6 People didn't learn the truth for decades. (until)

Not _____ people learn the truth.

7 We were late and our clothes were wet. (only)

_____ late, but our clothes were wet.

8 It didn't often rain so hard. (seldom)

_____ so hard.

**5 Complete the extract from a story using the correct form of the words in brackets. Add pronouns where necessary.**

A man out walking his dog had heard a commotion and called us to the house. ¹_____ (no sooner / arrive) than we noticed something was wrong. ²_____ (not only / be) the patio doors open, but the glass was broken. A pair of curtains flapped in the wind. Although I was an experienced detective with the South African Police Service, ³_____ (seldom / feel) in much danger – but I did then.

Everywhere, there were the signs of a struggle – broken ornaments and furniture. ⁴_____ (at our feet / lie) the remains of a vase – ⁵_____ (crunch / go) the pieces underfoot. ⁶_____ (no sooner / reach) the stairs than we heard strange sounds upstairs.

Two baboons came crashing out of a bedroom and down the stairs. ⁷_____ (rarely / these apes / come) near the centre of town, but there they were – baring their fearsome teeth at us. ⁸_____ (not for one moment / hesitate) – one glimpse of them was enough to make us turn and run!

## 2E Word Skills

# Compounds

*I can use a variety of compounds.*

**1 Complete the compounds with the words below.**

break  crack  hand  last  lift  strong  tax  tip  twenty
warm

1 _____-hearted      6 _____-off
2 _____-free          7 _____-down
3 _____-off           8 _____-storey
4 _____-made          9 _____-willed
5 _____-minute       10 _____-down

**2 Complete the compounds in the mini-dialogues.**

**Mandy**  Greg's a very ¹_____-going person. He never gets angry at anyone.

**Josh**  Yes, and he's very broad-²_____ too. He doesn't have any prejudices.

**Ricky**  Is that book good?

**Seth**  Well, it's a ³_____-selling novel by an award-⁴_____ writer, but I don't like it much. It's full of never-⁵_____ descriptions that go on and on. I prefer a book with more action.

**Man**  This machine is very ⁶_____-friendly.

**Woman**  Yes – you don't need to read the 300-⁷_____ guide that came with it to work it out.

**3 Complete the sentences. Use the verbs below and a suitable preposition to make compound nouns.**

break  check  make  rip  take  warm

1 Megan's left her boyfriend. He's very upset about the _____.

2 We were standing at the _____ desk when the flight was cancelled.

3 Do a _____ before you go for a run, or you'll hurt yourself.

4 The electrician was only here for five minutes, but he tried to charge me £200. What a _____!

5 There's nothing in the fridge, so let's get some _____ food on the way home.

6 The actress is still in the dressing room, putting on her _____.

**4 Complete the compounds in the text with the words below.**

award  educated  made  respected  three-minute  well
world  worldwide

# FAMOUS HOAXES

In 1912, an archaeologist called Charles Dawson presented some human-like bones at a meeting of the ¹_____-famous Royal Geological Society, in London. He claimed they were a fossil from Piltdown, England. Highly ²_____ scientists examined the bones, and decided that they belonged to a new species – an ancient ancestor of humans. But in fact, the fossil was a hoax. Dawson had made it out of modern human and orang-utan bones.

In April 1957 many people watched a ³_____ report on British TV about how spaghetti was 'grown' on a farm in Switzerland. It was broadcast on the ⁴_____-winning BBC *Panorama* programme, and was very believable. Spaghetti wasn't a ⁵_____-known food in Britain at the time, so many people believed the report. But it was broadcast on 1 April – April Fool's Day!

The tree octopus, which lives in the north-west United States has a ⁶_____ internet following, and there are campaigns to save this 'endangered creature'. You can watch well-⁷_____ videos about the tree octopus, and read all about it. The information is good enough to fool well-⁸_____ people, but it's just a joke. All octopus species live in the sea.

**VOCAB BOOST!**

A hyphen can indicate that two words form a compound adjective and are not unrelated words. The hyphen can change the meaning of the sentence.

**5 Read the *Vocab Boost!* box What is the difference between sentences A and B? Complete the sentence which follows with the sentences below.**

But we don't know who many undercover agents are.
Do I have to pay for it?   He's very famous.
His meal looked delicious.   I think it was a shark.
I don't want to buy beauty products with aluminium in them.

1 **A** I saw a man eating fish. _____
  **B** I saw a man-eating fish. _____

2 **A** Is this aluminium free? _____
  **B** Is this aluminium-free? _____

3 **A** Donnie Brasco is one of the best-known undercover agents. _____
  **B** Donnie Brasco is one of the best known undercover agents. _____

# *The Woman in White*, by Wilkie Collins
*I can understand and react to an extract from a 19th-century novel.*

**Revision:** Student's Book page 26

**1** Rewrite the sentences, replacing the <u>underlined</u> literary words with more modern equivalents.

1 Those doors lead to the King's private <u>chambers</u>.
2 <u>Pray</u> tell us all what you're thinking.
3 Why did you <u>steal</u> out of the house late last night?
4 Her eyes had a bluish-grey <u>hue</u>.
5 We would be happy to <u>receive</u> you at our house.
6 It's hard to explain my <u>sensations</u> at that moment.
7 I couldn't hear his words, but I could tell from his <u>earnestness</u> that it was a serious matter.

**2** Read the text. Are the sentences true or false? Find evidence in the text for your answers.

1 The narrator feels that he understands the woman and her motives. _____
2 She asks him a question which surprises him. _____
3 The woman and the narrator have a common acquaintance. _____
4 The narrator is unhappy with his own social status. _____
5 The woman loses her trust of him during the extract. _____

**3** Read the extract again and answer the questions.

1 What are the narrator's feelings at the beginning?
2 Why does he hesitate before answering the woman?
3 How does the narrator meet people 'of rank and title'?
4 What does the narrator speculate about the baronet?
5 Why does the woman want him to walk ahead?

**Reading Strategy**
Being able to summarise a text will enhance your awareness of how texts are organised and improve your ability to pinpoint the main ideas or events.

1 Start by dividing the text into sections. Mark the points where there is a clear change of ideas or events.
2 Underline the key points or events within each section.
3 Rewrite the key points or events in your own words. Be brief, keeping within the word limit if there is one.

**4** Read the Reading Strategy. Then write a short summary of the extract. Write no more than 50 words.

We set our faces towards London, and walked on together in the first still hour of the new day – I, and this woman, whose name, whose character, whose story, whose objects in life, whose very presence by my side, at that moment, were fathomless mysteries to me. It was like a dream. I was too bewildered – too conscious also of a vague sense of something like self-reproach – to speak to my strange companion for some minutes. It was her voice again that first broke the silence between us.

'I want to ask you something,' she said suddenly. 'Do you know many people in London?'

'Yes, a great many.'

'Many men of rank and title?' There was an unmistakable tone of suspicion in the strange question. I hesitated about answering it.

'Some,' I said, after a moment's silence.

'Many' – she came to a full stop, and looked me searchingly in the face – 'many men of the rank of Baronet?' Too much astonished to reply, I questioned her in my turn.

'Why do you ask?'

'Because I hope, for my own sake, there is one Baronet that you don't know.'

'Will you tell me his name?'

'I can't – I daren't – I forget myself when I mention it.' She spoke loudly and almost fiercely, raised her clenched hand in the air, and shook it passionately; then, on a sudden, controlled herself again, and added, in tones lowered to a whisper 'Tell me which of them YOU know.'

I could hardly refuse to humour her in such a trifle, and I mentioned three names. Two, the names of fathers of families whose daughters I taught; one, the name of a bachelor who had once taken me on a cruise in his yacht, to make sketches for him.

'Ah! you DON'T know him,' she said, with a sigh of relief. 'Are you a man of rank and title yourself?'

'Far from it. I am only a drawing-master.'

As the reply passed my lips – a little bitterly, perhaps – she took my arm with the abruptness which characterised all her actions.

'Not a man of rank and title,' she repeated to herself. 'Thank God! I may trust HIM.'

I had hitherto contrived to master my curiosity out of consideration for my companion; but it got the better of me now.

'I am afraid you have serious reason to complain of some man of rank and title?' I said. 'I am afraid the baronet, whose name you are unwilling to mention to me, has done you some grievous wrong? Is he the cause of your being out here at this strange time of night?'

'Don't ask me: don't make me talk of it,' she answered. 'I'm not fit now. I have been cruelly used and cruelly wronged. You will be kinder than ever, if you will walk on fast, and not speak to me. I sadly want to quiet myself, if I can.'

**GLOSSARY**

**fathomless** = deep and impossible to understand
**baronet** = the title of one type of member of the English upper class
**humour** (v) = oblige, grant someone their wish
**trifle** (n) = something unimportant

# Photo comparison

*I can compare and contrast photos.*

**1 Complete the sentences about photos A and B with the words below and your own ideas.**

common contrast difference hand obvious whereas

1 The most _____ similarity between the photos is that _____.
2 Another thing they have in _____ is that _____.
3 In _____ to the second photo, the people in the first photo are _____.
4 The clearest _____ between the photos is that one shows a _____.
5 The first photo shows a group of friends. On the other _____ the second photo shows _____.
6 There is a conversation in photo 1, _____ in photo 2 people _____.

**2 🎧 1.09 Listen to a student comparing the photos in exercise 1.**

Does the student have similar answers to your sentences in exercise 1? _____

**3 Complete the second sentences about photos A and B so that it means the same as the first. Use 3–5 words, including the word in brackets.**

1 This isn't the first time that they've met. (can't)
This _____ they've met.
2 They look relaxed. (appear)
They _____ relaxed.
3 I think the person speaking is telling a joke. (as if)
It _____ person speaking is telling a joke.
4 I think they are at a conference of some kind. (seem)
They _____ at a conference of some kind.
5 Someone certainly invited the presenter to speak. (must)
Someone _____ to speak.
6 Perhaps it took the speaker a long time to prepare for this event. (might)
It _____ the speaker a long time to prepare for this event.

**4 Complete the phrases to express opinions.**

1 Off the _____ of my head, I'd say that most people don't like public speaking. _____
2 We _____ to think that speaking to large groups is more difficult than speaking to a small group. _____
3 As I _____ it, it depends on the people that you're speaking to. _____
4 I'm of the _____ that some people are very shy. _____
5 I think it's true to _____ that nobody likes a conversation like a job interview. _____
6 All things _____, most people are most relaxed when they're in informal situations. _____
7 It would be _____ to argue that everyone is the same, because we aren't. _____

> **Speaking Strategy**
> The examiner might ask you a question about the photos which the other student has just compared. Listen carefully while the other student is speaking, and at the same time think about the photos and what you might say about them.

**5 🎧 1.10 Read the Speaking Strategy. Then listen to the examiner's follow-up question. Tick (✓) the statements from exercise 4 that you hear.**

**6 Look at photos C and D and make notes.**

Compare two pictures. Say what the people are doing, and how they might be feeling.

1 What do both photos have in common?
2 What is the main difference between the photos?
3 How do you think the people are feeling? Why?

**7 Do the exam task in exercise 6, then answer the follow-up question below.**

When is it wrong to stop a stranger in the street and ask them something?

## Writing
# Film review
*I can write a film review.*

**1** Read the Writing Strategy and the review. What kind of audience is the TV series suitable for?

**a** all ages     **b** teenagers     **c** adults

> **Writing Strategy**
> When you write a film review, you aren't being asked to write a straightforward description but to evaluate the film from a particular point of view, e.g. its suitability for a particular audience, how it affected you, or how it exceeded or failed to meet your expectations.

**2** Read the review and match paragraphs A–E with descriptions 1–5.

1 the main idea behind the series, and its influences _____
2 an overall impression and a note to readers _____
3 casting and the main characters _____
4 introducing the series and giving some basic facts _____
5 information about the setting and plot _____

**3** Replace the underlined words in the review with the correct form of the words and phrases below.

be disappointed by   enhance   rave reviews   short-listed
superbly cast

**4** Complete the sentences with the highlighted words in the review.

1 The character of Jack in your play is _____. He behaves just like all detectives in films.
2 Dreamworks' latest _____ film cost $65 million to produce.
3 The view from here is wonderful. It's just _____!
4 It isn't a _____ film – there isn't much action at all.
5 In the cinema this week there's a _____ new horror story by the director of *Watching from the Shadows*.
6 The film is a very _____ emotional drama. It makes a lot of people cry.

A language school wants to buy DVDs of a popular TV series for students to borrow and watch in their free time. Write a review of a TV series that you like, mentioning why it's a good series and who it would and wouldn't appeal to.

**5** Read the task, then plan your review. Make notes.

1 From what point of view are you writing the review?
2 What kind of TV series would be suitable?
3 What are the strong and weak points of the TV series?
4 Who would it appeal to?

# Something for everyone in CREEPY new sci-fi series

▶**A** The second season of American TV series *Stranger Things* has just begun. The first season received [1]a lot of praise from critics after it was released in 2016. It has won several awards, including a Screen Actors Guild Award, and was [2]considered for many others.

▶**B** The series is set in the 1980s in a small town called Hawkins, Indiana. This very ordinary setting [3]increases the tension by providing a contrast to the weird events that take place there. The first season begins with the disappearance of a teenage boy. Disturbing events begin to unfold when friends and family dig around for clues, taking us on a nail-biting journey into the unknown.

▶**C** The series concept is designed to appeal to a broad range of viewers, with its mix of gripping investigative drama, chilling supernatural horror and a touch of sci-fi. The formula owes a lot to film directors like Stephen Spielberg and John Carpenter, but it nicely avoids copying them

▶**D** Many of the leading actors are teenagers, so younger viewers have characters to identify with. Also, most of the teenage and adult actors are [4]very well chosen – particularly Winona Ryder as the tortured mother of the missing boy. However, I [5]didn't like the character of the sheriff, who appears very clichéd.

▶**E** To sum up, it's a well-made, big-budget TV series with a powerful concept, a fast-paced plot and some breathtaking special effects. I can recommend the series to both adult and teen viewers – as long as they are prepared for a fright!

**6** Write your review.

> **CHECK YOUR WORK**
> **Have you ...**
> ☐ organised your review into clear paragraphs?
> ☐ given readers a good idea of what the series is about and who it might appeal to?
> ☐ introduced and concluded the review?

## 2 Review Unit 2

## Vocabulary

**1 Complete the book review.**

*THE ROAD HOME*, by Rose Tremain, doesn't have a particularly fast-moving ¹p_____, but it captivates you from the start. The protagonist – a migrant worker called Lev – is a ²b_____ character, and you can easily ³i_____ with him and his struggle to adapt to life in a new land. The ⁴l_____ interest is a kind-hearted young chef, and she's also realistic. The ⁵d_____ between the main characters is very natural, and reveals Lev's increasing grasp of English. There are sad moments in the ⁶n_____, but there's also a fair amount of ⁷h_____. All in all, it's a really good read.

Mark: ____ / 7

**2 Match the literary forms below with the definitions.**

fable   fantasy   graphic novel   myth   play   poem

1 a piece of writing – often in verses – where the sound and rhythm of the words is important
2 a novel where the pictures are as important as the text
3 a traditional short story that teaches a lesson
4 a story from ancient times, often explaining ancient people's beliefs about the world
5 actors perform this story in a theatre
6 a story for adults or children that has magic or unreal characters

Mark: ____ / 6

**3 Choose the correct words to complete the extracts.**

*The Divide* is a ¹**compelling / chilling** novel – I couldn't put it down! Nicholas Evans's ²**set / portrayal** of his characters is faultless. (*Launchester Herald*)

A ³**thought-provoking / lightweight** book which made me reassess my own ⁴**narrative / point of view** on the ecology versus industry debate. (*Daily Review*)

An intriguing plot with many ⁵**red herrings / twists and turns**, which ultimately ⁶**opens / hinges** on the idea of broken trust. (*Waitangi News*)

Mark: ____ / 6

**4 Complete the idioms.**

1 I don't like the artwork on the front, but it's best not to judge a book _____.
2 I just couldn't _____ into the book, so I stopped reading it.
3 Reading between _____, you can tell that his biographer doesn't really approve of his actions.
4 That book's a real _____ – you won't be able to put it down.
5 Waterstones' bookshop is a great place to visit if you're a bit of _____!

Mark: ____ / 5

## Word skills

**5 Complete the sentences with the compound nouns below.**

award   best   crack   easy   lift   take

away   down   going   off   selling   winning

1 The police are _____ on people who drive fast.
2 This computer game is our _____ title.
3 There's nothing to eat at home, so let's get a _____.
4 Nothing ever bothers Martin – he's very _____.
5 I know it's an _____ novel, but I just didn't like it.
6 _____ is scheduled for 20.00 local time.

Mark: ____ / 6

**6 Complete the sentences.**

1 Off the top _____, I'd say you're right.
2 As I _____, it's good to have friends.
3 What both photos have _____ is that they show people doing things outdoors.
4 All things _____, I'd say that it's sometimes OK to lie.
5 In _____ to photo 1, photo 2 shows a formal situation.
6 The people in photo 2 seem tense. On the _____, the people in photo 1 are relaxed.

Mark: ____ / 6

**7 Complete the film review with the correct words.**

*Finest Hours* tells the ¹**powerful / far-fetched** true story of a ²**two-dimensional / nail-biting** rescue at sea that took place in 1952. The action never lets up in this ³**fast-paced / slow-moving** movie, as the coast guard braves 70-foot waves to rescue thirty sailors on a sinking ship. This is a no-expense-spared, ⁴**low-budget / big-budget** movie. Some of the characters aren't as ⁵**ground-breaking / well-rounded** as they could be, but Eric Bana puts in a great performance. And anyway, the real protagonist in this film is the wild, unforgiving Atlantic ocean!

Mark: ____ / 5

# 2 Review Unit 2

## Grammar

**8 Complete the sentences with the correct form of the verbs in brackets.**

1 We _____ (not be) at the back of the queue right now if we _____ (arrive) a few minutes earlier.
2 Supposing people _____ (not discover) antibiotics, _____ (doctors / be able to) treat infections?
3 I _____ (take) a book to read in case I _____ (need) to wait a long time for my appointment.
4 If it _____ (not be) for that traffic jam, we _____ (not miss) our flight.
5 We _____ (enjoy) last week's holiday in Ibiza more if it _____ (not rain) so much.
6 You _____ (not have) a bad stomach now if you _____ (not eat) that out-of-date pizza for lunch.
7 As long as we _____ (leave) in the next few minutes, we _____ (not be) late.
8 What if I _____ (tell) you Jake was coming to the party?

Mark: / 8

**9 Rewrite the sentences. Use the words below to start.**

hardly   in front of   little … know   no longer
not for one moment   should   so   under no circumstances

1 We never thought you were guilty of the crime.
_____
2 The match had only just started when they scored.
_____
3 It's totally forbidden for you to enter that building.
_____
4 Please call me if you need a lift home.
_____
5 I don't have to do that terrible job any more.
_____
6 I was totally unaware of how close I'd been swimming to a three-metre shark.
_____
7 I called the police because I was very worried.
_____
8 There was a tall, thin man standing in front of the house.
_____

Mark: / 8

## Use of English

**10 Complete the second sentence so that it means the same as the first. Use 3–6 words, including the word in brackets.**

1 Did Ryan fall asleep on the bus because he was very tired? (so)
Was Ryan _____ he fell asleep on the bus?
2 If my plane is delayed, I'll send you a text message. (should)
I'll send you a text message _____ delayed.
3 If I didn't have to revise, I'd come shopping with you. (fact)
If it _____ I have to revise, I'd come shopping with you.
4 I got home and turned on the football match straight away. (sooner)
No _____ I turned on the football match.
5 To sum up, I think the proposal is a good one. (considered)
_____, I think the proposal is a good one.
6 We didn't meet again for years. (until)
Not _____ we meet again.
7 I didn't help Kelly with her presentation because she didn't ask me. (had)
If Kelly _____, I would have helped her with her presentation.
8 You can go out if you finish your homework. (provided)
_____ your homework, you can go out.

Mark: / 8

Total: / 65

## I can …

Read the statements. Think about your progress and tick (✓) one of the boxes.

★ = I need more practice.          ★★★ = No problem!

★★ = I sometimes find this difficult.

| | ★ | ★★ | ★★★ |
|---|---|---|---|
| I can talk about books and stories. | | | |
| I can use a range of conditional sentences. | | | |
| I can predict the kind of information I need to listen for. | | | |
| I can use adverbials at the start of the sentence. | | | |
| I can use a variety of compounds. | | | |
| I can understand and react to an extract from a 19th-century novel. | | | |
| I can compare and contrast photos. | | | |
| I can write a film review. | | | |

# 1 Exam Skills Trainer 1

## Reading

**Strategy**
Read the gapped text first to gain an overall idea of the structure and meaning. To decide which paragraph fits in a gap, read the paragraphs before and after each gap to identify the context. Then read the paragraphs that have been removed, looking out for paraphrasing of vocabulary and connections between people, places and things.

**1** Read the Strategy above and the gapped text in exercise 2. Follow the instructions in the Strategy to find the paragraph that fits gap 1. What references to 'paper' are made in the missing paragraph? What connections exist between the missing paragraph and the paragraph after the gap?

**2** Read the text. Match paragraphs A–F with gaps 1–6.

### The story of paper

The Gutenberg printing press is regarded by many as the most important invention of the last millennium. Developed in Germany in the 1440s, the new machine revolutionised printing and brought about far-reaching changes in Europe. However, the press would never have existed were it not for a much earlier invention: paper.

**1** _____

Paper soon spread to the Arab world from Asia, but it did not take off in Europe because of a preference for parchment. Made from animal skin, parchment was rather expensive, but as there were so few people who could read and write at the time, this was not considered a problem.

**2** _____

The first paper was made from cotton soaked in water and chemicals to release cellulose from its fibres. This process is known as pulping, with pulp being the liquid in which the cellulose floats around. Once the cellulose was extracted from the pulp, it was left to dry in long flat sheets that were later cut into pieces.

**3** _____

But then disaster struck. The demand for paper in the West caused the supply of cotton and rags to dry up. So short of raw material were the paper mills that they used the bloodstained uniforms taken from dead soldiers on the battlefield to boost production. It was clear that an alternative to cotton was needed.

**4** _____

Today, the main raw material is paper itself, due to the practice of recycling. Aptly enough, much of the world's paper recycling takes place in China, the country of its birth. It's a hugely successful process which has helped to keep paper affordable and sustainable. However, new technologies have posed another threat to paper.

**5** _____

But then the printer came along, an invention that put paid to the idea. Recipients chose to print out important information on paper as a back-up instead of just saving it on their computers. Paper sales continued to boom and for a while it seemed that paper would be safe.

**6** _____

Old habits die hard, however, and some people prefer to read hard copy rather than text on a screen. For this reason, the demise of paper books seems extremely unlikely in the near future. For the time being, paper production will continue, although it will never be as profitable as it was in the past.

**A** Over the centuries, paper manufacturing was innovated time and time again with the aim of increasing efficiency and lowering costs. New machines were invented for pulping the cotton and different chemicals were added to the pulp. When paper was at its cheapest in 1702, the first daily newspaper, *The Daily Courant*, appeared.

**B** The 'paperless office' was first predicted in the 19th century by Thomas Edison. The concept gained momentum in the 1970s with the advent of computers, which would make it possible to visualise documents on a screen. Thanks to the new machines, paper appeared to be doomed.

**C** Developed by the Chinese around 2,000 years ago, this material was originally conceived for a very different purpose: to cover and protect valuable possessions. Once its potential as a writing medium was discovered, it soon replaced the much heavier bamboo and costlier silk that had previously been used for writing on.

**D** Not for long. In 2013, paper sales reached their peak and since then they have been falling due to the expansion of digital technologies. Lower prices have encouraged many to abandon paper books and newspapers in favour of cheaper online versions. It would seem that history is repeating itself, and digital is doing to paper what paper did to parchment at the end of the Middle Ages.

**E** At first, paper makers in Europe were blind to the solution in front of their eyes. The Chinese had been using wood to make paper for centuries, and as early as 1719, a French botanist had observed wasps making paper nests by chewing wood. It took another 130 years for wood to become an important source for paper production in Europe.

**F** The attraction of paper did not become apparent until the start of the Commercial Revolution in the late 13th century, when a cheaper medium for drawing up contracts and keeping accounts was required. As trade and commerce expanded, parchment was gradually replaced by paper, and Europeans began to manufacture it in earnest.

# 1 Exam Skills Trainer 1

## Listening

3 Read the Strategy above. Identify what you are listening for in questions 1–4 in exercise 4.

4 🎧 1.11 **You will hear two different extracts. For questions 1–4, choose the answer (A, B or C) which fits best according to what you hear.**

You hear a woman telling a friend about a book she's read.
1 What is she doing during the conversation?
   A expressing her admiration for the author
   B complaining about the unsatisfactory ending
   C admitting her ignorance of the book's theme
2 What is the man's criticism of moral issues in a novel?
   A Readers get an unbalanced view.
   B Authors are abusing their position of power.
   C It interrupts the flow of the narrative.

You hear two friends discussing ways of keeping up-to-date with the news.
3 Which aspect of TV news do they disagree about?
   A how tedious the programmes are
   B how biased the news is on different channels
   C how talented newsreaders are
4 What does the boy think of online newspapers?
   A They aren't very user-friendly.
   B The content is aimed at older readers.
   C They would benefit from fewer photos.

## Use of English

5 **Read the Strategy and question. Which words need changing so that they collate with the key word?**

As long as I explain the activity clearly, they will know what to do. **GIVE**
If I _____ the activity, they will know what to do.

6 **For questions 1–6, complete the second sentence so that it has a similar meaning to the first sentence, using the word given. Do not change the word given. You must use between three and six words, including the word given.**

1 We need to decide how we're going to the theatre. **MAKE**
   We need to _____ get to the theatre.
2 There needs to be a thorough revision of the guidelines for the treatment of bullies. **BE**
   The guidelines for the treatment of bullies _____.
3 By the end of the meeting, the workers had agreed on the next step. **REACHED**
   By the end of the meeting, an _____ about what to do next.
4 We didn't intend to return home until the building work had been finished. **HAD**
   We _____ until the building work had been finished.
5 There has been a gradual rise in car sales as the economy improves. **HAVE**
   Car sales _____ as the economy improves.
6 Shona expected a lot more of her new car. **LIVE**
   Shona's new car did not _____.

## Speaking

7 **Answer questions 1–4 using a variety of advanced language.**
   1 Have you read a good book lately?
   2 What stories are in the news at the moment?
   3 How often do you go to the cinema?
   4 Do you think you'd be happy if you were famous?

## Writing

8 **Read the Strategy above and the writing task below. Identify the target reader and the point of view in the task.**

You see this advert on an entertainment website for young adults:
*We're looking for reviews about a performance that you've seen recently. Tell us how suitable the performance was for people your age and make suggestions for how it could be improved.*

9 **Write the review (220–260 words) for the task above.**

# 3 Partners

## Vocabulary

### A Friendships
*I can talk about different kinds of relationships.*

**1 USE OF ENGLISH** Complete the second sentence so that it means the same as the first. Write no more than six words and include the word in brackets.

1 Sarah developed a strong friendship with Alison because of their passion for hockey. (bonded)
Sarah _____ their passion for hockey.

2 Katie continues to know about her former classmates through social media. (track)
Katie _____ through social media.

3 We used to be friends, but now our relationship has ended. (drifted)
We used to be friends, but now we _____.

4 I met an old friend by chance while I was queuing up at the box office. (ran)
I _____ while I was queuing up at the box office.

5 Paul became friends with Ben when he joined the drama club. (struck)
Paul _____ when he joined the drama club.

6 My sister has argued with her boyfriend because of his friends. (fallen)
My sister _____ over his friends.

**2** Read the sentences and choose the correct answer.

1 The police were **baffled** / **honoured** by the crime. They had no idea of the motive.

2 Roseanna was **gobsmacked** / **gutted** when she got the job. It was exactly what she wanted.

3 Owen was **perturbed** / **devastated** when he didn't get into university. It had been his greatest dream.

4 My brother was **impervious** / **perplexed** to the noise the car was making and carried on driving.

5 The reason why we were **aggrieved** / **elated** was that we were completely ignored at the party.

6 I feel **gutted** / **privileged** to have so many good friends – not everyone is so lucky.

7 I was **unconcerned** / **stunned** when I heard about the wedding. I didn't even know they were going out together!

8 Doctors are **outraged** / **troubled** by the speed at which the new disease is spreading.

**3** Compete the relationships idioms.

A They don't see eye to _____ over something.
B They get on like a house on _____.
C They go back a long _____.
D Despite their different backgrounds, they hit it _____.
E They know each other inside _____.
F They stick together through thick and _____.
G They're like chalk and _____ at the start.
H They talk about someone behind their _____.

**4** 🎧 1.12 Listen to two students talking about friendships in films. Number the films 1–5 in the order they are mentioned. Which film does the girl choose to write about?

**5** 🎧 1.12 Listen again. Match the films in exercise 4 with sentences A–H in exercise 3. There are three sentences you do not need.

1 _____  4 _____

2 _____  5 _____

3 _____

# Reporting structures

*I can report direct speech in a variety of ways.*

**1 Put the words in the correct order.**

1 offered / home / to / me / Mandy / take

_____

2 study / encouraged / medicine / to / They / him

_____

3 denied / Leo / having / for / I / feelings

_____

4 having / I / to / not / book / read / confessed / the

_____

5 laptop / blamed / breaking / Callum / She / for / her

_____

6 the / recommended / Luc / we / fish / order

_____

7 were / us / staying / They / where / asked / we

_____

**2 Read the sentences and choose the correct answer(s). One, two or three of the options may be correct.**

1 The police officer insisted on _____ a statement.
  **a** me making  **b** I make  **c** my making

2 My sister refused _____ me her new leather jacket.
  **a** lend  **b** to lend  **c** lending

3 They enquired _____ we needed a taxi.
  **a** if  **b** that  **c** whether

4 His lawyer warned him _____ anything to anybody.
  **a** against say  **b** against to say  **c** against saying

5 Martin admitted _____ to Jessica.
  **a** lying  **b** to lie  **c** having lied

6 I suggested _____ a different restaurant for a change.
  **a** we try  **b** trying  **c** that we should try

7 The teacher reminded _____ for the exam.
  **a** to study  **b** us to study  **c** studying

**3 Complete the sentences with the past simple form of the verbs below.**

accuse  advise  apologise  mention  propose  threaten  wonder

1 He _____ us to go to the police.

2 He _____ they meet again the following week.

3 She _____ me of copying the homework.

4 I _____ having seen her the day before.

5 I _____ if she would be staying for dinner.

6 They _____ to arrest him if he didn't cooperate.

7 We _____ for not calling in advance.

**4** 🎧 **1.13 Complete the dialogue. Write one word in each space. Then listen and check.**

**Becky** Rosie, what happened between you and Ben last night?

**Rosie** Well, it all started when I arrived at the club where he'd taken his friends.

**Becky** What happened?

**Rosie** He didn't like it. He asked me ¹_____ made me think he'd be happy to see me, and demanded to know why I'd insisted ²_____ following him.

**Becky** So, what did you say?

**Rosie** Well, it wasn't true, so I ³_____ following him.

**Becky** And what did he say?

**Rosie** He accused me ⁴_____ spying on him.

**Becky** That's not fair!

**Rosie** I know. Anyway, I confessed ⁵_____ being upset that he'd gone out with his friends, not me, and I told him I just felt like seeing him. Then I apologised ⁶_____ being so jealous, but he ⁷_____ to accept my apology.

**Becky** What then?

**Rosie** He said he'd warned me ⁸_____ trying to stop him seeing his friends and that he regretted ever ⁹_____ met me. He blamed me ¹⁰_____ having to split up and he said he never wanted to see me again.

**Becky** Oh Rosie, I'm sorry!

**5 Write the highlighted reported speech 1–10 in exercise 4 as direct speech.**

1 What _____?

2 Why _____?

3 I _____!

4 You _____!

5 I _____.

6 I'm _____.

7 I won't _____.

8 I _____.

9 I wish _____.

10 It's your fault _____.

# Successful business partnerships

*I can understand and react to a radio programme about successful business partnerships.*

**Revision:** Student's Book page 33

**1 Match 1–8 with a–h.**

1 Our potential partners pulled out _____
2 Their new product took _____
3 Somehow, we got off on the _____
4 Karen and Nikki share a _____
5 Last year, the directors witnessed a _____
6 Tony dropped _____
7 I'm toying with the _____
8 My boss has talked _____

a out of university to take over his father's business.
b wrong foot, so I wonder if we can start again.
c me into working late on Friday night.
d of the deal at the last moment.
e off almost as soon as it was launched.
f passion for vintage clothes.
g milestone when their company reached its tenth anniversary.
h idea of setting up my own company.

**Listening Strategy**

To help you choose the correct answer, remember that the words in the options in the task will be paraphrased in the recording. This means that the speakers will use different words to express the same idea.

**2 Read the Listening Strategy. Then look at the question below. Rewrite options a–d, paraphrasing the meaning of the sentence.**

How does the speaker feel about her business partner?

a She's devastated at her decision.

_____

b She's troubled by her lack of commitment.

_____

c She's aggrieved at her demands.

_____

d She's baffled by her behaviour.

_____

**3** 🎧 1.14 **Listen to a woman talking about a bad experience with a business partner. Look at exercise 2 again and choose the correct answer. How was the option phrased in the recording?**

_____

**4** 🎧 1.15 **Listen to a radio programme about how to create a successful business partnership. Choose the best answer a–d.**

1 According to Hilary, the only people who should be considered as business partners are those with
   a a large fortune to invest.
   b an extraordinary talent to offer.
   c an essential contribution to make.
   d a list of contacts to exploit.

2 Hilary suggests you shouldn't go into business with someone
   a you can't speak your mind to.
   b you don't share the same qualities with.
   c you haven't worked with before.
   d you've never learned anything from.

3 What does Hilary think business partners should agree on from the outset?
   a How they will go about selling their products.
   b Which of their skills will be required.
   c Who will be responsible for money matters.
   d How they envisage the venture developing.

4 Hilary thinks that business partnerships between husband and wife can succeed if
   a they keep out of each other's way.
   b they separate their business and private lives.
   c they each have their own space.
   d they divide responsibilities equally.

5 Hilary believes that a partnership agreement
   a should be flexible.
   b should concentrate on financial issues only.
   c should outline the growth of a company.
   d should be made for a fixed amount of time.

6 Hilary explains that the main purpose of exit clauses is to specify
   a how much money each of the partners should get if they leave.
   b how to proceed if there is a change in the partnership.
   c who should take over the partnership if both partners pull out.
   d how the profits should be shared at each stage of the partnership.

# Comparative and superlative structures
*I can compare partners-in-crime from the past.*

**1 Correct the sentences.**

1 They took longer that planned.

_____

2 Your bag isn't half as heavier as mine.

_____

3 It's as a reliable car as you'll ever have.

_____

4 It's getting more difficult and more difficult to find a job.

_____

5 This exam was ten times harder as last year's.

_____

6 He isn't such good a player as he thinks.

_____

7 We spent more on drinks than we are on food.

_____

8 The further you walk, fewer people you'll meet.

_____

**2 Complete the sentences with *as* or *like*. Sometimes both answers are possible.**

1 I failed the last exam, _____ did most of my class.

2 Andy hopes to become an architect, _____ his sisters did before him.

3 _____ her brothers and sisters, Amelia is bilingual.

4 _____ a doctor, my father is expected to treat medical emergencies whenever they occur.

5 _____ you, I'm looking forward to the holidays.

6 _____ a student, her scholarship only covers her tuition fees.

7 We could get a taxi home together _____ we did last time.

8 My dad's an excellent cook, _____ is my grandad.

**3 Complete the second sentence so that it means the same as the first. Write no more than six words and include the word in brackets.**

1 She gradually became less interested in her old friends as her fame spread. (and)
As her fame spread, she became _____ in her old friends.

2 Both the thief and his accomplice served ten years in prison. (did)
The thief served ten years in prison, _____ accomplice.

3 Matt thinks he's a good driver, but he isn't. (as)
Matt isn't _____ he thinks he is.

4 Holly arrived late yesterday, but she arrived even later today. (than)
Holly arrived _____ yesterday.

5 A guesthouse in Brighton is half the price of a hotel. (expensive)
A hotel in Brighton _____ as a guesthouse.

6 Daisy and nearly all her friends are political activists. (most)
Daisy is a political activist, _____ her friends.

7 My brother has to wear a uniform because he's in the police. (officer)
_____, my brother has to wear a uniform.

8 I've never experienced a more frightening ride. (as)
It's _____ I've ever experienced.

**4 USE OF ENGLISH Complete the text. Write one word in each gap.**

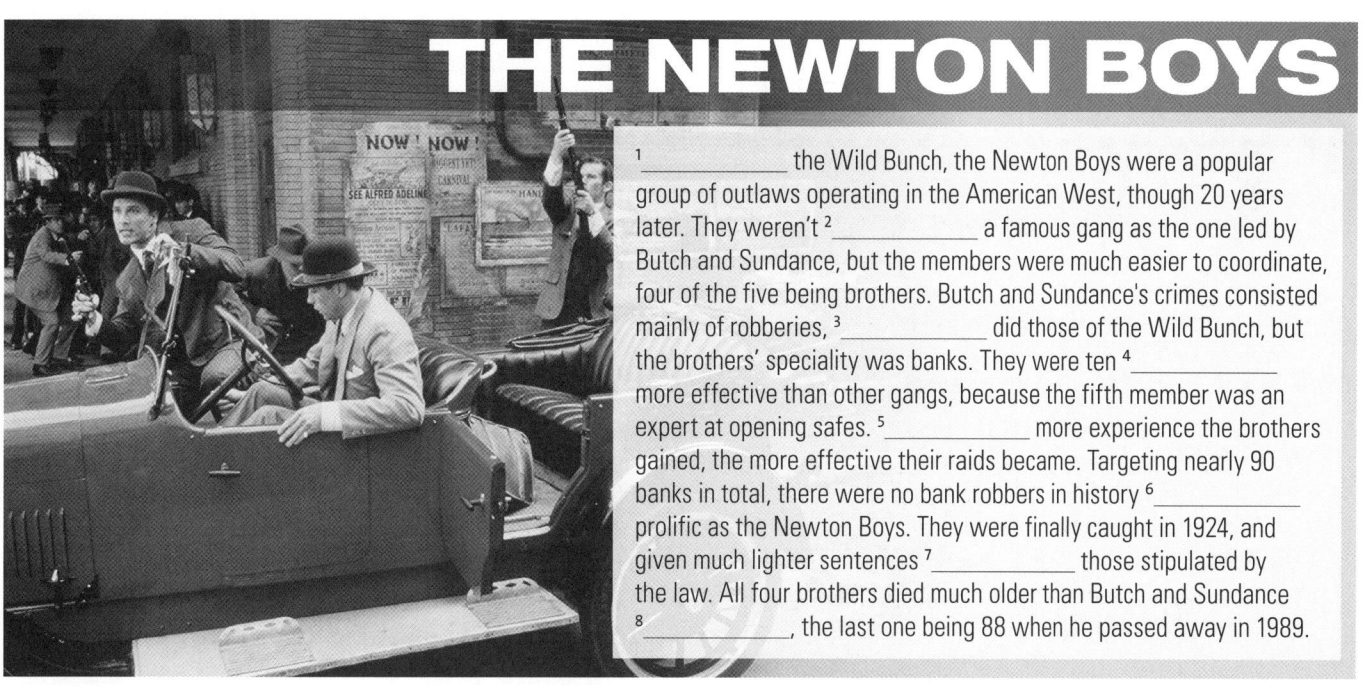

# THE NEWTON BOYS

[1] _____ the Wild Bunch, the Newton Boys were a popular group of outlaws operating in the American West, though 20 years later. They weren't [2] _____ a famous gang as the one led by Butch and Sundance, but the members were much easier to coordinate, four of the five being brothers. Butch and Sundance's crimes consisted mainly of robberies, [3] _____ did those of the Wild Bunch, but the brothers' speciality was banks. They were ten [4] _____ more effective than other gangs, because the fifth member was an expert at opening safes. [5] _____ more experience the brothers gained, the more effective their raids became. Targeting nearly 90 banks in total, there were no bank robbers in history [6] _____ prolific as the Newton Boys. They were finally caught in 1924, and given much lighter sentences [7] _____ those stipulated by the law. All four brothers died much older than Butch and Sundance [8] _____, the last one being 88 when he passed away in 1989.

# Metaphors and similes

*I can use metaphors and similes to make comparisons.*

**1 Complete the metaphors with the words below.**

broken heart   bumpy ride   disaster area   mirror
plain sailing   prison

1 Once we'd got through the rush hour traffic, it was all
_____.

2 When his wife passed away, my elderly neighbour died of a
_____.

3 Her house was a _____ until she had fully
recovered from the accident and could walk again.

4 The surface of the water is a _____ in which the
palace and its surroundings are reflected.

5 No wonder you can't find anything in your room – it's a
_____!

6 He had a _____ through his first year at university
because he split up from his girlfriend.

**2 Complete the sentences with similes made from the words
and pictures below.**

blind   cry   eat   fit   light   quiet

1 I was _____ when I came in so as not to
wake anybody up.

2 These shoes are extremely comfortable. They
_____.

3 My niece is _____, so I don't mind carrying
her.

4 Sad films really upset me. I always _____ at
the end.

5 I don't know why you're so slim – you _____.

6 You need to get your eyes tested – you're
_____.

**3 Complete the second sentence so that it means the same
as the first. Use similes. Write no more than six words and
include the word in brackets.**

1 Last night I had a very good sleep. (like)
I _____ last night.

2 My grandad is very hard of hearing. (post)
My grandad is _____.

3 Your mum looks really angry. (face)
Your mum's got _____.

4 That woman is always on the go. (busy)
That woman is _____.

5 My twin brothers are very similar. (pod)
My twin brothers are _____.

6 He seemed calm, despite his arrest. (cool)
He was _____ despite his arrest.

> **VOCAB BOOST!**
>
> Most metaphors, similes and idioms are listed in a
> dictionary under the first word in the phrase, e.g. *plain
> sailing*, (as) *cool* as a cucumber, *sleep* like a log. Expressions
> with very common words, such as *good* or *run*, are listed
> under the other important word, e.g. (as) *good as* **gold**, *run
> like the* **wind**.

**4 Read the *Vocab Boost!* box and the dictionary extract. Then
replace the words in bold with an idiom in the correct form.**

> **IDM** at 'heart used to say what sb is really like even though they may seem to
> be sth different: *He's still a socialist at heart.* break sb's 'heart to make sb
> feel very unhappy: *She broke his heart when she called off the engagement.*
> By 'heart ℓ (*BrE also* off by 'heart) using only your memory: *I've dialled the
> number so many times I know it by heart.* ◇ *She's learnt the whole speech off
> by heart.* close / dear / near to sb's 'heart having a lot of importance and
> interest for sb from the (bottom of your) 'heart in a way that is sincere: *I beg
> you, from the bottom of my heart, to spare his life.* Give sb (fresh) 'heart to
> make sb feel positive, especially when they thought that they had
> no chance of achieving sth give your 'heart to sb to give your love to
> one person have a 'heart! (*informal*) used to ask sb to be kind and/or
> reasonable

*From Oxford Advanced Learner's Dictionary 9e, 2015.*

1 She thanked him **very sincerely** for all he'd done for her.
_____

2 Paul told Holly that he **loved only** Amelia.
_____

3 Women's rights is an issue that is **of great importance
to her.** _____

4 The warm soup **made the hikers feel more positive**.
_____

5 **Be reasonable!** We don't need to get up at 6 a.m. on a
Saturday! _____

6 He told us to learn our lines **using our memories** before the
next rehearsal. _____

7 My sister's boyfriend **made her very unhappy** when he
finished with her. _____

8 She may seem quite sweet, but she's **really a radical**.
_____

# Animal partnerships

*I can understand and react to an article about symbiosis.*

**Revision:** Student's Book page 36

**1** Replace the standard adjectives in bold with six of the emphatic adjectives below.

captivating daunting doomed frenetic miniscule profound rigid startling

1 There's a **tiny** crack in that glass. _____
2 Adolescence is a period of **great** change. _____
3 Zumba can be quite **energetic**. _____
4 He came to an **astonishing** conclusion. _____
5 They have a **strict** exercise regime. _____
6 He fell for her **attractive** smile. _____

**Reading Strategy**

When you are doing a gapped-paragraph task, read the text quickly, ignoring the gaps, to get a general idea of what it is about. Then read the paragraphs before and after the gap carefully to find out what the topic of the missing paragraph is. Read through the options A–G to find the paragraphs about that topic. Try each paragraph in the gap until you find the one that fits grammatically.

**2** Read the Reading Strategy. Then read the first two paragraphs of the text and decide what the topic of the missing paragraph should be.

_____

**3** Read through options A–E. Which is the correct option?

_____

**4** Read the text. Match paragraphs A–E with the gaps 2–4. There is one extra paragraph. Remember to follow the procedure in the Reading Strategy.

**A** While the dogs and their owners experienced a significant rise in what is known as the 'happiness' chemical, no change at all was detected in the wolves or their owners. This could explain the attachment that humans feel for dogs, sometimes treating them like children.

**B** The researchers found that all the dogs displayed more brain activity when faced with the reward stimuli than the control. This suggests that dogs actively seek the companionship of humans, probably as a result of their evolution together.

**C** Dogs are certainly one of the first animals to ever interact with humans, although at the time as a species of wolf. The first contact was probably made between 30,000 and 40,000 years ago, when a group of Eurasian grey wolves approached a human settlement in search of food.

**D** More than 2,300 dogs around the country are helping children to improve their reading. Children who are uncomfortable reading aloud to people are able to practise with a companion who will not judge them, and are more likely to practise words they do not immediately recognise.

**E** Much research has been done into the extent of this bond. One study conducted by Emory University in the US has succeeded in demonstrating the sociability of dogs in relation to humans.

# Man's best friend

Humans have collaborated with all kinds of animals throughout history, from cows as livestock to horses for transport. So why is it the dog that has gained the title of man's best friend?

**1** _____
The modern dog appeared around 20,000 years later. By this stage, a mutual understanding had developed between the two, by which humans provided shelter and protection in return for the animals' help with hunting. From then on, humans and dogs continued evolving together and became increasingly dependent on each other.

**2** _____
In the experiment, thirteen dogs were trained to associate three different objects with different outcomes. A blue toy knight signalled verbal praise, a pink toy truck signalled a treat, and a hairbrush signalled no reward, and was a control. During the study, each dog was tested 32 times to monitor its neural activity.

**3** _____
No less fascinating is the effect that dogs have had on humans. Scientists at Azabu University in Japan have recently shown that looking into a dog's eyes activates the same hormonal response that bonds us to human babies. Dogs and wolves were used in the research, which involved the owners and the animals staring into each other's eyes for a set amount of time while their levels of oxytocin were monitored.

**4** _____
Today, dogs are not just companions, but assistance animals too, helping children with learning difficulties and adults with mental-health issues. In this way, they most definitely fulfil the role of a best friend.

## 3G Speaking
# Collaborative task
*I can maintain the interaction in a collaborative task and reach an agreement.*

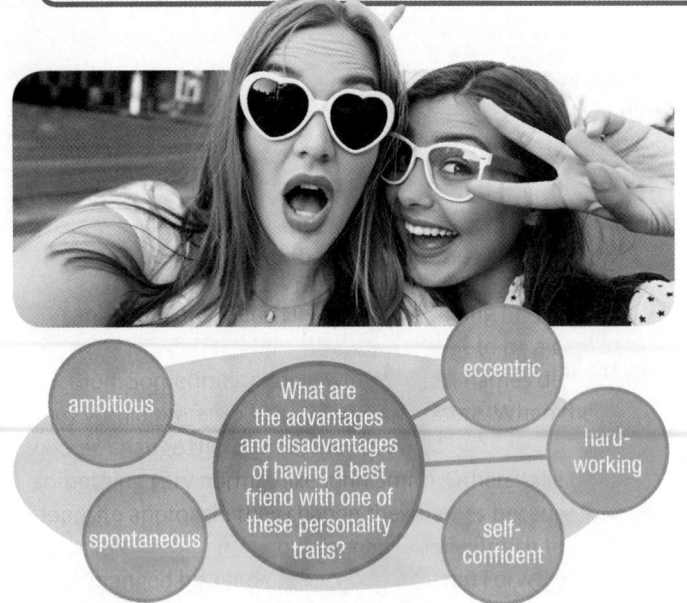

**What are the advantages and disadvantages of having a best friend with one of these personality traits?**
- ambitious
- eccentric
- hard-working
- spontaneous
- self-confident

**1** 🎧 **1.16** Read the task and listen to two students doing the task. Which qualities do they talk about? In general, do they find the quality more positive (+) or more negative (–)?

| Quality | more + or –? |
|---------|--------------|
|         |              |
|         |              |
|         |              |

**Speaking Strategy (1)**
In the discussion phase of a collaborative task, avoid repeating the words in the question. For example, when you are asked to discuss advantages and disadvantages, use synonyms for these words:

*It's a plus for me having a friend to study with.*

*I find it difficult to stay focused when I study with a friend, so for me, it's a minus.*

**2** Read the Speaking Strategy. Then choose the best word below to replace *advantage(s) / disadvantage(s)*.

benefits bonus downside drawback plus pros

1 Weighing up the advantages and the cons.
2 The disadvantage of … is … (while the upside could be …)
3 There are many other advantages to the plan.
4 For me, it's a(n) advantage (but for others it may be a minus).
5 One major disadvantage is …
6 The added advantage of … would be …

**3** 🎧 **1.16** Listen again and tick (✓) the phrases you hear.

Which personality trait would affect a friendship the most?

**4** 🎧 **1.17** Read the question above and listen to the same students doing the second part of the task. Which quality do they choose? Why?

**Speaking Strategy (2)**
When you are discussing the different options in this task, you and your partner may not share the same opinions. In this case, you should negotiate to try to reach an agreement. You can:
**a** disagree politely and justify your opinion.
**b** ask for a reaction to the new justification.
**c** concede a point.
**d** conclude the discussion.

**5** Read the Speaking Strategy. Match phrases 1–12 with categories a–d in the Strategy.

1 Would you be happier if … _____
2 I can't help thinking that … _____
3 Let's wrap this up, shall we? _____
4 Yes, I suppose you're right. _____
5 Would you go along with that? _____
6 That's one way of looking at it, I suppose, but … _____
7 Fair enough. I can accept that. _____
8 So, have we come to a decision? _____
9 Maybe, but I just wonder if … _____
10 Good point. I hadn't thought of that. _____
11 Which one are we going for, then? _____
12 You wouldn't disagree with that, would you? _____

**6** 🎧 **1.17** Listen again and tick (✓) the phrases you hear.

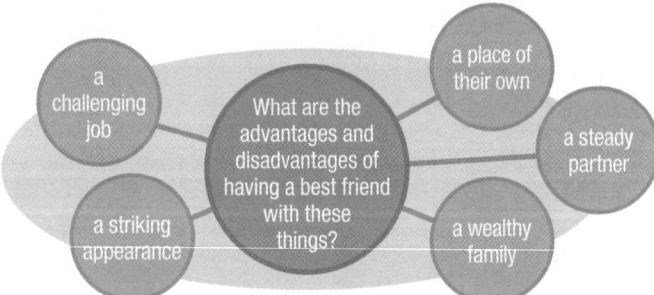

**What are the advantages and disadvantages of having a best friend with these things?**
- a challenging job
- a place of their own
- a steady partner
- a striking appearance
- a wealthy family

**7** Look at the task. Make notes about the advantages and disadvantages of each option.

| option | advantage | disadvantage |
|--------|-----------|--------------|
|        |           |              |
|        |           |              |
|        |           |              |
|        |           |              |
|        |           |              |

Which characteristic would affect the friendship the most?

**8** Read the question above. Make a note of your choice and your reasons.

**9** Now do the task using your notes from exercises 7 and 8.

You and your classmates feel that your school does not offer sufficient opportunities for students to practise the foreign language they are studying. Write a proposal to the head teacher, describing what opportunities currently exist, suggesting further opportunities for practising the language and saying how your suggestions might benefit the rest of the school community.

1 Read the task and the proposal below. How many opportunities to practise a foreign language does the writer suggest?

# Speak up!

### Introduction

This proposal is intended to outline the possibilities students have to speak their chosen foreign language, make some recommendations as to how the situation could be improved and explain how the improvements might be good for the whole school.

### Current situation

Comments made during focus groups show that students do not feel confident about speaking the foreign language they are learning. They mentioned that the only chance they had to practise was when answering their teachers' questions in class.

### Key needs to be addressed

Students learning a foreign language should have the opportunity to listen to and repeat new vocabulary to perfect their pronunciation. It would also help if they could practise with a native speaker. What would motivate them even more, however, is the opportunity to interact with foreign students of their own age.

### Recommendations

I would like to suggest the following:

- Some language classes should be held in the IT department so that students can use computer software to improve their pronunciation.
- At least one native speaker should be employed in our school to help students with speaking.
- The school should start an exchange programme to give students the opportunity of speaking a foreign language with people of their own age. This would benefit the whole school as it would give all the students a chance to learn about another culture. Also, the teachers could refresh their own knowledge of the language by travelling once a year to the country concerned.

If these recommendations are carried out, the integration of new students is bound to be smoother.

2 Put the phrases in the correct group.

Following a survey of ... it was revealed that ...
I recommend that ...   There ought to be ...
If these recommendations are carried out ...
In this proposal, I will present ...

**Stating the purpose**

1 The main aim of this proposal is to ...
2 This proposal is intended to ...
3 _____

**Background information**

4 Comments made during focus groups show that ...
5 Feedback from ... suggests that ...
6 _____

**Making recommendations and suggestions**

7 _____
8 _____
9 ... *need / should* + passive infinitive

**Final recommendation**

10 Unless these ideas are implemented, it is unlikely ...
11 The results of ... suggest that ... would be the best option.
12 _____

3 Which of the phrases in exercise 2 are in the proposal?

> **Writing Strategy**
>
> A proposal follows a clear structure. It has a title and four paragraphs each with a sub-heading.
>
> **Paragraph 1:** states the purpose of the proposal.
> **Paragraph 2:** gives background information.
> **Paragraph 3:** describes the existing problems.
> **Paragraph 4:** suggests improvements to be made.

4 Read the Writing Strategy and the task. Make notes under the headings: Current opportunities, Further opportunities and Benefits to the wider school community.

You and your classmates feel that your school does not offer sufficient opportunities for students to do sport. Write a proposal to the head teacher, describing what opportunities currently exist for students, suggesting further opportunities for them to do sport and saying how your suggestions might benefit the rest of the school community.

5 Write your proposal (220–260 words) using your notes from exercise 4.

> **CHECK YOUR WORK**
>
> **Have you ...**
>
> ☐ followed the structure in the Writing Strategy?
> ☐ included phrases for writing proposals?
> ☐ checked the spelling and grammar?

**3**

# Review Unit 3

## Vocabulary

**1 Complete the text with the words below.**

bonded   drift   fall   inseparable   keep going   stay in touch
struck   wreck

It's easy to $^1$_____ out with friends. Stupid arguments can $^2$_____ a good friendship, and people who were once $^3$_____ can develop different interests and social circles, and slowly $^4$_____ apart. If people move to different areas and don't regularly $^5$_____ with each other, then it can be hard to maintain a friendship. In short, friendship dies if some of the reasons why you $^6$_____ up the friendship in the first place go away. A team at an Ohio university who interviewed hundreds of people found three things that make the difference between a passing acquaintance and a friendship that will $^7$_____ for life. According to the study, a life-long friend is someone that you can always talk to, depend on and enjoy being with. If you can describe your friend in these terms then the chances are that you have $^8$_____ with that person for life.

Mark:  / 8

**2 Replace the underlined words with the feelings below. There are two extra words.**

aggrieved   ecstatic   gobsmacked   gutted   impervious
perturbed   privileged   unconcerned

1 I feel quite upset that Harry lied to me. _____
2 We were totally amazed when we heard the news. It was hard to believe at first. _____
3 Mandy was desperately upset when Gary broke up with her. _____
4 I feel very fortunate to be friends with a great musician, who has helped to kick-start my career. _____
5 Sally was overjoyed when she won the gold medal.
   _____
6 Josh seemed to be deaf to the criticism. _____

Mark:  / 6

**3 Complete the idioms in the mini-dialogues.**

**Leo** Kelly and Simon are so different. They're like
$^1$_____, but they're great friends. They get on like a $^2$_____.

**Ali** Yes, they $^3$_____ a long way – they've known each other since primary school.

**Jen** You and my new boyfriend didn't really
$^4$_____ off very well, did you?

**Sam** I just think we aren't on the same
$^5$_____ really.

**Jen** No, probably not. I don't think you'd see
$^6$_____ on a lot of issues.

Mark:  / 6

## Word skills

**4 Complete the sentences. Write 1–3 words.**

1 The fire spread quickly because – after weeks without rain – the forest was as dry _____.
2 All relationships have their up and downs. It's never always plain _____.
3 You need to put on some weight, Keira. You're as light _____.
4 The company had a _____ ride for a year or two, and nearly went out of business. But now it's OK.
5 Detectives tried to scare Beth into talking. But she sat there as cool _____ and refused to speak.
6 Athletes have their running shoes specially made for their feet, so they fit _____.
7 I'm not surprised the band broke up after all the arguments they had. They used to fight like _____.

Mark:  / 7

**5 Complete the emphatic adjectives in the sentences.**

1 Tom gave up his summer job at a busy restaurant because he couldn't cope with the f_____ pace of work.
2 It was s_____ that the climber fell 80 metres and somehow survived.
3 The beauty of the place was c_____ – it took my breath away.
4 Safety rules at the factory must be very r_____ to protect people. There can't be any flexibility.
5 The deer had no way to escape the hungry lions. It was d_____.
6 Walking right across Antarctica was a d_____ task, but they managed to reach the South Pole on foot.

Mark:  / 6

**6 Choose the correct words to complete the sentences.**

1 Weighing up the **pros and cons / drawbacks and benefits**, I'd say that this is the best thing to do.
2 The advantages of this proposal clearly **benefit / outweigh** the disadvantages.
3 Let's **wrap / end** this discussion up, shall we?
4 Have we **reached / got to** a decision?
5 The main **recommend / purpose** of this proposal is to improve recycling at school.
6 When developing its new product, the company held **focus / survey** groups with ordinary consumers.
7 Your idea has a lot of advantages, but the main **benefit / drawback** is the high cost.
8 If the recommendations in this proposal are **revealed / implemented**, we think they will benefit all students.

Mark:  / 8

## Grammar

7 Report the sentences using the past simple of the verbs in brackets. If more than one option is possible, use the more formal option.

1 'I haven't done anything wrong.' (deny)
Jane _____.

2 'I'm sorry that I'm late.' (apologise for)
Rob _____.

3 'Yes, I have changed my mind.' (confess)
The minister _____.

4 'The team should practise more.' (suggest)
Chloe _____.

5 'I won't help the boys tidy up after their party.' (refuse)
Gary _____.

6 'Don't go into that building.' (order / them)
The policeman _____.

7 'To be honest, I've lied to you.' (admit / us)
Lucy _____.

8 'It's your fault that we missed the film, Rick.' (blame / Rick)
Mel _____.

Mark: ____ / 8

8 Choose the correct words to complete the text.

In 2015, husband and wife Joseph and Jenny Carrier robbed five banks in five US states in just one month. Jenny comes from Quincy, Massachusetts, [1]**so / as** does her husband, and in October they began what would become a series of [2]**more and more / more than** daring robberies, committed up and down the East Coast. Despite the fact that they drove a known car, stolen from Jenny's former workplace, it was harder to track down the couple [3]**than you would / like you** think – perhaps because they moved around so much.

The [4]**longest / longer** the robberies went on, [5]**more than / the more** the media began to compare the Carriers to that famous 1920s outlaw couple, Bonnie and Clyde. The Carrier's exploits quickly became [6]**by far / as much as** the most reported crime story of the year. In the end, of course, [7]**as / like** Bonnie and Clyde, their luck ran out. The fugitive couple were finally captured after a high-speed police chase on the outskirts of Philadelphia. Joseph could now be in prison for up to 20 years, [8]**as could / more like** Jenny.

Mark: ____ / 8

## Use of English

9 Complete the text with one word in each gap.

It's quite hard to [1]_____ track of the Zhou brothers' astounding creative output, which ranges from huge paintings and innovative sculptures to stunning live art performances. The multi-talented brothers have become two of the art world's biggest celebrities.

ShanZou and DaHuang Zhou were born in the 1950s and studied art in Shanghai and Beijing. The brothers produced their first work together, *The Wave*, in 1973. Critics loved it, and suggested [2]_____ the Zhou brothers were rising talents to watch. Although working together probably had its pros and [3]_____, the benefits have far outweighed any disadvantages. And the [4]_____ the brothers worked and exhibited together, the more daring and innovative their art became. By the mid-eighties they were national heroes in China. But then they took by [5]_____ the biggest risk of their careers – they moved to the USA, where nobody knew them or their art.

Finding their feet in America proved to be easier than the brothers [6]_____ feared. They soon began to receive awards and critical acclaim, and they also got acquainted [7]_____ many American artists, celebrities and politicians. Today, the brothers live and work in Chicago and Beijing. They are inseparable, and they claim to have never seriously fallen [8]_____.

Mark: ____ / 8

Total: ____ / 65

## I can ...

Read the statements. Think about your progress and tick (✓) one of the boxes.

★ = I need more practice.          ★★★ = No problem!

★★ = I sometimes find this difficult.

| | ★ | ★★ | ★★★ |
|---|---|---|---|
| I can talk about different relationships. | | | |
| I can report direct speech in a variety of ways. | | | |
| I can understand and react to a radio programme. | | | |
| I can compare partners-in-crime from the past. | | | |
| I can use metaphors and similes to make comparisons. | | | |
| I can understand and react to an article. | | | |
| I can maintain the interaction in a collaborative task and reach an agreement. | | | |
| I can write a proposal. | | | |

**Vocabulary**

**A** **Changing world**
*I can talk about global issues.*

**1 Complete the sentences with the words below.**

armed conflicts   climate change   epidemics   famine
global capitalism   life expectancy   poverty   refugees

1 Most scientists attribute the rising number of violent storms to _____.
2 In 2015, scientists battled to control the spread of two global _____, Ebola and Zika.
3 In the UK, average _____ is 81.
4 Although _____ has made some countries richer, widespread inequality remains.
5 The number of _____ has fallen in recent years, but more people are killed in them.
6 Education offers these children a chance to escape the _____ they were born into.
7 When violence erupted, thousands of _____ were forced to flee.
8 In this region, another year without rain has made _____ almost inevitable.

**2 Circle the word which has a completely different meaning from the other three.**

1 tumble   nose-dive   crash   mushroom
2 outpace   plateau   surpass   outstrip
3 level off   fluctuate   plateau   flatline
4 surge   rocket   mushroom   plunge

**3 Circle the word which makes better sense in these verb phrases.**

1 gradually **evolve** / **revise**
2 make a tiny **adjustment** / **conversion**
3 completely **adjust** / **transform**
4 **adapt** / **vary** widely
5 undergo genetic **amendments** / **mutations**
6 make an **accidental** / **ingenious** modification

**4** 🎧 **1.18** **Listen to six speakers. Complete each summary with the correct form of the verb phrases from exercise 3.**

1 Speaker 1 says that reactions to his invention have _____ but he is still hopeful.
2 Speaker 2 says that the village she lives in is _____ into a tourist resort.
3 Speaker 3 says that the new head teacher has _____ his school.
4 Speaker 4 says that she has saved a lot of money by _____ to the heating in her home.
5 Speaker 5 says that he has _____ to his son's wheelchair.
6 Speaker 6 says that, over millions of years, this cave-dwelling fish _____ which led to its loss of sight.

**5 USE OF ENGLISH Choose the correct words (a–d) to complete the text.**

**IN 2000**, the United Nations set out some ambitious goals which they hoped the world would achieve over the next few decades. One of these was that the number of people living in poverty in the developing world should [1]_____ from 43% to 21% by 2015 – a 50% reduction. In fact, the number [2]_____ so quickly that this target was met in 2010. Having [3]_____ everyone's expectations, the United Nations has now [4]_____ its goal. Its new aim is to eradicate world poverty completely by 2030. This is certainly very ambitious, but many experts believe it is achievable. Over the past three decades, economic growth has been the main driving force behind the reduction in poverty. In China, for example, poverty rates have [5]_____ from 84% to 10% since the 1980s. Provided growth does not [6]_____, the number of people living in poverty worldwide should continue to [7]_____. However, equality is also an important factor. As economies grow, governments must make sure that the poorest in society do not [8]_____ the rest.

| | | | |
|---|---|---|---|
| 1 a soar | b overtake | c plateau | d plummet |
| 2 a outpaced | b plunged | c rocketed | d mounted |
| 3 a mushroomed | b surpassed | c crashed | d levelled off |
| 4 a evolved | b varied | c converted | d revised |
| 5 a plateaued | b tumbled | c mounted | d soared |
| 6 a flatline | b overtake | c surpass | d escalate |
| 7 a dwindle | b outstrip | c mushroom | d rocket |
| 8 a fluctuate | b level off | c crash | d lag behind |

# Compound future tenses

*I can use compound future tenses for predictions and suppositions.*

**1** Choose the correct compound future tense in these sentences.

1 At the end of this month, I'll **be / have been** looking for a job for exactly one year.
2 By the time my brother leaves school, I'll **have finished / have been finishing** university.
3 In fifty years, nobody will **be using / have been using** cash any longer.
4 If Chelsea win the final, how many times will they **have won / be winning** the FA Cup?
5 You can take my bike in the morning. I won't **be using / have used** it tomorrow.
6 Sam's train will **be arriving / have been arriving** at 4 p.m.; let's meet him at the station.
7 There won't be any food left if you arrive at 9 p.m. – we'll **be eating / have eaten** it all by then.
8 I'll be tired when I reach the hotel, as I'll **have been travelling / be travelling** since 5 a.m.

**2** Read about the 'eco village'. Then use the prompts to write sentences in the future perfect simple or continuous or the future continuous.

## ECO VILLAGE

○ **2028**
Designs finalised
○ **2030**
Building work starts
○ **2035**
Half the homes finished
○ **2036**
First residents arrive
○ **2040**
All homes finished

1 (2029 / start building work)
*In 2029, they won't have started the building work.*
2 (2033 / build / three years)
_____
_____
3 (2036 / half the homes / be finished)
_____
_____
4 (2036 / first residents / arrive)
_____
_____
5 (2038 / the whole village / be built / yet)
_____
_____
6 (2042 / the project / be complete)
_____
_____

**3** **USE OF ENGLISH** Complete the second sentence so that it means the same as the first. Include a compound future tense.

1 I expect my brother has arrived in Spain by now.
My brother _____ in Spain by now.
2 I don't imagine Luke is enjoying the camping trip.
Luke _____ the camping trip.
3 I doubt they've been able to find the thieves.
They _____ the thieves.
4 I expect all the students have been sent home.
All the students _____ home.
5 I imagine she's studying hard for her exams.
She _____ her exams.
6 I don't expect this bike has been used much.
This bike _____ much.

**4** Complete the dialogue. Use the future continuous, future perfect simple or future perfect continuous of the verbs in brackets. Include the adverbs, where given.

**Sarah** I can't believe Owen missed the train. Now we
¹_____ (spend) the night here in Milan while he's still stuck in Bergamo.

**Ted** It doesn't matter. He can get a train in the morning. We ²_____ (definitely / not leave) for the airport until the afternoon.

**Sarah** He was in the café next to the station. What happened? Did he forget the time?

**Ted** I guess so. He ³_____ (most likely / read) his book. You know what he's like …

**Sarah** Now he's all alone.

**Ted** I'm sure he's fine. He ⁴_____ (no doubt / find) a hostel in Bergamo by now.

**Sarah** But why isn't he replying to my messages?

**Ted** Oh, he ⁵_____ (turn off) his phone by now. He always turns it off when he goes to bed.

**Sarah** That's so annoying. Now I ⁶_____ (probably / worry) about him all night.

**Ted** Relax! Owen ⁷_____ (not worry); he ⁸_____ (sleep) peacefully!

# Change.org

*I can infer information which is implied rather than overtly stated.*

**Revision:** Student's Book page 45

**Listening Strategy**

Sometimes information can be implied rather than clearly stated. For example, a subsequent contrast or concession can make the speaker's opinion clear:

*We spent the morning shopping for souvenirs, but then we had a relaxing afternoon at the beach.* (Implication: the morning was not relaxing.)

**1** 🎧 **1.19** **Read the Listening Strategy. Then listen to six speakers and decide which of the two options (a or b) is being implied.**

**1** Speaker 1 implies that the campsite they stayed at last month
   **a** did not have very good facilities.
   **b** was not near the sea.

**2** Speaker 2 implies that her visit to Hyde Park yesterday
   **a** was not the first time she has been there.
   **b** was not as enjoyable as her first visit.

**3** Speaker 3 implies that his Thai meal
   **a** was nicer than he'd expected.
   **b** was spicier than he'd expected.

**4** Speaker 4 implies that her attitude to running
   **a** has changed since meeting her husband.
   **b** is more negative than her husband's.

**5** Speaker 5 implies that he doesn't usually
   **a** go to bed early.
   **b** watch TV in the evenings.

**6** Speaker 6 implies that she would prefer not to
   **a** stay very late at Misha's party.
   **b** walk home after Misha's party.

**2 Circle the correct verb in these phrases.**

**1** **put** / **reduce** taxes so that …
**2** **bring** / **reverse** the trend towards …
**3** **bring** / **initiate** a project to …
**4** **bring** / **initiate** in legislation …
**5** **cut** / **reverse** the red tape surrounding …
**6** **make** / **provide** funding for …
**7** **make** / **raise** it illegal for people to …
**8** **provide** / **put** a stop to …

**3 Read the text. Complete the gaps with four of the phrases from exercise 2.**

Founded in July 2015, the UK Parliament petitions website allows people to create petitions which may, if enough signatures are collected, be debated in Parliament. One successful petition persuaded the government to ¹_____ related to sugar levels in processed food and drinks. But most petitions fail – like the one which wanted the government to ²_____ every family in the UK to buy a piano, or another which aimed to ³_____ talk in a 'quiet' carriage on trains. Some are rejected before they are even published, because they relate to personal rather than national issues. For example, one petition demanded direct flights from Birmingham Airport to Sibiu in Romania, because 'we're going there next year'. Another e-petition wanted to ⁴_____ e-petitions completely, on the grounds that too many of them were not serious.

**4** 🎧 **1.20** **Listen to five people talking about e-petitions. Which speakers started their own petition?**

_____

**5** 🎧 **1.20** **Listen again. For questions 1 and 2, choose from the list (A–H). There are three extra sentences. Write your answers below.**

**1** What is the aim of the petition each speaker refers to?
   **A** to improve the local transport provision
   **B** to save an important building
   **C** to allow year-round access to a communal facility
   **D** to ban dangerous substances used in buildings
   **E** to force dog-owners to act responsibly
   **F** to protect a wild animal
   **G** to increase the number of people with internet access
   **H** to prevent the building of a new facility

| Speaker | 1 | 2 | 3 | 4 | 5 |
|---------|---|---|---|---|---|
|         |   |   |   |   |   |

**2** How does each speaker explain the failure of the petition to attract many signatures?
   **A** a lack of concern for 20th-century architecture
   **B** a prejudice against people who can't drive
   **C** a lack of interest beyond the local community
   **D** the misleading wording of the petition
   **E** the selfish nature of the petition
   **F** people's aversion to the animal concerned
   **G** the fact that the petition was not publicised
   **H** people's concerns about wasting energy

| Speaker | 1 | 2 | 3 | 4 | 5 |
|---------|---|---|---|---|---|
|         |   |   |   |   |   |

# Quantity
*I can use articles and quantifiers correctly.*

**1 Complete the sentences with *some, any* or *no*.**

1 Scientists have struggled to find _____ evidence that this type of particle even exists.
2 _____ experts believe hypnosis is effective, but others dispute this.
3 Nobody has _____ reason to doubt the results of the study.
4 The match did not take place because _____ suitable venue was available.
5 This essay is very good, considering you hardly spent _____ time on it!
6 _____ university would offer you a place if you failed all of your exams.

**2 Complete the second sentence so that it means the same as the first. Use the quantifiers below.**

all  both  either  every  many  neither  no  none
very few

1 Nearly all of the applicants were women.
_____ of the applicants were men.
2 Neither of his parents has a job.
_____ of his parents are unemployed.
3 We found both of the hotels unsatisfactory.
We didn't find _____ of the hotels satisfactory.
4 Both of his parents were out last night.
_____ of his parents was at home last night.
5 There aren't any good reasons to stay here.
There are _____ good reasons to stay here.
6 He sends birthday cards to each of his cousins.
He sends birthday cards to _____ cousin.
7 He spent the whole holiday staring at his phone!
He spent _____ holiday staring at his phone!
8 A large number of his projects have failed.
_____ of his projects have failed.
9 They didn't publish any of his poems during his lifetime.
_____ of his poems was published during his lifetime.

**3 Circle all of the quantifiers that can go with these nouns.**

1 **a good deal of / each / lots of / no** messages
2 **a little / much / several / some** people
3 **each / either / much / no** classroom
4 **a large amount of / each / less / a little / lots of** confidence
5 **a lot of / half / any / many** bread
6 **every / both / no / little** emails
7 **none of / either / a few / the whole** film
8 **loads of / little / many / a large number of** time
9 **a great deal of / many / half of / no** work
10 **few / each / all of the / several** lawyers

**4 Complete the text with the correct option, a or b.**

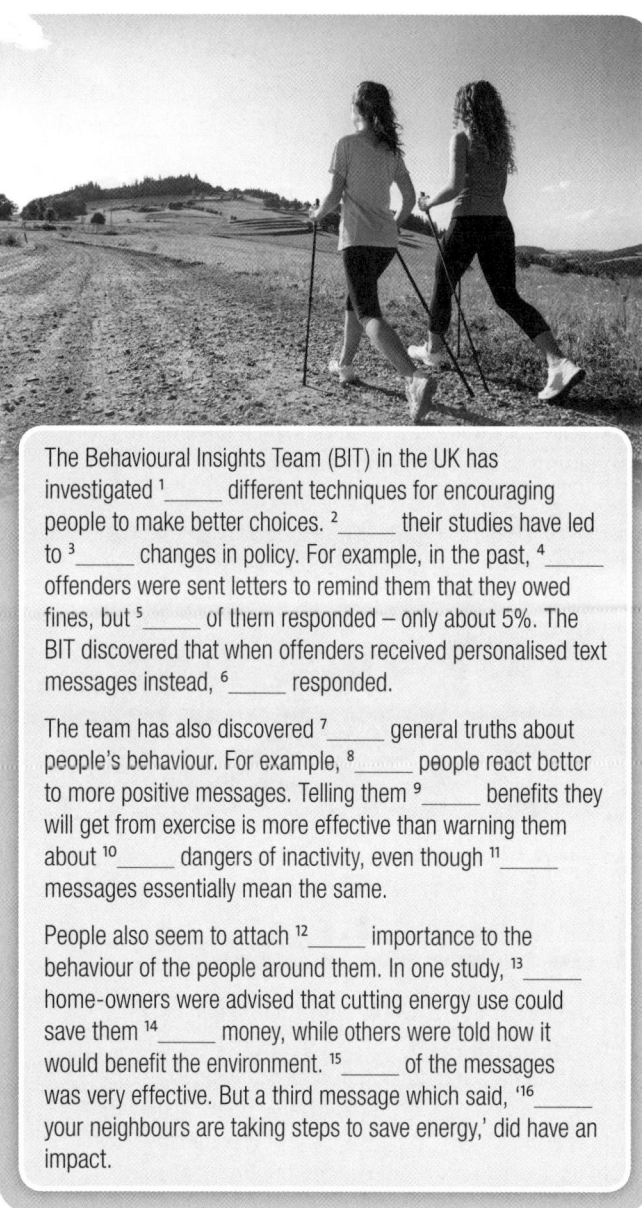

The Behavioural Insights Team (BIT) in the UK has investigated ¹_____ different techniques for encouraging people to make better choices. ²_____ their studies have led to ³_____ changes in policy. For example, in the past, ⁴_____ offenders were sent letters to remind them that they owed fines, but ⁵_____ of them responded – only about 5%. The BIT discovered that when offenders received personalised text messages instead, ⁶_____ responded.

The team has also discovered ⁷_____ general truths about people's behaviour. For example, ⁸_____ people react better to more positive messages. Telling them ⁹_____ benefits they will get from exercise is more effective than warning them about ¹⁰_____ dangers of inactivity, even though ¹¹_____ messages essentially mean the same.

People also seem to attach ¹²_____ importance to the behaviour of the people around them. In one study, ¹³_____ home-owners were advised that cutting energy use could save them ¹⁴_____ money, while others were told how it would benefit the environment. ¹⁵_____ of the messages was very effective. But a third message which said, '¹⁶_____ your neighbours are taking steps to save energy,' did have an impact.

| | | | |
|---|---|---|---|
| 1 | a a large amount of | b a large number of |
| 2 | a Any of | b Some of |
| 3 | a several | b several of the |
| 4 | a all | b every |
| 5 | a a few | b few |
| 6 | a a third of them | b third of them |
| 7 | a a few | b few |
| 8 | a most | b most of the |
| 9 | a all of the | b the whole |
| 10 | a all | b all the |
| 11 | a both | b either |
| 12 | a a great deal of | b a large number of |
| 13 | a some | b some of the |
| 14 | a a large amount of | b much |
| 15 | a Neither | b None |
| 16 | a Most | b Most of |

**Word Skills**

# Binomial pairs
*I can use a two-part set phrase correctly.*

**1** Complete the binomial expressions with the words below.

aches born by hard here high ins make more pick short sooner thick touch trial wear

1 _____ and large
2 _____ and sweet
3 _____ and go
4 _____ and fast
5 _____ or break
6 _____ and bred
7 _____ and error
8 _____ and outs
9 _____ and choose
10 _____ and dry
11 _____ and thin
12 _____ and tear
13 _____ and there
14 _____ or less
15 _____ and pains
16 _____ or later

**2** Complete the text with nine of the expressions from exercise 1. Choose expressions which have a similar meaning to the words in brackets.

MONTGOMERY'S **DOUBLE**

**THE YEAR WAS 1944.** World War II had been raging for five years. ¹_____ (at some point) it had to end, but the outcome was still ²_____ (uncertain). The British were preparing a ³_____ (crucial) invasion of northern France, but wanted the Germans to believe they were planning to invade from the south instead. Their plan to deceive the Germans involved an Australian-born soldier called ME Clifton James, who looked ⁴_____ (almost) identical to Bernard Montgomery, one of the most senior officers in the British Army. James spent a few days with Montgomery learning the ⁵_____ (details) of his behaviour. He then travelled to Algeria, where, acting as Montgomery, he toured the region, appearing ⁶_____ (in various places) with senior officers. A few days later, the Allied invasion of northern France began. ⁷_____ (in general), the mission was a success, in that nobody guessed James was an impostor. However, it seems that James's starring role in the war was ⁸_____ (brief). When the invasion began, he was apparently left ⁹_____ (abandoned) in an Algerian hotel and never received the credit he deserved.

**3** Complete the sentences with the expressions below.

rant and rave dos and don'ts peace and quiet through and through neat and tidy fair and square sick and tired live and learn

1 My grandfather has a tendency to _____ whenever somebody mentions the local council.
2 I'm _____ of finding litter in our garden.
3 I didn't realise you could reserve seats on this train. Oh well, you _____.
4 Unlike her brother, Milly always keeps her bedroom _____.
5 You can't complain – I won, _____.
6 He may live in Spain but he's Irish _____.
7 Before we were allowed into the cave, we had to read a list of _____.
8 After a week in New York, I'm ready for some _____ in the mountains.

**4** What part of speech are the expressions from exercise 3: noun, verb, adjective or adverb? There are two of each part of speech.

| | noun | verb | adjective | adverb |
|---|---|---|---|---|
| 1 rant and rave | | | | |
| 2 dos and don'ts | | | | |
| 3 peace and quiet | | | | |
| 4 through and through | | | | |
| 5 neat and tidy | | | | |
| 6 fair and square | | | | |
| 7 sick and tired | | | | |
| 8 live and learn | | | | |

**VOCAB BOOST!**

When you come across new binomial expressions, write them as part of a sentence, not on their own. It is easier to understand and learn these phrases in context. Make sure the sentences help to show the meaning of the phrases.

*Mistakes are **part and parcel** of learning languages.*

*We used some old bricks to make a **rough and ready** barbecue.*

**5** Read the *Vocab Boost!* box. Then write sentences that include the expressions below.

cut and dried hit and miss safe and sound ups and downs

1 _____
2 _____
3 _____
4 _____

**Reading**

# How time changes us

*I can understand a text about how personality changes over time.*

**Revision:** Student's Book page 48

**1** Read the text. Find words in the text which match the definitions below.

a believe without proof

b weaken

c affect, influence

d likely to show or possess

e receive advantage, profit, improve

f be permanent and not change

**Reading Strategy**

Remember that multiple-choice questions about a text:

- always follow the order of the text.
- sometimes specify what part of the text they refer to by mentioning a paragraph.
- may relate to the overall meaning of the text rather than to a specific part. (If so, this will be the final question.)

**2** Read the Reading Strategy. Then look at questions 1–5. Which questions refer to a specific paragraph? Which question refers to the text as a whole?

# Your true self

**①** Most of us consider our personality to be an integral and unchanging part of who we are, and for decades psychologists have more or less assumed that our main personality traits are fixed by the age of 30. But now mounting evidence is undermining that notion; personality is far more mutable than we thought. That may be a little unsettling, but it's also good news for the almost 90% of us who wish our personalities were at least a little different.

**②** There's no doubt that personality is partly genetic, but experiences in childhood also shape our personalities. Research shows that young children become more extroverted and work harder when surrounded by other kids with these traits. Parental behaviour has an impact, too. Jerome Kagan at Harvard University has found that if parents encourage timid infants to be sociable and bold, they grow up to be less shy and fearful.

**③** Genes and environment interact in complex ways to shape our personality, and this process doesn't stop when we reach adulthood. It's becoming clear that major life events can have long-lasting impacts on personality at any age. For example, going through a divorce makes women more extroverted and more open to experience, while men become less conscientious, according to one US study.

**④** Becoming unemployed can have a dramatic effect on well-being. 'It's probably the life event that has the biggest impact,' says Christopher Boyce at the University of Stirling, UK. And he has found that the impact on personality is twice as big, tending to

**3** Read the text. Choose the correct option (a–d).

**1** The idea that our personality does not change much after the age of 30 is one which

a psychologists have always doubted.

b most people find uncomfortable.

c has been undermined by advances in genetics.

d is not supported by the results of research.

**2** According to the study mentioned in paragraph 3, the experience of getting divorced tends to

a affect men and women differently.

b have a bigger effect than genetics.

c make people generally more outgoing.

d affect people differently depending on their age.

**3** The effect on your personality of losing your job is

a less dramatic than moving house.

b as profound as its effect on your well-being.

c the same as the effect of moving to New York.

d far bigger than its effect on your well-being.

**4** The research in paragraph 5 suggests that your personality

a becomes more unstable as you get older.

b is different at different points in your life.

c is more affected by environment when you are young.

d only becomes fixed when you reach your seventies.

**5** Overall, the main point of the text is that

a you cannot escape the personality that you are genetically destined to have.

b scientists still know very little about how our personalities are formed.

c your personality can change during adulthood and you may be able to affect the process.

d people are becoming generally more neurotic than they used to be.

make people less conscientious and less agreeable. Moving to a new town or country might influence your personality too – people living in New York tend to be highly neurotic, for example, while Londoners score low on agreeableness.

**⑤** The extent to which environmental factors shape our characters over a lifetime is remarkable. In work published last year, psychologist Wendy Johnson and her colleagues at the University of Edinburgh compared results from personality tests taken by people when they were aged 14 and again at 77. 'We couldn't find any evidence for stability in individual personality characteristics,' she says.

**⑥** There is also growing evidence that we can actively shape our own personality – and would benefit from doing so. Psychologists continue to debate the extent to which personality is plastic in adulthood, but there is now no doubt that it can and does change. And that's good news for all of us. Knowing that you are not 'set' by 30 is empowering. You can think: 'I'm not stuck with who I am. I can change,' says Boyce.

# Discussion

*I can discuss a topic and express opinions.*

**1** Circle the adjective which has a different meaning from the other two.

1 Intelligent robots will cause **dramatic / marginal / momentous** changes in society.

2 Robots will lead to a **drastic / marked / minimal** reduction in people's fitness.

3 For disabled people who want to live independently, robots will bring about a **cosmetic / profound / radical** improvement.

4 Robots would make a **radical / subtle / sweeping** difference to how much time people have for leisure activities.

5 There is only a **marginal / minimal / fundamental** risk that robots will cause accidents in the home.

**2** Match the beginnings and endings of the key phrases for acknowledging a point.

1 That's a fair ... _____
2 True, but what it really ... _____
3 Maybe so, but what it really boils ... _____
4 Perhaps, although in ... _____
5 I see what you mean, but at ... _____
6 That may be the case, but ... _____

a my view ...
b comes down to is ...
c the end of the day ...
d point, but I still think ...
e for me, it's more about ...
f down to is ...

**3** 🎧 **1.21** Listen to two students and answer the questions.

1 Which opinion from exercise 1 (1–5) does each student express?
girl: _____ boy: _____

2 Which phrases from exercise 2 (1–6) do the students use?
girl: _____ boy: _____

**4** 🎧 **1.21** Read the Speaking Strategy. Then listen again and complete the rhetorical questions used by the students. Write the implied answers.

1 But *who wants to* clean toilets?
*Nobody.*

2 I mean, _____ pets in the house?
_____

3 But _____ to go wrong?
_____

4 How _____ the future?
_____

### Speaking Strategy

When you are expressing opinions, you can use rhetorical questions to emphasise your points. Remember:

- rhetorical questions do not require answers, but you can sometimes add an answer in order to emphasise your view. If you do not give an answer, it must be clear what answer you have in mind:
  *What have you done to help today? (Nothing!)*
  *Would you let a child watch that video? (Of course not!)*
  *How much time do people waste on the internet? (Far too much!)*
- do not over-use rhetorical questions.

**5** Read the task and the questions. Then make notes.

How will intelligent robots affect what jobs people can do? Will the effect be positive or negative?

What types of jobs will robots be able to do?
_____
_____

Will robots make it harder for some people to find work? Why / Why not?
_____
_____

Are there certain jobs that nobody wants to do? Will robots be able to do them?
_____
_____

Are there some jobs that robots will never be able to do, in your opinion? What are they? Why won't robots be able to do them?
_____
_____

Would it be dangerous to make robots that are more intelligent than humans? Why / Why not?
_____
_____

**6** Now do the task using your notes from exercise 5.

# 4H

## Letter to an editor

*I can write a letter about a local improvement scheme.*

**1** Read the task and letter below. In which paragraph (1–5) does the writer:

**a** mention a point in favour of the proposal? _____

**b** sum up their opinion? _____

**c** explain the reason for writing the letter? _____

**d** talk about leisure activities? _____

**e** mention environmental concerns? _____

You have read about plans to redevelop an area of woodland near your home as a large housing estate. Write a letter to the editor of a magazine explaining your objections to this proposal.

To the editor,

1  After reading in your magazine about the proposal to build 1,500 new homes on a site which is currently woodland, I felt compelled to write in order to express my opposition to the scheme. Not only is the proposal unnecessary, but it would also prove very unpopular with the local community, I reckon.

2  I do recognise that there is a housing shortage in this part of the country and that a degree of development is inevitable. But important as new homes are, I firmly believe that there are loads of sites in this area which would be better suited to redevelopment.

3  The proposed site is a valuable piece of woodland which is extremely popular with off-road cyclists and dog-walkers. At no point have local people had the opportunity to express how much they appreciate this communal facility. It is particularly important to those in the area who are a bit short of money to spend on leisure pursuits.

4  I am also pretty concerned about the impact which the proposed development would have on the environment. Cutting down so many trees to make way for housing is sure to have a negative impact both on wildlife and on air quality. Only by protecting our woodlands can we ensure a healthy and attractive environment for generations to come.

5  To sum up, I feel that this proposal is entirely unsuitable, and the sooner it is abandoned the better. In no way does it meet the needs of the local community, nor is it sensitive to the local environment. In short, it is rubbish.

**Writing Strategy**

In a formal letter, in addition to avoiding inappropriately colloquial language, you should:

- avoid using rhetorical questions.
- use inversion to add emphasis: *Only rarely have they allowed the public to visit.*
- include passive forms to make the style more impersonal.
- emphasise your opinions using formal expressions like *What is clear / undeniable is that … , I have no doubt that …* and *I firmly believe that … .*

**2** Read the Writing Strategy. Then, for each paragraph of the letter (1–5):

**1** underline one example of inversion.

**2** find a word or phrase which is inappropriately colloquial and suggest a more formal alternative.

You have read about plans to redevelop a riverside area and popular open-air swimming location into a luxury hotel. Write a letter to the editor of a newspaper explaining why you are strongly against this proposal.

**3** Read the task above and think about your objections to the proposal, and one or two points in its favour. Make notes using the prompts below to help you.

**Loss of a communal facility**

_____

**Environment – pollution, etc.**

_____

**Job opportunities**

_____

**Tourism – local economy**

_____

**4** Plan your letter using the letter in exercise 1 to help you.

**5** Write your letter (220–260 words), using your notes and plan from exercises 3 and 4.

**CHECK YOUR WORK**

**Have you …**

- ☐ written 220–260 words?
- ☐ used appropriately formal language, including syntax?
- ☐ checked the spelling and grammar?

**4**

# Review Unit 4

## Vocabulary

**1 Choose the correct words to complete the news stories.**

### New car-maker implicated in emissions scandal

Shares in Chrysler [1]**crashed / skyrocketed** today, losing $2.3 billion, after it emerged that the company had concealed the true amount of polluting gases emitted by its cars. The revelations come months after a similar scandal at Volkswagen, which saw their sales [2]**mushroom / flatline** as consumers refused to buy new models. Car companies are now coming under [3]**tumbling / mounting** pressure to alter the way that they measure emissions.

### REFUGEE CRISIS – TURKEY STRUGGLING TO COPE

The number of refugees entering Turkey from Iraq and Syria recently [4]**escalated / tumbled** as more people have been forced to flee the intense fighting. An estimated 3.5 million refugees are now in the country – and in border towns like Kilis, refugee numbers will soon [5]**plateau / overtake** the local population. Economic problems – a wildly [6]**fluctuating / mushrooming** currency and [7]**mounting / plummeting** exports – are adding to the pressure on the government, making it harder to cope with the huge influx of people.

Mark: / 7

**2 Write the words to match the definitions.**

1 when people don't have enough money to pay for basic needs like food and housing: p_____
2 how long the average person in any community will live: l_____ e_____
3 when an infectious disease spreads through a community: e_____
4 a change in global or regional weather patterns: c_____ c_____
5 when people attack and kill civilians for political or religious reasons: t_____
6 when a lot of people have very little food to eat: f_____

Mark: / 6

**3 Complete the sentences with the correct form of either the verbs below, or nouns made from those verbs.**

adapt alter amend evolve mutate transform

1 Genetic _____ happen by accident, but they can change the way an animal develops.
2 In 20 years, Belfast has been _____ from a depressed city to a lively tourist destination.
3 As the world's weather changes, many animals will either _____ to the changing environment or die out.
4 The government illegally _____ the figures to make unemployment look lower than it really was.

5 We have proposed an _____ to the constitution to allow people aged over sixteen to vote.
6 The works at the Picasso Museum show how Picasso's style gradually _____ over many decades.

Mark: / 6

## Word skills

**4 Replace the underlined words in the sentences using a two-part set phrase. Use the words in brackets.**

1 I have some problems at work, but generally I like my job. (large) _____
2 If you drive that fast, eventually you'll have an accident. (sooner) _____
3 Mandy has gone travelling, stopping in some places to do temporary jobs. (here) _____
4 I'm glad that the things I ordered online arrived in one piece, without any damage. (sound) _____
5 Before you abseil for the first time, I'll explain some safety rules. (dos) _____
6 You have to choose from Menu A or Menu B – you can't mix them up. (pick) _____

Mark: / 6

**5 Choose the correct words to complete the sentences.**

1 It's the same product. We've just made some small **radical / cosmetic** changes to make it look newer.
2 The government has begun a **sweeping / cosmetic** review of health policy, covering all aspects of the health system.
3 Unless we make **fundamental / marginal** changes to the way we live, global warming will get worse.
4 I photographed the same scene twice. The two pictures are nearly the same, but with **sweeping / subtle** differences.
5 This discovery will affect us in a **profound / minimal** way. Life will never be the same again.
6 A fairly small change in the climate could have a **minimal / drastic** effect, creating a global catastrophe.

Mark: / 6

**6 Complete the sentences with the correct form of the words below.**

come down end even so mean point view

1 Yes, globalisation creates jobs – that's a good _____. But it also exploits poor people.
2 I see what you _____, but I don't agree with you completely about this issue.
3 At the _____ of the day, poverty will continue because people are unwilling to share resources equally.
4 In my _____, most armed conflicts are about competition for resources, not ideology.

5 What population growth really _____ to is the fact that more and more people are living longer.

6 Life expectancy has increased a lot, but _____, many people still die of preventable diseases.

Mark: ☐ / 6

## Grammar

7 **Choose the correct words to complete the text.**

Two hundred years from now, humans will [1]**have lived / be living** in a very different world. By the year 2220 we will [2]**be using / have been using** computers for over 250 years, and they will [3]**have developed / be developing** beyond recognition. Self-aware computers will probably [4]**be doing / have done** many of the jobs that people do today. We'll no doubt have [5]**found / been finding** cures to many diseases too, and I imagine that someone will [6]**be discovering / have discovered** a way to copy the trillions of connections in a human brain. This procedure will allow people to live on after the death of their physical bodies. However, only rich people will probably be able to afford to have their brains copied. It's unlikely that human nature will [7]**have changed / be changing** much, so there will still be huge inequality — and we will still [8]**have fought / be fighting** wars. I expect that in the future many people will [9]**be / have been** struggling to survive, while the lucky few enjoy huge wealth.

Mark: ☐ / 9

8 **Choose the correct quantifiers to complete the text.**

# A simple way to improve your memory

Do you wish you were [1]**enough / a little** better at remembering things? [2]**Many / Half** people forget names a [3]**few / lot of** minutes after hearing them, and can't remember a(n) [4]**all / whole** shopping list unless they write it down. There are [5]**several / few** techniques which you can use to improve your memory without [6]**much / many** effort, but perhaps the easiest of these is placing the items to remember in a well-known location. Imagine walking into your living room and seeing [7]**more / all** of the furniture covered with spaghetti, then watching [8]**some / any** oranges roll down the stairs. Such vivid mental images are hard to forget. Using the location technique, people who previously remembered less than [9]**enough / half** of a shopping list were easily able to recall nearly [10]**every / each** item without any difficulty.

Mark: ☐ / 10

## Use of English

9 **Choose the correct words to complete the text.**

| 1 | a evolve | b alter | c amend |
|---|----------|---------|---------|
| 2 | a deal | b lot | c type |
| 3 | a any | b much | c some |
| 4 | a be | b have | c want |
| 5 | a lot | b many | c whole |
| 6 | a marked | b cosmetic | c sweeping |
| 7 | a Much | b Every | c Most |
| 8 | a later | b after | c better |
| 9 | a be | b have | c being |

The technology of neural implants involves attaching computer chips to brain or nerve cells in order to [1]_____ the way they function. A good [2]_____ of research has been done into this technology, which has already been used in [3]_____ people with medical problems like epilepsy, paralysis or blindness. Soon doctors will [4]_____ using neural implants to treat a [5]_____ array of medical conditions. But what about using them to give healthy people [6]_____ improvements in their abilities? Imagine a future where neural implants gave us better memories, or the ability to find our way by sensing the Earth's magnetic field. [7]_____ scientists avoid this kind of research for ethical reasons, but the chances are that sooner or [8]_____, someone will try it. Perhaps in a hundred years' time, humans will [9]_____ evolved into a super species – part man and part machine.

Mark: ☐ / 9

Total: ☐ / 65

## I can ...

Read the statements. Think about your progress and tick (✓) one of the boxes.

★ = I need more practice.     ★★★ = No problem!

★★ = I sometimes find this difficult.

| | ★ | ★★ | ★★★ |
|---|---|---|---|
| I can talk about global issues. | | | |
| I can use compound future tenses for predictions and suppositions. | | | |
| I can infer information which is implied rather than overtly stated. | | | |
| I can use articles and quantifiers correctly. | | | |
| I can use a two-part set phrase correctly. | | | |
| I can understand texts about languages and the brain and about how personality changes over time. | | | |
| I can discuss a topic and express opinions. | | | |
| I can write a letter about a local improvement scheme. | | | |

## 2 Exam Skills Trainer 2

## Reading

**Strategy**
In the cross-text multiple-matching task, you should read the texts first to determine the general attitude of each writer. As you read, underline parts of the text which give an opinion or an attitude and look for agreement and disagreement between the texts.

1 **Read the strategy above and the question below. Follow the instructions in the strategy to answer the question.**

Which expert has a different view from B about the possibility of producing enough meat in the future?

2 **You are going to read four extracts from articles in which experts give their opinions on what would happen if the world decided to go meat free. For questions 1–4, choose from the experts A–D. The experts may be chosen more than once.**

**Which expert**

1 expresses a different view to A about the range of vegetarian food available.
2 shares C's opinion about the impact of giving up meat on one of the world's natural resources?
3 has a different view from the others about the effect of global vegetarianism on health?
4 has a different view from D about the repercussions on air quality of not keeping farm animals?

### Meat-free world

*Four experts comment on the consequences if the world suddenly went vegetarian*

**A** Becky Thomas *nutritionist*
First and foremost, I think we have to bear in mind the health benefits of a meat-free diet. While consuming meat in moderation isn't necessarily bad for you, too much can have a detrimental effect. The World Health Organisation has warned that consuming 50g of processed meat a day greatly increases the risk of cancer. Moreover, a change in the world's eating habits would be good for the environment. We could use our valuable water supply for human consumption rather than having to reserve so much for the cattle we keep. Turning to more practical issues, supermarkets stock a variety of meat-free options these days, and it's much easier to eat out. In general, the pros of giving up meat far outweigh the cons, so I fail to understand why more people don't do it.

**B** Nigel Bentley *environmentalist*
While it's clear that a vegetarian diet can prevent harmful medical conditions, a meat-free diet might become a necessity in the future. World population is set to exceed nine billion by 2050, which would entail having to produce 200 million tonnes of meat, which would be completely impossible to produce. If the current rate of population growth continues, we will be obliged to reduce our meat intake and we may have to become vegetarians, because the meat industry will become unsustainable. Of course, a smaller amount of livestock would also have a far-reaching effect on the planet: there would be a massive fall in greenhouse gas emissions, because there would be fewer cows releasing huge quantities of methane into the air.

**C** Kiera Reed *anthropologist*
What concerns me most about a meat-free world is the effect it would have on our ability to resist illness. A vegetarian diet would not necessarily give people the nutrients they have until now obtained from meat, which would lead to more sickness and disease in the world. At the very least, people would require education about where to find these nutrients elsewhere. There are an estimated two billion undernourished people in the world today, but that figure would only grow if we all became vegetarians. Having said that, keeping fewer animals would help us save water. Apparently, giving up meat for one day saves the same amount of water used daily by nine people. There are so many different aspects to world vegetarianism, that it is difficult to say whether it would benefit us or not.

**D** Michael Townsend *chef*
While I accept that a meat-free diet may reduce the chances of developing certain illnesses, I wonder whether people might be exaggerating the effect it would have on the environment. Regarding the pollution generated by agriculture, surely, the fumes from a greater number of harvesting and processing machines would outweigh the lack of gases produced by cows? As for struggling to produce enough meat to feed the world's population, there are several cultures that have a meat-free diet, so less meat would be needed than certain figures suggest. I am sure the food industry could cope with the increase in meat production. The thing that worries me most is the lack of choice at mealtimes. For me, the pleasure of dining is in contemplating the variety of wonderful dishes available. If the world became vegetarian, there would only be salad on the menu!

## Listening

**Strategy**
In the sentence-completion task, the answers are usually the exact words you hear on the recording. However, the wording of the questions paraphrases the actual recording. Read the question carefully and listen for what they are paraphrasing to help you identify the correct answer.

3 **Read the Strategy and the short extract and complete the sentence below. How are the words around the gap paraphrased in the extract?**

The Dead Sea has not lost its appeal for tourists, despite the fact that it is shrinking. However, hotels that were built on the lake in the 1980s now lie around 2 km from its banks. To reach the current water level, visitors have to climb down some rocks, cross a busy main road, make their way through a line of marshy plants and pass over a vast mud flat.

Hotel guests must negotiate a number of obstacles to arrive at the Dead Sea, including a wide expanse of _____.

4 **🎧 1.22 You will hear a talk about the changes experienced by the Aral Sea. For questions 1–8, complete the sentences with a word or short phrase.**

**A Changing World**

Covering parts of Kazakhstan and Uzbekistan, the Aral Sea used to be roughly half as big as $^1$_____. Before it began to disappear, fish from the lake were distributed all over what used to be $^2$_____. The water supply to the Aral Sea was interrupted when the rivers were redirected for the $^3$_____ crop. A system of dams, reservoirs and $^4$_____ was built to irrigate the land. As the level of water in the lake dropped, the amount of $^5$_____ rose. Part of what used to be the South Aral Sea has turned into a $^6$_____. The North Aral Sea has been saved by the construction of a new $^7$_____. Today, the North Aral Sea offers nearby residents more $^8$_____ and jobs than in recent years.

## Use of English

**Strategy**

In the open cloze task, some gaps can be filled by referring just to the immediate phrase or sentence surrounding the gap. However, others require understanding of the paragraph or whole text. Always read through the text before you attempt the task to make sure you understand the story or message.

5 **Read the Strategy above and the text in exercise 6. Choose the sentence which best summarises the message of the text.**

a Scientists have found a less painful method for diabetes sufferers to obtain blood for testing.

b A new technique has been developed which will improve the lives of diabetes patients.

c A recent medical discovery is likely to prolong the lives of people with diabetes.

6 **Complete the text with one word in each space.**

**A medical breakthrough**

Diabetes is a medical condition patients can live with $^1$_____ that they check their blood sugar levels regularly. This is usually done by pricking a finger and placing a drop of blood on a testing strip attached $^2$_____ a meter. But now, a team of researchers at Harvard and MIT have come $^3$_____ with an alternative method for checking the blood. Using a special

ink, they have developed a kind of tattoo that will make the process much $^4$_____ invasive in the long term. Not $^5$_____ does the ink detect the presence of sugar in the blood, but it is also able to track other substances. Too much glucose and the tattoo turns brown; an excess of sodium and it goes green. Pinks and purples indicate a change $^6$_____ pH levels.

The main advantage of the new method is that diabetes patients won't have to $^7$_____ extracting blood for testing any more. For this reason the tattoos will probably catch $^8$_____ quickly once they have passed all the necessary medical trials.

## Speaking

**Strategy**

In the collaborative task, you may need to use the following techniques to speculate about the prompts:

• use synonyms of 'think': *I reckon, I suppose*
• use modal verbs of speculation: *must, might*
• use verbs that indicate impression: *look, appear*
• use set phrases: *there's a chance, in all probability*

7 **Read the Strategy and add examples to the techniques.**

8 **Work in pairs. Do the task below. Use the ideas in the Strategy to speculate about the prompts.**

How might these changes affect a teenager's life?

• going to school abroad for a year
• acquiring a motorbike
• having a new baby brother or sister
• inheriting some money
• starting a new school

## Writing

**Strategy**

When you write a proposal, you will be expected to demonstrate appropriate use of two or more functions in your answer, such as describing, expressing opinion, giving reasons, persuading, or recommending. These functions will be specified in the task.

9 **Read the Strategy above and the task below. Which functions from the Strategy are specified in the task?**

Your local council is concerned about the rising number of young people hanging around the streets at night in your town. Write a proposal for the council in which you outline the current facilities available for young people, make suggestions for new facilities, and explain how your suggestions might affect people of other ages in your town.

10 **Write the proposal (220–260 words) for the task in exercise 9.**

# 5 Battles

## A  War and conflict
*I can talk about military conflicts.*

**1  Choose the correct words to complete the texts.**

| | a | b | c |
|---|---|---|---|
| 1 | troops | guerrillas | terrorists |
| 2 | guerrilla | occupation | special |
| 3 | allies | terrorists | troops |
| 4 | security | atrocities | coalition |
| 5 | asymmetric warfare | invasion | insurgency |
| 6 | leader | government | coalition |
| 7 | allies | leaders | civilian governments |
| 8 | insurgency | occupation | security |
| 9 | border | security | civilian government |
| 10 | terrorists | civilians | forces |
| 11 | invasion | atrocity | guerilla raid |
| 12 | insurgency | ally | asymmetric warfare |

## HOTEL SIEGE OVER

Malian government ¹_____, assisted by elite ²_____ forces from other countries, have retaken the Radisson Blu Hotel in Bamoko, Mali. 170 hostages were rescued nearly three days after two ³_____ entered the building and began shooting. Many of the hostages were foreign aid workers, and this attack brings into question the ⁴_____ of aid organisations in the country.

## Rebuilding Proves Difficult in Iraq

More than fifteen years after the ⁵_____ of their country by the United States and a ⁶_____ of its ⁷_____, life is still very difficult for the people of Iraq. The military ⁸_____ of Iraq has now ended, but the ⁹_____ is very weak, and many people still lack jobs and basic amenities.

## ELN Guerrillas Attack in Colombia

ELN guerrillas have ambushed a police convoy, injuring five police officers and three ¹⁰_____, Colombian television reports. The well-planned ¹¹_____ took place late last night on a busy road in the capital, Bogotá. The government has been fighting the ELN ¹²_____ on and off since 1964.

**2  Complete the sentences with the correct form of a verb and a noun below.**

come  deploy  go  launch  lie  withdraw

ambush  attack  force  force  power  war

1  Police caught the terrorists as they _____ in _____ outside an army base, ready to attack.
2  Our army has _____ a new _____ on the rebel-held city.
3  The Prime Minister _____ to _____ last year, after winning the election.
4  Britain is going to _____ a small _____ of military police to Jordan to help train local recruits.
5  'We don't want to _____ to _____,' the Defence Minister said, 'but we have to defend ourselves.'
6  America has _____ all of its _____ from Iraq.

**3  🎧 2.02  Listen to a talk about a war in Liberia. Complete the sentences with a word or short phrase.**

1  Liberia was a democracy until a soldier called Samuel Doe _____ in 1980.
2  There were many _____ when fighting broke out after troops loyal to Charles Taylor attacked the capital, Monrovia.
3  In 1999, another civil war started when a number of groups _____.
4  An international UN force of 15,000 _____ to Liberia between 2003 and 2013.
5  Their role was to secure Liberia's borders and provide training to its _____.
6  Many people witnessed awful _____ during the war.

**4  Complete the sentences with the correct form of the verbs below.**

break  inflict  occupy  put up  stage  station  supply

1  The army _____ heavy casualties in the operation.
2  Foreign troops _____ the country ten years ago.
3  A surprise attack finally _____ the stalemate.
4  Our company _____ arms to the security forces.
5  Troops _____ on this island to protect it.
6  People _____ a protest about the government's plans.
7  Our troops _____ a lot of resistance right now, but we may have to withdraw from the city.

# 5B Grammar
## Passive structures
*I can use passive structures.*

**ARGO – THE REAL STORY**

In 1979, during the Iranian Revolution, the American embassy in Tehran ¹_____ (occupy) by revolutionaries, and embassy staff became hostages. America ²_____ (see) as an enemy by the new government, and any American ³_____ (caught) on the streets could ⁴_____ (arrest). Five diplomats managed to escape and hide after ⁵_____ (help) by citizens of Canada and other countries. Then the CIA came up with a rescue plan.

Fake Canadian passports ⁶_____ (produce) for the diplomats, along with a story to explain why they were in Iran: they were a Canadian film crew in Tehran to find locations for a new film. For their story ⁷_____ (believe), Hollywood writers ⁸_____ (ask) to produce a real film script for the operation. They came up with a science-fiction film called *Argo*, ⁹_____ (set) in an alien city that looked exactly like Tehran – the story was probably too strange ¹⁰_____ (doubt)!

On 27 January 1980, the diplomats used their fake identities to get through security at Tehran's airport and board a flight to Switzerland. After months in hiding, they were free!

**1 Complete the text with the correct passive forms.**

**2 Write passive sentences from the cues.**

1 I / never like / be / tell / what to do by others
_____

2 years ago, Tom / give / a small part in a Bond movie
_____

3 today Amy Adams / regard / as a great actress
_____

4 the film / direct / by JJ Abrams / cost / $50 million
_____

5 give / a role in any film / you / need / audition
_____

6 we / wake up / this morning by a loud noise outside
_____

**3 Rewrite the sentences using a passive form of the verbs in brackets.**

1 They presented the film at the film festival. (show)
_____

2 Undercover CIA agents often risk death. (kill)
_____

3 People say that Josh is getting divorced. (rumour)
_____

4 People invented that story – it's not true. (make up)
_____

5 If you want them to select you for the Olympic team, you need to train harder. (choose)
_____

6 A reporter was talking to me when we heard the explosion. (interview)
_____

**4 Complete the sentences using the auxiliary passive and the phrases below.**

~~a medal / present~~   a strange package / deliver
bag / steal   my phone / confiscate   my bank card / take
our army boots / give   the trick / explain
our wedding dinner / cook

1 The soldier *had a medal presented* to her for bravery in battle.

2 I _____ because I was using Whatsapp in class.

3 We _____ for us by a celebrity chef.

4 Tessa _____ to her, but she still couldn't work out how the magician had done it.

5 I _____ from me by the cash machine. Maybe I used the wrong pin code.

6 We _____ to us by an officer in the store room.

7 At the start of the film, a killer _____ to a complete stranger – inside it, there was a gun and a photo.

8 I _____ when I left it under a café table and went to get a drink.

**5 Rewrite the incorrect sentences. Tick (✓) the correct ones.**

1 Have you had everything explained you yet?
_____

2 Jack had his photo took for the film poster.
_____

3 I had an amazing trick was played on me by a magician.
_____

4 We had checked our passports twice at the airport.
_____

5 I'm having flowers sent to my mum for her birthday.
_____

6 Why don't you have tidied your garden?
_____

# Arguments

*I can understand people talking about arguments.*

**Revision:** Student's Book page 55

**1 Choose the correct words to complete the sentences.**

1 The government **conceded** / **doubted** / **boasted** that they weren't winning the war.
2 Gary **dismissed** / **reminded** / **insisted** that it wasn't his fault.
3 Tom **informed** / **recommended** / **argued** that we see the film.
4 I **argued** / **reminded** / **observed** that Max was worried about something.
5 Many people **complained** / **protested** / **insisted** in the streets against the government's plans.
6 Our investigation **revealed** / **advised** / **enquired** that the minister was lying.
7 I **resent** / **regret** / **deny** having to do all the housework – you should help me!
8 Did I **warn** / **inform** / **mention** to you that I had an argument with Harry yesterday?

**2 Complete the sentences with the correct form of the verbs below.**

announce   deny   fear   object   remind   threaten

1 Terrorists _____ to attack the festival.
2 Mandy _____ that she had taken the money, but I saw her do it.
3 I'm glad that Janet _____ me to call Fran on her birthday – I'd completely forgotten.
4 Rob wasn't answering his phone. Sam began to _____ that he'd had an accident, but she didn't tell anyone.
5 The police _____ that they had arrested the criminal. They said they would charge him with murder.
6 A lot of people _____ strongly to the plans for building a shopping centre on protected land.

**Listening Strategy**
Listening tasks often include language that reports or summarises things people say in the recording. It is important therefore to have a good knowledge of reporting verbs, adjectives and adverbs that describe feelings, and verbs that report opinions.

**3 🎧 2.03 Read the Listening Strategy. Then listen to eight people talking. Choose the correct answer (1–8).**

Which speaker:

A reveals something about their past _____
B proposes a celebration _____
C announces something important _____
D complains about something _____
E boasts about their talent _____
F reminds someone to do something _____
G denies taking something _____
H questions what someone says _____

**4 🎧 2.04 Listen to three conversations and choose the correct answers. There are two questions for each conversation.**

**Conversation 1:** you hear two people talking about an argument.

1 Matt's friend insisted that ...
   A her party was the best.
   B Matt should help her to give out leaflets.
   C Matt should take part in the election.
2 Matt objected to ...
   A being told he was irresponsible.
   B his friend walking out of the room.
   C someone trying to change his political ideas.

**Conversation 2:** you hear two people talking about an art exhibition.

3 The man regrets ...
   A going to the exhibition.
   B expressing a strong opinion about the exhibition.
   C telling his friend something.
4 The woman recommends ...
   A apologising.
   B not speaking to his friend for a while.
   C talking to his friend about art.

**Conversation 3:** you hear two people talking about a damaged laptop.

5 The woman concedes that ...
   A she was fully to blame.
   B she lied about it.
   C she might have been more careful.
6 The man ...
   A proposes talking to Stephen about the damage.
   B recommends that she buy him a new laptop.
   C advises her to ignore Stephen's complaints.

**Grammar**

# Uses of *it*

*I can use a range of structures with* it.

**1** Complete the text with *it* and the correct form of the words below.

be / well worth   be accepted / a fact   be easy / enjoy
be important / be good   be / incredibly difficult   like / when
~~regard / as~~   take / a lot of training

**ARE YOU READY FOR THE RAT RACE?**

The Rat Race Coast-to-Coast is a two-day race across Scotland that takes place every September – ¹*it is regarded as* one of the most difficult races in Britain. The route takes athletes through some of Scotland's most stunning scenery, but of course ²_____ the view when you're pedalling uphill on a racing bike!

The race involves long-distance walking, running, canoeing and cycling, so ³_____ at all these disciplines. ⁴_____ that the weather in Scotland is usually wet and cold, so runners also have to be prepared for that too. People who ⁵_____ they have a bit of comfort can enter the race in the 'Challenger' category. These athletes are allowed to stop for a night and rest in a campsite. 'Expert' racers, on the other hand, just keep on going all night!

⁶_____ to get ready for this kind of race – and even then, ⁷_____ to actually finish. Many competitors drop out on the way. But for the ones who reach the finishing line ⁸_____ all the effort!

**2** Complete the sentences using *it* and the words below.

accept / a fact   find / surprising   hate / when   love / if
regard / as

1 Josh _____ that a dish called 'Bombay Duck' is actually made of fish.
2 We really _____ we have to get up early in the morning.
3 I _____ people do remember my birthday, but I don't get upset if they forget.
4 Scientists _____ that the universe is getting bigger all the time.
5 Art critics _____ one of her best paintings.

**3** Rewrite the sentences with preparatory *it*, and the words or phrases in brackets.

1 We don't know who'll win. (anybody's guess)
_____
2 You were wrong to leave without saying goodbye. (rude of you)
_____
3 You can go home, I'll stay behind and lock up the shop. (leave)
_____
4 We had difficulty passing the test. (not easy)
_____
5 I don't care who started the argument. (important)
_____

**4** Complete the sentences with a word from each box, and *it*. Use the correct form of the verb.

appreciate   hate   make   regard   take

not shake   push   say   train   watch

1 I'd really _____ if people _____ 'thank you' more often.
2 _____ hard work _____ for a marathon.
3 _____ me too scared _____ horror films at night.
4 We _____ as an insult that he _____ our hands.
5 I _____ when people _____ in front of me in a queue.

**5** Put the words in the correct order, beginning with *it* or a pronoun.

1 a goal / it / love / score / we / when / I
_____
2 wasn't / it / in / weather / easy / get / for / us / here / to / this
_____
3 you / of / it / was / bring / to / present / me / kind / a
_____
4 was / fun / it / running / race / in / the
_____
5 the / up / appreciate / if / you / tidied / I'd / classroom / it
_____

**6** Tick (✓) the correct sentences and rewrite the others, changing 1–3 words.

1 I see it's a waste of time that we're completing all these forms.
2 I don't like it that you make jokes about me.
3 It's unusual for you being up so early in the morning.
4 It was really stupid of me to forget the door keys.
5 It's really pain to have to rewrite my English essay.

# Dependent prepositions
*I can use a range of dependent prepositions.*

**1** Complete the sentences with the correct prepostions. Then match 1–8 to a–h.

for  from  in  of  of  on  to  to

1  My parents disapprove _____ me ... ____
2  Troops opened fire on civilians, showing ... ____
3  We have to limit ourselves _____ ... ____
4  The government is resorting _____ ... ____
5  A building company is intent _____ ... ____
6  The fighting is putting ... ____
7  That lawyer helps to get compensation for ... ____
8  Respect the law and the police. We discourage ... ____

a  the victims _____ industrial accidents.
b  peaceful civil disobedience, and not be violent.
c  the lives of everyone trapped inside the city _____ danger.
d  destroying our neighbourhood to build skyscrapers.
e  attending the protest march, but I'm going to go.
f  anyone _____ taking the law into their own hands.
g  cheating in order to win the election.
h  a complete disregard _____ human life.

**2** Complete the text with suitable prepositions.

**ROD CORONADO – ECO-WARRIOR**

Rod Coronado is a highly controversial figure: a hero to some but a dangerous criminal to others, including the FBI. On 9 November 1989, Coronado was responsible [1]_____ attacking and sinking two 430-tonne ships being used to hunt whales in Reykjavík, Iceland. In 1995, he took part in an arson attack on a university to protest [2]_____ testing on animals. This action resulted [3]_____ him being sent to prison for 57 months.

Unlike environmental organisations like Greenpeace, eco-warriors like Coronado aren't opposed [4]_____ acts like sabotage and criminal damage. They argue that although peaceful actions are preferable [5]_____ more violent steps, they are often not as effective. A lot of people have some sympathy [6]_____ people like Coronado, and think that he is justified [7]_____ what he does. Others are opposed [8]_____ this kind of action, and they call him an 'eco-terrorist'.

**3** Choose the correct words to complete the sentences.

1  My political opinions differ **about** / **from** Mel's, but we're still good friends.
2  There's been a slow improvement **of** / **in** environmental laws.
3  Sci-fi has never appealed **for** / **to** me very much.
4  We put up notices to warn people **about** / **against** pickpockets.
5  I hope I can improve **on** / **in** my performance in the last election, and win this time.
6  The police have appealed **for** / **about** the public to come forward with information about the crime.

**4** Rewrite the sentences using the words in brackets and a suitable dependent preposition.

1  The company says that their chemicals aren't dangerous for wildlife. (a threat)
2  Civil disobedience is better than violent protest. (preferable)
3  We'll try to persuade Jenny not to take a job with a company that cuts down trees. (discourage)
4  I think I was right to break an unjust law. (justified)
5  Our lack of civil rights doesn't mean that you can resort to violence. (excuse)
6  All kinds of violence are wrong. (any form)

> **VOCAB BOOST!**
> Some dependent prepositions are more common than others. When you come across sentences which contain dependent prepositions, record them as examples under the preposition.

**5** Read the *Vocab Boost!* box, then complete the sentences with the correct noun or verb form of the words below.

approve  base  concentrate  concern  confine  depend  prepare  refer  reply

1  A  The film _____ **on** an award-winning novel.
   B  I can't _____ **on** my work because of the protest outside.
   C  You must play in the match – we _____ **on** you to win.
2  A  The government has given its _____ **for** the new motorway.
   B  Have you finished _____ **for** the party?
   C  The government shows a lack of _____ **for** our problems.
3  A  Protestors _____ **to** a small area by the police all day.
   B  The FBI _____ **to** Coronado in one of its reports, and called him 'dangerous'.
   C  Why don't you _____ **to** my emails?

## 5F

# 'Why?' 'Because it's there!'
*I can understand a text about ballooning.*

**Revision:** Student's Book page 59

1 **Complete the sentences with an intensifying adverb formed from one of the two words in brackets.**

1 Reading the book, I was _____ struck by how lethal high-altitude ballooning can be. (compel / force)

2 The Eiger is so difficult to climb because of its _____ steep rock faces. (tantalise / ferocious)

3 We were _____ close to the summit when we had to turn back. (tantalise / force)

2 **Read the text quickly, ignoring the gaps. What is its main purpose?**

A To give an introduction to the history of ballooning.

B To review a recent book.

C To explain the events of a ballooning accident.

**Reading Strategy**

In gapped text tasks, you sometimes have to choose carefully between two paragraphs and decide which is the most logical to fill the particular gap. Look for words and phrases which indicate the logical development of the text, e.g. adverbs of time and reason, words that express contrast, pronouns that point forwards or backwards to nouns, paraphrasing of vocabulary, repetition of names or ideas and the use of verb tenses.

3 **Read the Reading Strategy. Then read the text and match the missing paragraphs A–E with the gaps 1–4. There is one extra paragraph which you do not need.**

A As the balloon lost air, it descended. Glaisher came round, and calmly started taking readings again. After landing in a field, the two men walked seven miles to the nearest pub – no doubt still feeling the effects of acute hypoxia.

B They were alarmingly unprepared for the journey, and took off wearing light tweed jackets. Ascending quickly, they took readings and made entries in a log book.

C It turns out that the history of early ballooning is one of daring, ingenuity and often breathtaking stupidity. As I read the book, I was forcibly struck by how fairly ordinary people had taken extraordinary risks – in the name of science, exploration or plain one-upmanship.

D The history of scientific exploration is full of unlikely heroes, and also of rogues who wish to profit from the work and reputations of others. Sometimes, the people who achieved the most received scant recognition.

E By now, they were shivering uncontrollably and gasping for air. Frostbite was setting in on their exposed hands and faces. The men could no longer see well enough to read their instruments. Then Glaisher blacked out.

# Falling Upwards

In the weeks before my one-and-only balloon flight in 2017, a friend gave me Richard Holmes's seminal work about the history of ballooning, *Falling Upwards: How we Took to the Air.* Holmes's beautifully written account takes readers from the early balloon flights of the 1780s to the first successful round-the-world attempt in 1999.

1 _____

The book contains a wealth of such extraordinary tales, but my personal favourite is that of scientists Coxwell and Glaisher's near-fatal flight in 1862. The two men proposed to take measurements of temperature, pressure and humidity at different altitudes. They took off on 5 September, intending to reach the upper atmosphere. Even Coxwell – an experienced balloonist – was completely ignorant about the dangers they faced.

2 _____

After nineteen minutes aloft, the pair had reached an altitude of two miles, and the temperature was dropping fast. At four miles, hypoxia – a lack of oxygen in the blood – was taking its toll. They could hardly function well enough to write in their log. But amazingly, they kept going to their planned altitude of five and a half miles.

3 _____

Holmes's breathtaking account of what happens next reveals the desperate courage of a man facing death. With Glaisher unconscious, Coxwell perilously climbed out of the basket and up the rigging even though he was about to black out. Unable to use his hands, he pulled himself up by the elbows, opening the gas value with his teeth.

4 _____

Like many people in Holmes's inspiring book, Coxwell and Glaisher illustrate the naivety of early aerial pioneers. These men may have stepped out into the unknown blissfully unaware of the risks, but having read the book, I was acutely aware of them when I finally stepped into a basket. I was also comically overdressed!

# 5G

# Photo comparison

*I can describe, compare and speculate about photos.*

**Speaking Strategy**

You should accustom yourself to:

- speaking for a minute on a subject without interruption
- using fillers (*Well, ...*) and paraphrasing (*It's kind of ...*) to help you keep pauses to a minimum.
- listening to other students speak for a minute and then commenting or asking questions based on what you have heard.

**1** Read the Speaking Strategy. Then complete the table with the phrases below.

Actually, ...   er / um ...   How do you say?   I suppose
if you see what I mean   it looks a bit like a ...
it's similar to a ...   Let's see   those things that you ...
What else? ...   What I mean is ...   you know   You use it to ...

| Fillers to gain time | Paraphrasing when you don't know a word |
|---|---|
| _____ | _____ |
| _____ | _____ |
| _____ | _____ |
| _____ | _____ |
| _____ | _____ |
| _____ | _____ |

**2** Look at photos A and B and the task below. List the points that you would mention about each photo.

Compare the photos and say what challenges you think these people face every day. What personal qualities might they have?

**3** 🎧 **2.05** Listen to a student comparing photos A and B. Does she mention similar points to you?

**4** 🎧 **2.05** Complete the sentences from the listening with 1–2 words. Then listen again and check your answers.

1 My initial _____ is that the photos appear to be quite different ...

2 ... in all _____ she's one of the construction workers.

3 It's highly _____ that there are many women working on her construction site ...

4 The _____ are that she suffers from prejudice ...

5 I _____ he runs into problems like this all the time.

6 ... I _____ if he gets very frustrated sometimes.

7 ... my _____ would be somewhere in Britain.

**5** Look at the task and photos C and D and make notes.

Compare the photos and say what challenges you think these people face in their jobs. What personal qualities might they have?

_____
_____
_____
_____

**6** Do the exam task using your notes from exercise 5.

# 5H

## Writing
## For and against essay
*I can write a for and against essay.*

### Writing Strategy

Make sure your essay has a clear, logical structure.

**Paragraph 1:** Introduction. Rephrase the question and/or give an example of the situation it describes to show that you have understood it.

**Paragraph 2:** Give two or three pros (arguments for). Include evidence and/or examples where appropriate.

**Paragraph 3:** Give two or three cons (arguments against). Include evidence and/or examples where appropriate.

**Paragraph 4:** Conclusion. Sum up the most important or convincing arguments and give your opinion.

**1 Read the Writing Strategy. Then read the task and essay.**

1 How many pros and cons are mentioned?

2 Which arguments are backed up by examples or evidence?

Some people think that one year's military service should be compulsory for everyone when they leave full-time education. What are the advantages and disadvantages of military service?

Many people believe that young men – and possibly women – should complete a year of military service after leaving school. There are some advantages to this, but also many drawbacks.

To begin with, <u>it is sometimes argued that</u> military service helps to build character by teaching people the military ethos of protecting others and working together for the greater good. <u>By the same token</u>, people often learn skills that they use in later life. For example, many people first get their driver's licence – or learn to cook and clean – in the military. Last but not least, some nations need manpower to defend themselves against hostile neighbours. Scrapping military service would jeopardise their security.

<u>By contrast</u>, many people maintain that military service prevents millions of young people from getting on with their lives. The reasoning is as follows: understandably, some people stay in higher education for years to avoid doing military service. <u>Similarly</u>, many employers are reluctant to give people permanent jobs until they've done their military service. <u>In other words</u>, military service has a much bigger impact on a person's life than the year they actually spend in uniform. Another compelling argument against military service is the obvious fact that people can be sent to war. There is a strong argument for saying that people who go to war should be career soldiers, who have accepted the risk.

<u>To sum up</u>, compulsory military service has some benefits for both countries and individuals. But overall, I feel that these benefits are outweighed by the serious impact on young people's lives.

**2 Match the <u>underlined</u> words in the text with the words and phrases below.**

In conclusion   in the same way   likewise   on the other hand   people sometimes think that   to put it another way

**3 Complete the sentences with the words below.**

case   compelling   least   maintain   place   reasoning

1 Some people _____ that having nuclear weapons is a good thing, but I disagree.

2 The _____ for my argument against military service is as follows.

3 Why don't I want to go out? Well, in the first _____, it's pouring with rain.

4 Jess is a great colleague, a brilliant scientist, and last but not _____ – a true friend.

5 The fact that you could die is, in my view, a _____ reason not to join the army.

6 There's a strong _____ for compulsory military service in countries that share borders with hostile nations.

**4 Read the task and make notes under the headings below. Think about pros and cons for the community as well as for people doing community service.**

Some people argue that everyone should do a year of community service at some point in their lives. Discuss the advantages and disadvantages of compulsory community service.

1 Advantages of compulsory community service

_____

_____

_____

2 Disadvantages of compulsory community service

_____

_____

_____

3 Your opinion

_____

_____

_____

**5 Write your essay (220–260 words) using your notes from exercise 4.**

**CHECK YOUR WORK**

**Have you ...**

☐ followed all the advice in the Writing Strategy?

☐ used some of the phrases from exercises 2 and 3?

☐ checked your spelling and grammar?

# 5 Review Unit 5

## Vocabulary

**1 Match the words and phrases with the definitions.**

asymmetric warfare   atrocities   border   insurgency
special forces   terrorists

1 people who use violence against ordinary people to achieve political or religious aims _____
2 when two sides fight using very different weapons, manpower and strategies _____
3 unnecessary and cruel acts in a war – often involving killing or hurting civilians _____
4 the line that divides two countries or areas _____
5 when a group fights against the government and tries to take control of the country _____
6 troops who have extra training, weapons and skills

_____

Mark: ____ / 6

**2 Complete the text with the correct form of the words below.**

catch   come under   deploy   fall   inflict   mount   put up
wage

Afghan government soldiers in Mazar-e-Sharif
¹_____ attack earlier today from Taliban fighters. A group of fighters ²_____ the attack after entering a heavily fortified base dressed as soldiers. Many troops were ³_____ in an ambush as they left Friday prayers at the base. The Taliban fighters ⁴_____ heavy casualties in the first hours of the attack. Although most of them are now dead, the remaining Taliban are still ⁵_____ fierce resistance. Afghan special forces have now ⁶_____ to the base.

Mazar-e-Sharif, in Balkh province, is the third-largest city in Afghanistan. The Taliban have ⁷_____ a war on Afghan forces in the area ever since the Taliban-led government ⁸_____ from power in 2001.

Mark: ____ / 8

**3 Choose the correct words to complete the mini-dialogues.**

**Glen** Reece ¹**mentioned / recommended** that you were really angry with me. It isn't true, is it?

**May** Yes, it is, actually. Sorry Glen, but I really ²**complain / object** to you spreading gossip about me.

**Ben** I ³**doubt / object** that we can go sailing this weekend. The weather's going to be bad.

**Max** I know. The sailing club ⁴**argued / advised** people not to go out sailing today.

**Dana** Did you ⁵**complain / resent** to the teacher that Rich had copied your essay?

**Liam** Yes, I did. But when she asked him about it, he ⁶**protested / denied** everything. In fact, he ⁷**claimed / conceded** that I had copied his essay!

Mark: ____ / 7

## Word skills

**4 Complete the sentences with the correct prepositions.**

1 Who is responsible _____ this scandal?
   a on      b for      c of
2 The threat _____ big fines deters people from speeding.
   a of      b from      c for
3 Peaceful protest is preferable _____ more violent actions.
   a to      b with      c against
4 The police warned people _____ damaging property.
   a for      b against      c from
5 You'll have to improve _____ that performance if you want to stay in the team.
   a with      b on      c about
6 I differ _____ Mandy on my view of eco-terrorism.
   a to      b against      c with

Mark: ____ / 6

**5 Complete the extracts from a student's photo-description task with the words below.**

a kind of   actually   not sure   suppose   what else
what I mean

The people in photo 1 are meeting in a park and relaxing or exercising. I ¹_____ it's early in the morning because of the light. The people are all dressed casually, and a couple of them are playing a game. I'm ²_____ what the sport is in English, but it's ³_____ badminton without a racket – if you see ⁴_____. ⁵_____, this sport is very popular in Shanghai, where I come from. Um … ⁶_____? I imagine they come here often, and …

Mark: ____ / 6

**6 Choose the correct words to complete the extracts from students' photo-description tasks.**

'My initial ¹**expression / impression** of the photo is that it's terrifying because the workers are up so high. But no ²**doubt / chance** they're used to working on high buildings.'

'The man's ³**impression / expression** suggests that he's thinking hard about something. My best ⁴**imagine / guess** would be that he's just received some important news.'

'It's not ⁵**daresay / clear** where the photo is taken, but my guess would be Ukraine. I think the people in the photo know each other. The ⁶**chances / doubts** are they're great friends.'

Mark: ____ / 6

## Grammar

**7** Complete the sentences with the correct passive form of the verbs in brackets.

1 I really hate _____ (make) to wait for a table at a restaurant.
2 You _____ (give) a pay rise after six months if you perform well in the job.
3 _____ (name) FIFA Footballer of the Year is a great honour, even for a world-famous player like Ronaldo.
4 Ai Weiwei _____ (see) as one of the most important artists living today.
5 The film *La La Land*, _____ (write) by Damien Chazelle, is a hugely successful romantic musical.
6 It _____ (rumour) that Stephen Spielberg is working on a top-secret new film project.

Mark: ___ / 6

**8** Complete the sentences with the correct form of the words in brackets. Use the auxiliary passive.

1 I _____ (everything / explain) to me earlier, so I know what I have to do.
2 Rachel _____ (her bag / steal) last year so now she always keeps it in her locker.
3 We _____ (the email / translate / for us) by a friend because it was in Japanese.
4 I often order books on the internet, and I _____ (them / send) to my home address.
5 The Queen _____ (her portrait / paint) this week. It'll take several days to complete.
6 They're a local band, but they're really good – they _____ (their concert / show on TV / last year).

Mark: ___ / 6

**9** Complete the second sentence so that it means the same as the first. Use *it* and the words in brackets.

1 We really enjoyed getting to know you. (lovely)
_____ meet you.
2 If you love the warm weather, why not go on holiday to Thailand? (like / hot)
If _____, why not go on holiday to Thailand.
3 We must get here on time tomorrow. (necessary / arrive)
_____ on time tomorrow.
4 I think it's impolite for people to spit in the street. (see / very rude)
I _____ that people spit in the street.
5 It isn't easy for Tim to sleep when it's hot. (find / difficult)
Tim _____ when it's hot.
6 You should apologise to Jack. (owe / to Jack)
You _____ to apologise.

Mark: ___ / 6

## Use of English

**10** Choose the correct words to complete the text.

| | | | | | |
|---|---|---|---|---|---|
| 1 a from | b to | c against |
| 2 a What | b It | c When |
| 3 a of | b from | c for |
| 4 a that | b has | c when |
| 5 a was | b are | c had been |
| 6 a is regarded | b was made | c printed |
| 7 a to take | b to take | c taken |
| 8 a of | b from | c for |

Mexican photographer Javier Manzano is opposed ¹_____ violence of any kind, but he has risked his life to record conflict in Mexico and in Afghanistan and Syria.

In 2011, Manzano documented the vicious fighting between rival Mexican drug gangs. ²_____ was very risky to get close to the Mexican underworld – whose members are responsible ³_____ hundreds of murders every year – but Manzano's work won him the World Press Photo Award.

A year later, Manzano was running down alleys and dodging snipers in Aleppo, Syria. It was here ⁴_____ he took an iconic photograph of two soldiers of the Free Syrian Army fighting in a dark, ruined building. The men were illuminated by shafts of light coming through holes which ⁵_____ shot through a metal wall. Manzano won the prestigious Pulitzer Prize for this image, which ⁶_____ as one of the best photos ⁷_____ during the fighting in the city. Today, Manzano still travels to conflict zones, photographing the civilian victims ⁸_____ wars, and the young soldiers who fight and die in them.

Mark: ___ / 8

Total: ___ / 65

## I can ...

Read the statements. Think about your progress and tick (✓) one of the boxes.

★ = I need more practice.  ★★★ = No problem!
★★ = I sometimes find this difficult.

| | ★ | ★★ | ★★★ |
|---|---|---|---|
| I can talk about military conflicts. | | | |
| I can use passive structures. | | | |
| I can understand people talking about arguments. | | | |
| I can use a range of structures with *it*. | | | |
| I can use a range of dependent prepositions. | | | |
| I can understand texts about mountaineering and ballooning. | | | |
| I can describe, compare and speculate about photos. | | | |
| I can write a for and against essay. | | | |

# 6 Dreams

## A Life's too short
*I can talk about dreams and ambitions.*

**1** Cross out the verb in each sentence that does not collocate with the noun.

**A** She **met / reached / realised** her target of competing in an international sports event.

**B** He **accomplished / achieved / met** his aspiration of performing on the stage.

**C** He **attained / fulfilled / reached** his goal of successfully conducting an experiment.

**D** He **achieved / accomplished / completed** his mission of setting up his own company.

**E** She **accomplished / attained / completed** her objective of making two records.

**F** She **fulfilled / met / realised** her dream of sailing single-handedly around the world.

**G** He **achieved / reached / realised** his ambition of exhibiting some of his work.

**H** She **achieved / attained / fulfilled** her aim of becoming a member of parliament.

**2** 🎧 **2.06** Listen to a radio programme about people who achieved important goals early in life. Write their ages at the time they achieved these goals.

1 Gaten Matarazzo, aged _____
2 Vanessa-Mae, aged _____
3 Kieron Williamson, aged _____
4 Jamie Edwards, aged _____
5 Shubham Banerjee, aged _____
6 Proscovia Alengot Oromait, aged _____
7 Laura Dekker, aged _____
8 Gaurika Singh, aged _____

**3** 🎧 **2.06** Listen again and match people 1–8 in exercise 2 with sentences A– H in exercise 1.

1 _____   2 _____   3 _____   4 _____
5 _____   6 _____   7 _____   8 _____

**4** Complete the second sentence so that it means the same as the first. Use a time idiom. Write no more than six words and include the word in brackets.

1 We enjoyed ourselves very much in Ibiza. (lives)
   We _____ in Ibiza.
2 I dislike people who shout a lot. (no)
   I _____ people who shout a lot.
3 We got to the hospital just before something bad happened. (nick)
   We got to the hospital _____.
4 Harry got the job as he was in the best position to take advantage of the opportunity. (right)
   Harry got the job as he was in the _____.
5 You'll eventually learn to accept the situation. (in)
   You'll learn _____.
6 My aunt didn't travel in her youth, but she's compensating now for the wasted years. (lost)
   My aunt didn't travel in her youth, but she's
   _____ now.
7 Getting the project done is going to be something that has to be done quickly. (race)
   Getting the project done is going to be
   _____.
8 People expected that musician to have died by now. (borrowed)
   That musician _____.

**5** Replace the verbs in bold with the synonyms below.

circumnavigate   conduct   endure   master   pilot   retrace   scale   traverse

1 Naomi James was the first woman to **sail around** the world single-handed. _____
2 Junko Tabei was the first woman to **climb** Everest.
   _____
3 Koko the gorilla is the first animal to **learn** sign language.
   _____
4 Ernest Shackleton was not the only explorer to **lead** an expedition to the Antarctic. _____
5 Robert Scott had to **suffer** great hardship in his attempt to reach the South Pole. _____
6 Amelia Earhart was the first woman to **fly** a plane solo across the Atlantic ocean. _____
7 Harriet Chalmers Adams was one of the first explorers to **follow** the steps of Christopher Columbus in Haiti.
   _____
8 Sir Ranulph Fiennes was the first person to **cross** Antarctica on foot. _____

**Grammar**

# Relative clauses and reduced relative clauses

*I can use relative clauses and reduced relative clauses.*

**1** Join the sentences with a suitable relative clause. Omit the pronoun where possible.

1 The London Marathon is held in spring. It's a fundraising event.

_____

2 That's the woman. She gave me lift home.

_____

3 They've set up a crowdfunding site. It has raised over £2,000 so far.

_____

4 Angelina Jolie's most famous role is Lara Croft. She is also a film director.

_____

5 We bought some bracelets. The local women had made them.

_____

**2** Rewrite the sentences beginning with the words in bold. Use relative clauses and an informal style, where possible.

1 The thieves broke into **the house**. It's owned by a wealthy banker.

_____

2 **The people** let me down. I'd been doing the project with them.

_____

3 The books hadn't been written in. **We gave** them to the teacher.

_____

4 **The flat is shared by four students**. They're all studying music.

_____

5 I've been looking forward to **the party** all week. It's at Beth's house.

_____

6 **My aunt gave me two books for my birthday**. I'd read both of them before.

_____

**3** Complete sentences 1–6 with the clauses below. Use relative pronouns and make any other changes. Add commas where necessary.

he had been hired at the last moment
it is based on a true story
it is playing in the background
it was given last night   it was light at first
they were waiting at the stage door

1 The profits from the concert _____ are all going to charity.
2 The comedian _____ turned out to be hilarious.
3 The song _____ is by one of my favourite bands.
4 His new film _____ will be released in the autumn.
5 The fans _____ were unaware that the musicians had already left.
6 The rain _____ soon became a deluge, and the audience had to run for cover.

**4** Rewrite the sentences in exercise 3 using reduced relative clauses.

1 _____
2 _____
3 _____
4 _____
5 _____
6 _____

**5** Complete the text. Write one word in each space.

On 15 March 2017, Vine and Snapchat star Jérôme Jarre got a call from a volunteer in Somalia, [1]_____ had seen a little girl die of thirst. This is not uncommon in the East African country as it is prone to famine, the worst [2]_____ which occurred in 2011, when 260,000 people died. Jarre's response was to record a message on Twitter [3]_____ which he outlined his 'crazy plan' to fill a plane with food and send it to Somalia. Discovering that Turkish Airlines is the only airline [4]_____ flies there, Jarre asked his followers to lobby the airline under #TurkishAirlinesHelpSomalia. His message reached actor Ben Stiller and sportsman Colin Kaepernick, to

[5]_____ Jarre's idea did not seem so absurd. Together, they started the crowdfunding page Love Army For Somalia. Meanwhile, vlogger Casey Neistat, [6]_____ YouTube channel is subscribed to by millions, created a video about the campaign, [7]_____ was published on 17 March. Later the same day, Turkish Airlines agreed to provide a plane, setting 27 March as the day [8]_____ which the flight would be made. By that date, Love Army For Somalia had raised over $2.5 million. The food delivery was made just two weeks after Jarre's initial plea.

# Against all odds

*I can understand and react to a radio programme about female explorers in history.*

**1 Circle the two synonyms that complete each sentence correctly.**

1 Mary Kingsley travelled to Africa when it was thought **becoming** / **fitting** / **improper** / **unsuitable** for women to travel alone.

2 Marco Polo must have had numerous **dismal** / **dreary** / **hair-raising** / **thrilling** adventures during the 24 years he spent travelling through Asia.

3 Annie Smith Peck was criticised heavily by the **intolerant** / **liberal** / **narrow-minded** / **unbiased** press for the trousers she wore when climbing.

4 Mary Moffat was the **cowardly** / **fainthearted** / **fearless** / **valiant** wife of David Livingstone, who accompanied her husband on many of his travels.

5 Captain James Cook was commissioned to lead a voyage to the Pacific because of his reputation as a/an **distinguished** / **great** / **insignificant** / **unknown** sailor.

6 Dutch explorer Alexandrine Tinné began her first expedition **alone** / **chaperoned** / **escorted** / **unaccompanied** by her mother and aunt.

**Listening Strategy**

In a true or false listening task, the statements may contain words that are synonyms or antonyms of words in the recording. While you are listening, look out for synonyms and antonyms for the key information.

**2** 🎧 **2.07** **Read the Listening Strategy and listen to a short biography of American explorer Fanny Bullock. Are the sentences true or false?**

1 Fanny Bullock had never tried climbing until she met her husband. _____

2 Once they were married, the couple moved to a more mountainous state in the US. _____

3 Fanny Bullock's husband was rather narrow-minded. _____

4 Fanny was renowned for her fearless approach to climbing mountains. _____

**3** 🎧 **2.08** **Listen to a radio documentary about globetrotter Annie Londonderry. What three means of transport did she use on her world trip?**

1 _____

2 _____

3 _____

**4** 🎧 **2.08** **Listen again. Are the sentences true (T) or false (F)?**

1 Annie Londonderry was escorted by her husband on her trip around the world. _____

2 She initially obtained money for the trip through advertising. _____

3 Cycling wasn't yet fashionable at the end of the 19th century. _____

4 Annie made little progress at the start of her journey as she was too big for her bike. _____

5 She had to get off the ship every time it stopped to complete the stipulated number of kilometres she had agreed to ride. _____

6 Annie was a very talented businesswoman. _____

7 She wasn't always truthful about her exploits when she spoke in public. _____

8 The speaker considers Annie's headline dramatic, but not misleading. _____

**5 Complete the pairs of sentences with the same verb in a different form, either as a present participle, a past participle or a perfect participle. Use the verbs below.**

buy know leave lose take wear

1 a _____ the hint, we finished our drinks and left.
  b _____ by a professional, the photos can be purchased online.

2 a _____ his voice, he cancelled the performance.
  b _____ in thought, she didn't hear my question.

3 a _____ the suit only once, he'd now like to sell it.
  b _____ high heels, she walked carefully down the stairs.

4 a _____ tickets for the concert, I bumped into my neighbour.
  b _____ in advance, concert tickets are usually cheaper.

5 a _____ the stage, she tripped and fell.
  b _____ the stage, she changed out of her costume.

6 a _____ Tom, he'll be at the front of the queue.
  b _____ for his antics, the guitarist did not disappoint.

# Modal verbs: speculation

*I can speculate about different possibilities.*

**1** Complete the sentences with the correct modal verbs in brackets.

1 That _____ be my mum calling. I didn't tell her I was going to be late. (can / can't / will)

2 I'd take a jacket if I were you. It _____ get cold later on. (must / may / can't)

3 Carl _____ still be playing football. The match finished ages ago. (can't / may / will)

4 You _____ have no problems passing. Physics is your best subject. (could / must / should)

5 The weather _____ be rather unpredictable here. One minute the sun's out and the next it's raining. (can / could / will)

6 I suppose Lisa _____ be waiting at the other exit. We didn't say exactly where we'd be. (can / might / must)

7 Your dad _____ have a very demanding job. He always looks exhausted. (might / must / should)

8 Let's watch the documentary on TV tonight. It _____ be interesting. (can / can't / could)

**2** Complete the sentences with the words in brackets. Use the modal verb with a perfect, perfect continuous or passive infinitive.

1 Look at all those puddles. It _____. (must / rain)

2 Why didn't you say you had a problem? I _____ you. (could / help)

3 I'm surprised her sister isn't here. She _____. (can't / invite)

4 Where's Ian? He _____ by now. (should / arrive)

5 I can't find my wallet. I think it _____. (may / steal)

6 Of course she didn't pick up the phone. She _____ (will / drive) home from work!

7 I think I _____ my keys in the front door. (might / leave)

**3** Complete the second sentence so that it means the same as the first. Use the modal verbs below. Write between three and six words.

can  can't  may not  must  should  won't

1 I'm sure you weren't listening to me.
You _____.

2 It's freezing! I'm sure you left a window open.
It's freezing! You _____.

3 Their plane is due, so I expect they're landing now.
Their plane is due, so they _____.

4 In spring, it's common to see lambs in the fields.
In spring, lambs _____.

5 It's possible they haven't received your application.
Your application _____.

6 I know they haven't marked our exams yet.
Our exams _____.

**4** **USE OF ENGLISH** Complete six of the gaps in the text with the modal verbs below and two of the gaps with additional words.

can  can't  could  must  should  will

# The Crystal Palace Fire

Built to house the Great Exhibition of 1851, Crystal Palace [1]_____ have been an impressive sight when it was finished. The opening ceremony, performed by Queen Victoria, [2]_____ certainly have drawn crowds from all over the country and beyond. On the evening of 30 November 1936, however, disaster struck when the general manager, Sir Henry Buckland, was walking his dog. Sir Henry may [3]_____ been admiring the Palace from a distance when he noticed a red glow. Rushing inside, he found two employees trying to extinguish a small fire. Because of its size, the three men thought they [4]_____ be able to put it out by themselves. It [5]_____ have been as easy as they expected, however, because they had to call the fire brigade an hour later. By then, the fire had rapidly spread. Generally, old buildings [6]_____ contain a great deal of flammable material, and the old dry timber flooring of the Palace will have [7]_____ consumed in minutes. Soon the building was utterly destroyed. The cause of the fire has never been ascertained, but some say there's a chance it [8]_____ have been arson. The only thing for sure is that a beautiful building was lost to the world that night.

# 6E Word Skills

## Phrasal verbs (2)

*I can recognise and use literal and idiomatic phrasal verbs correctly.*

**1** Read the sentences. Do the phrasal verbs have a literal meaning (L) or an idiomatic meaning (I)?

1 I've made a list of people to invite to my party. I hope I haven't left anyone out! _____

2 My little sister was really excited when her first tooth fell out. _____

3 I didn't manage to get up in time to walk to school, so I got the bus instead. _____

4 Daisy isn't really upset; she's putting it on to get some sympathy. _____

5 I think that chicken has gone off; it smells funny. _____

6 Did you remember to switch off all the electrical appliances before we left home? _____

**2** Rewrite the underlined phrases as phrasal verbs. Use the correct form of six of the verbs below.

get on   get over   go down   make up   put out   settle down
take in   take off

1 I tried to <u>invent</u> a good excuse for being late, but I couldn't think of one.

_____

2 I'm not ready to <u>start having a quieter way of life</u> and have a family yet.

_____

3 The Prime Minister has <u>published</u> a statement denying accusations of corruption within the party.

_____

4 His parents invested a lot in his education in the hope that he would <u>be successful in a career</u>.

_____

5 Starting a new company was hard, but we <u>dealt with</u> our difficulties as best we could.

_____

6 Her singing career <u>became successful</u> when she appeared on a TV talent show.

_____

**3** Complete the sentences with the correct form of the phrasal verbs in exercise 2. Remember the phrasal verbs have a different meaning.

1 I wanted to ask David about his job interview, but he _____ before I had the chance.

2 It took my grandmother longer than she expected to _____ her knee operation.

3 There's no need to give me a lift home. I don't want to _____ you _____.

4 When I'm revising, it gets to the point that I can't _____ any more _____.

5 My joke _____ very well. Nobody laughed!

6 Sam's parents are worried because he _____ very well at school this year.

7 The teacher waited for us to _____ before starting the class.

8 I _____ for having a day off by studying all weekend.

> **VOCAB BOOST!**
> Phrasal verbs often have multiple idiomatic meanings. When you look up a phrasal verb in the dictionary, read through all the meanings and write an example sentence for each one.

**4** Read the *Vocab Boost!* box. Then look at the two phrasal verbs below. Match definitions 1–8 with sentences A–H.

*come up*

1 be going to happen very soon _____
2 be mentioned or discussed _____
3 happen _____
4 rise _____

A Your name came up in conversation yesterday.
B She's excited because her birthday's coming up.
C The room is filled with light as the sun comes up.
D Something's come up so I can't see you tonight.

*get through*

5 deal with something difficult _____
6 be connected by phone _____
7 finish doing something _____
8 be successful in an exam _____

E I finally got through to Jenny on her mobile.
F If the animals can get through the winter, they will reproduce in spring.
G We got through the exams without any problems.
H We got through everything early and went home.

# I have a dream

*I can understand and react to the opinions of four people on a historic decision.*

**Revision:** Student's Book page 70

**1** Match words 1–8 with their synonyms a–h.

| | | | |
|---|---|---|---|
| 1 condemn _____ | | a | attitude |
| 2 consternation _____ | | b | be a sign of |
| 3 converge _____ | | c | come together |
| 4 demeanour _____ | | d | criticise |
| 5 dire _____ | | e | insignificant |
| 6 foreshadow _____ | | f | make strong again |
| 7 negligible _____ | | g | critical |
| 8 revive _____ | | h | anxiety |

**2** Skim the text quickly. Which of the four experts are pro-Brexit?

_____

### Reading Strategy

In this task you have to read four texts to identify similar or different opinions and attitudes. Take each question in turn and follow the procedure below:

1 Underline the key words in the question.
2 Note whether you need to find a similar or a different opinion.
3 Find and underline the opinion in the text specified in the question. If no text is specified, read all the texts.
4 Find and underline the same opinion in the other three texts.
5 Compare the opinions and choose the correct answer.

**3** Read the Reading Strategy. Follow the instructions in the Strategy to match the experts A–D with questions 1–4. The experts may be chosen more than once.

Which expert ...

1 disagrees with George Phillips about the value for money of being in the EU? _____
2 has a different opinion from Chris Holmes about the nature of future trade deals with non-EU members? _____
3 shares the same view as Sylvia Chalmers about the importance of rigorous checks at ports and airports? _____
4 disagrees with Chalmers about the possibility of a beneficial trade agreement between the UK and the EU?

_____

## Four experts give their opinions on the pros and cons for the UK of leaving the EU.

**A CHRIS HOLMES**

In my view, Brexit will have a devastating effect on the UK economy. Granted, membership of the EU wasn't cheap, but access to the single market, which exempts member states from paying tariffs on imports and exports within the EU, more than made up for the expense. Now, a whole new set of agreements will have to be drawn up. A free-trade deal with Europe is unlikely, as the EU will want to deter other member states from breaking away. Having left the union, the UK will also have lost much of its bargaining power to establish agreements with other world powers.

**C GEORGE PHILLIPS**

As far as I can see, the UK will be much better off without the EU. Not only did it cost a fortune to be a part of Europe – some estimates put the figure at around £200 billion – but being a member state also had other drawbacks. For over four decades, the UK had to go along with wasteful and expensive EU regulations, such as those of the Common Agricultural Policy. I believe Brexit will bring some clear-cut advantages to the UK, such as favourable trade agreements with influential countries like China, India and the US and renewed control over fishing rights around its coast.

**B SYLVIA CHALMERS**

Weighing up the pros and cons, I am inclined to come down on the side of Brexit. In my opinion, concerns about trade agreements are unfounded because of the large deficit the UK has with the EU. The fact that the UK imports more than it exports means that it is in Europe's interest to maintain tariff-free trading if the UK leaves the single market. A more pressing issue for me is border security and the question of who and what should be allowed to enter the country. Leaving the EU will allow the UK to regain control of its borders and determine who and what can and can't come in.

**D AMANDA SHAW**

The most disastrous effect of Brexit for me is the threat it poses to freedom of movement. Until now, EU residents have been able to live and work freely anywhere else in the bloc, not only increasing their job opportunities but also broadening their horizons. While security at customs is obviously an issue to be taken seriously, immigration to the UK appears to have created a more diverse national culture and a better-qualified workforce. Since Brexit, however, both the EU citizens currently working in the UK and the Brits settled in other EU member states are fearful about their future.

# Debate

*I can use a range of discourse markers to give my opinion in a debate.*

'All of our dreams can come true if we have the courage to pursue them.'
Walt Disney

**1** Read the quote. Do you agree or disagree with the statement?

> **Speaking Strategy**
> In a debate, you have some time to plan your answer. Decide if you are for or against the statement and think of four or five arguments to support your view. Start with one of your weaker arguments and move onto the stronger ones as the conversation progresses.

**2** 🎧 2.09 Read the Speaking Strategy. Then listen to a student giving his view about the quote in exercise 1. Does he agree or disagree with the statement? Complete his arguments.

1 _____
2 _____
3 _____
4 _____
5 _____

**3** Which do you think is the speaker's weakest and strongest argument?

Weakest argument: _____
Strongest argument: _____

**4** Cross out the incorrect discourse marker in each group. Add it to the correct group.

**1 Adding further information**
As well as that. ... For one thing, ...
What's more, ... _____

**2 Announcing the subject in advance**
As for ..., As far as ... is concerned,
It's true, ... _____

**3 Clarifying**
I mean, ... Still, ...
in other words, ... _____

**4 Concession**
Regarding ..., Certainly, ...
Of course, ... _____

**5 Counter-argument**
All the same, ... Even so, ...
that is to say, ... _____

**6 Explaining the reason for something**
As a result, ... Because of this, ...
Broadly speaking, ... _____

**7 Generalising**
On the whole, ... By and large, ...
Besides, ... _____

**8 Structuring**
To start with, ... For another thing, ...
Consequently, ... _____

**5** 🎧 2.09 Listen again and circle the phrases you hear.

**6** Read the speech disagreeing with the quote in exercise 1. Complete the speech with a suitable discourse marker. More than one answer may be possible.

> ¹_____, I'd like to say that I don't agree with the statement. ²_____, it helps to have courage when pursuing your dreams, but other qualities are also necessary. ³_____, I believe it is hard work that can make your dreams come true. If you work hard at school, you will be successful. ⁴_____, the doors to many careers will be open to you. ⁵_____, you will have to keep up the hard work. ⁶_____ the dream itself, this must be realistic, ⁷_____, it must be achievable. ⁸_____, you must have a clear idea of the path you need to follow in order to achieve it.

**7** Read the quote. Decide if you agree or disagree with the statement. Make notes on four or five points to support your argument.

'Keep true to the dreams of the youth.' (Friedrich Schiller, German playwright)

_____
_____
_____
_____
_____

**8** Now do the task using your notes from exercise 7.

## Writing
# An informal email
*I can show empathy in an informal email.*

You have received an email from an English friend.

*As for starting work next month, I'm dreading it! I'm terrified I won't fit in. What about you – how are you feeling about your new job? Are you doing anything special to prepare for the first day – if so, what?*

Write your email in reply.

**1** Read the task and the email. <u>Underline</u> the two questions in the task and the answers in the email.

To: chris@email.com

Hi Chris,

Thanks for your email – it was great to hear from you! So good to hear you passed all your exams – congratulations on doing so well!

I know what you ¹_____ about dreading starting work. If it ²_____, I feel exactly the same way. I keep on waking up in the middle of the night and wondering how I'll get through the first day. If it's any ³_____, you aren't the only one who'll be getting up at the crack of dawn to trek across town! I still haven't decided yet whether to drive or go on public transport. At least if I get the train, I won't have to sit in a traffic jam for hours.

I see where you're ⁴_____ from with the preparations – there's an awful lot to think about! I don't ⁵_____ about you, but I've spent a fortune on clothes, because I really want to look the part. I've bought a new suit, a couple of shirts, a tie and some smart shoes. Apart from that, I've been thinking of questions I can ask my new colleagues when I meet them. I'm desperate to make a good impression and I really don't want to put my foot in it if I can avoid it.

Well, Chris, it's time for me to go. Enjoy your last week of freedom and try to stay cool. I'm sure ⁶_____ will turn out all right in the end.

Let me know how it goes on Monday.

Best wishes,

Mike

**2** Read the email again and complete the highlighted phrases for showing empathy 1–6.

**3** Read the Writing Strategy. Then find expressions in the email to replace the phrases below.

1 manage to complete _____
2 very early in the morning _____
3 too much _____
4 have the right appearance _____
5 say or do the wrong thing _____
6 remain calm _____

**Writing Strategy**
- Emails follow the same rules as letters: an opening greeting, clear paragraphing and a closing phrase.
- The style depends on the target reader. In the case of a friend, the style should be informal, but the language should be as sophisticated as in a letter. Use contractions instead of full forms, and a wide range of:

1 phrasal verbs: *put up with* (tolerate)
2 idioms: *have stars in your eyes* (dream of being famous)
3 set phrases *Break a leg!* (Good luck with your acting!)

**4** Complete the informal expressions.

1 Let's cross that _____ when we come to it.
2 Get _____ to me as soon as you can.
3 I guess it's time to call it a _____.
4 We're all in the same _____.
5 Give it your best _____ and see what happens.
6 I'm scared that I won't make the _____.
7 She's always a _____ wreck before exams.
8 I'm going to _____ at it until I can do it.

**5** Read the task. Make notes about how you could answer the two questions.

You have received an email from an English friend.

*As for going travelling next month, I'm quite looking forward to it, but I'm afraid I'll get very lonely. How are you feeling about your trip? Are you doing anything special to prepare for the journey – if so, what?*

Write your email in reply.

**6** Write your email (220–260 words), using your notes from exercise 5.

**CHECK YOUR WORK**

**Have you ...**
- ☐ used four paragraphs?
- ☐ used the appropriate informal style?
- ☐ included phrases for giving advice and showing empathy?
- ☐ checked the spelling and grammar?

# 6 Review Unit 6

## Vocabulary

**1 Complete the film review with the words below.**

against time   for lost time   in time   no time   nick of time
of their lives   on borrowed time

*Me, Earl and the Dying Girl* is a hugely successful comedy film about a relationship that becomes a race [1]_____. Greg's mother gives him the unenviable task of befriending Rachel and trying to 'cheer her up' after she's been diagnosed with an incurable disease. But since Rachel is living [2]_____, she doesn't want to waste her last days hanging around with a boy whom she hardly knows.

At first, Rachel has [3]_____ for Greg. But then, [4]_____, a friendship slowly develops. Wishing they had got to know each other earlier, they begin to make up [5]_____ by hanging out together every day. Then, along with Greg's buddy Earl, they have the time [6]_____ making comically bad home movies.

*Me, Earl and the Dying Girl* is a great film with some hilarious moments. Ultimately, dying tragically young doesn't fit well with the film being a comedy – so expect a late twist in the plot to arrive in the [7]_____ for Rachel.

Mark: ___ / 7

**2 Complete the sentences. Choose the correct words from the pairs of antonyms below.**

chaperoned / unaccompanied   distinguished / insignificant
dreary / hair-raising   fearless / fainthearted
liberal / intolerant   unsuitable / fitting

1 That politician has _____, racist views.
2 It isn't _____ to wear shorts to a formal wedding.
3 Ida Laura Pfeiffer was a brave, _____ explorer.
4 Thousands turned out for the funeral of the _____ Nobel-prize-winning scientist.
5 For a few _____ moments during the climb, Iva was left hanging by one hand above a 50-metre drop.
6 Small children must be _____ when they travel.

Mark: ___ / 6

**3 Circle one or two options to complete the sentences.**

1 I've managed to _____ most of my goals in life – with a lot of hard work and a little luck.
   a reach       b attain       c meet
2 Suzie was able to _____ a long-standing dream when she finally met Miley Cyrus.
   a reach       b fulfil       c meet
3 Special-forces soldiers were able to _____ their mission and return safely.
   a attain       b complete       c accomplish

4 After years of incredibly hard work, Salma _____ her ambition of competing in the Olympic Games.
   a realised       b completed       c achieved
5 Few of us are able to _____ all of our aspirations, but it's still important to set ourselves goals.
   a complete       b achieve       c meet
6 In order to win the competition, you have to _____ all the objectives that we set for you in 24 hours.
   a reach       b complete       c meet

Mark: ___ / 6

## Word skills

**4 Complete the sentences. Use each phrasal verb twice.**

fall out   get over   go off   take off

1 We don't know how the prisoner managed to _____ a four-metre-high wall and escape.
2 The fire alarm _____, so we left the building.
3 The doctor told me to _____ my shirt.
4 Lucy and Tom aren't speaking. They've _____.
5 Don't eat that cheese. It's _____.
6 It took a while for our company to _____, but it's doing well now.
7 My younger brother _____ of a tree and broke his arm.
8 _____ the death of my pet dog wasn't easy at all.

Mark: ___ / 8

**5 A student is discussing a quote by a famous person. Complete their words, writing one word in each gap.**

To [1]_____ with, I don't really agree with the quote. As far as I'm [2]_____, it's not true that only imagination limits our aspirations. By and [3]_____, people's aspirations aren't met because of external factors. For one [4]_____, people need to earn money, marry, have children and so on. [5]_____ of this, they often have to put their dreams to one side. Besides, you can have aspirations that you simply don't have the talent to achieve. That is to [6]_____, if you're a mediocre musician, you'll never be a rock star. Even [7]_____, I do think that imagination can help us to achieve more of our goals.

Mark: ___ / 7

## Grammar

**6 Write the two sentences as one with a relative clause.**

1 The film is about an old man. His life changes when he meets a refugee.

   _____

2 Did you book that holiday? You were telling me about it last week.

   _____

# 6

## Review Unit 6

**3** We'd been trekking non-stop for eight hours. At that point, we were exhausted.

_____

**4** At the end of the film, we see a coffee tin. There are Edward's ashes inside it.

_____

**5** People tend to worry about a lot of things. Most of them aren't very important in the end.

_____

**6** There may be a train strike. In that case, Dad will drive us.

_____

**7** 'Hello' won a Grammy award in 2017. It's still one of my favourite songs.

_____

Mark: ___ / 7

**7** Write sentences using reduced relative clauses.

**1** the play / be / show / today / is a romantic comedy

_____

**2** this / be / a memorial to soldiers / kill / in the war

_____

**3** the film / tell / the story of a man / kidnap / by gangsters

_____

**4** it / be / always great / see / someone / fulfil / their dream

_____

**5** the film / direct / by Ang Lee / star / Suraj Sharma

_____

**6** my mum / love / old photos / take / in black and white

_____

Mark: ___ / 6

**8** Choose the correct words to complete the dialogues.

**Leya** Gavin ¹**can hardly have** / **will have** forgotten about band practice because I sent him a text.

**Abi** He ²**could have** / **might not have** got it.

**Leya** No, he got it – he replied straight away.

**Abi** He ³**can** / **could** be stuck in traffic or something?

**Leya** No, he always cycles here, so it ⁴**can't** / **could** be the traffic. There ⁵**may** / **must** be another explanation.

**Man** The museum alarms ⁶**should have** / **may have** gone off, but they didn't. I think the robbers ⁷**can have** / **may have** hacked into the system.

**Guard** They ⁸**may** / **can't** have entered our museum through this hole in the wall, because it's too small. There ⁹**must** / **could** be another way in.

**Man** Unless the robbers ¹⁰**will** / **could** have made that hole for a drone!

Mark: ___ / 10

## Use of English

**9** Choose the correct words to complete the text.

| | | | | | | |
|---|---|---|---|---|---|---|
| **1** | a quoting | **b** to quote | **c** quoted |
| **2** | a completing | **b** fulfilling | **c** reaching |
| **3** | a go off | **b** look forward | **c** get over |
| **4** | a what | **b** that | **c** which |
| **5** | a locating | **b** located | **c** it's located |
| **6** | a may have | **b** can't have | **c** could have |
| **7** | a who | **b** whom | **c** they |
| **8** | a can't have | **b** must have | **c** should have |

'Live your dreams!' It's a piece of advice often ¹_____ but seldom followed. We all talk vaguely about ²_____ the dreams on our 'bucket list', but how often do we actually ³_____ and do it? I have a book with photos of some of the world's most amazing places, very few of ⁴_____ I've seen. But last year, on my 50th birthday, I did something crazy – I asked a friend to open the book and pick any place at random, promising I would go there. She picked the Rainbow Mountains of Zhangye Danxia, ⁵_____ in remote north-western China!

I ⁶_____ asked her to pick somewhere closer to home, but something told me that visiting that place would change me. So, two months later, I found myself on a wind-blown hilltop, staring at those beautiful, surreal mountains. Next to me was a local guide ⁷_____ seemed more interested in his tea than the staggering view. He ⁸_____ seen these mountains every day of his life, but I was gobsmacked. There and then I made a decision to make up for lost time and see more of the world.

Mark: ___ / 8

Total: ___ / 65

## *I can ...*

Read the statements. Think about your progress and tick (✓) one of the boxes.

★ = I need more practice.  ★★★ = No problem!

★★ = I sometimes find this difficult.

| | ★ | ★★ | ★★★ |
|---|---|---|---|
| I can talk about dreams and ambitions. | | | |
| I can use relative clauses and reduced relative clauses. | | | |
| I can understand and react to a radio programme about female explorers in history. | | | |
| I can speculate about different possibilities. | | | |
| I can recognise and use literal and idiomatic phrasal verbs correctly. | | | |
| I can understand and react to the opinions of four people on a historic decision. | | | |
| I can use a range of discourse markers to give my opinion in a debate. | | | |
| I can show empathy in an informal email. | | | |

# 3 Exam Skills Trainer 3

## Reading

**Strategy**

In the multiple-choice task you should first read the whole text to get an overall impression of it. Then you should read each question and underline the part of the text that refers to that question. You should then look at the options and decide which one answers the question.

1 Read the Strategy and the text in exercise 2. Which part of the text refers to question 1? Which option best answers the question?

2 Read the text and choose the correct answers (A, B, C or D).

### New device to clear landmines

Every year between 15,000 and 20,000 people are killed by landmines, and many more are injured. The UN has identified 78 countries where around 110 million of these highly dangerous explosives still lie hidden in the ground, one of the worst affected being Afghanistan. Little wonder, then, that the inventors of the latest device intended to rid the world of this curse are two Afghan brothers.

It was in the mid-1990s that Massoud and Mahmud Hassani were smuggled out of the war-torn country by their anxious mother. After trekking through Pakistan and Uzbekistan, they eventually reached Europe, and ultimately the Netherlands, where they settled and were granted Dutch citizenship. Here the brothers resumed their education before going on to gain university degrees and founding their own company, Hassani Design BV.

The brothers' original design for an anti-mine device was based on a toy they used to make as children. They would hunt in the rubbish for the right materials to make a ball that would roll along the ground in the wind. Once the toy was ready, they would race it against others made by their friends to see whose travelled fastest. The game was frequently interrupted because if the toys left the path, the children could not go after them for fear of stepping on a landmine.

The Mine Kafon (kafon is short for kafondon, 'something that explodes' in the brothers' native Dari language) is a giant version of this toy. With over a hundred bamboo sticks as 'legs', and circular 'feet' made out of biodegradable plastic, the ball rolls along in the wind and detonates any landmines it falls on. The device can detonate up to four mines before too many lost 'legs' renders it ineffective. Relying on wind power, however, means that the user has no control over the instrument's path, so it is never certain that an area has been completely cleared of mines.

The brothers' latest device looks far more promising, however. The Mine Kafon Drone is a flying machine containing a computer, on-board GPS, and a robotic arm. The system works in three stages: mapping, detecting and destroying mines. First, it maps the terrain using a 3D camera. Then, it sweeps the mapped area with a metal detector, hovering around 4 cm above the ground and pinpointing any mines with the GPS coordinates. Finally, it places a small explosive on each mine and then triggers the charge remotely from a safe distance.

So far, several prototypes of the machine have been tested successfully, and the drone has met with the approval of the Dutch military, who have promised to help with further testing. The key phase will be to carry out tests in the field in Afghanistan. Having witnessed the effect of landmines first-hand as children, Massoud and Mahmud Hassani are keen to return to their homeland with a viable solution to the problem.

1 The writer thinks the nationality of the inventors of the latest anti-mine device is
   A appropriate.
   B bizarre.
   C irrelevant.
   D surprising.

2 The hardest part of the brothers' journey to Europe was
   A avoiding areas of conflict.
   B crossing inhospitable countryside.
   C dodging opportunistic criminals.
   D leaving close family behind.

3 The writer describes a child's toy in the third paragraph to
   A give an example of a typical Afghan game.
   B indicate how dangerous life is in Afghanistan.
   C show what a happy childhood the brothers had.
   D explain the origin of the brothers' inspiration.

4 Why wasn't the original Mine Kafon entirely successful?
   A It was blown up too many times.
   B Its design is too intricate for mass production.
   C Its route cannot be determined accurately.
   D The raw materials are difficult to source.

5 The Mine Kafon Drone flies over each area three times to
   A carry out each of its different functions.
   B get an accurate picture of the land.
   C ensure that no mines are left undetected.
   D check the GPS coordinates on the computer.

6 With respect to their future visit to Afghanistan, the Hassani brothers are
   A concerned they may not be able to afford it.
   B hopeful of being able to help their countrymen.
   C fearful that their invention may not work.
   D eager to see their childhood friends once more.

## Listening

**Strategy**

In the multiple-matching task, you should listen for gist meaning rather than detail. You may not understand every word, but you should be able to identify one of the following for each of the tasks: speaker's main point; speaker's feeling; speaker's attitude; speaker's opinion.

# Exam Skills Trainer 3

3 Read the Listening Strategy and the two tasks in exercise 4. Which of the gist meanings in the Strategy do you have to identify in

1 task one? _____    2 task two? _____

4 (🎧 2.10) You will hear five short extracts in which people are talking about a day they had really been looking forward to.

For speakers 1–5, choose an activity from the list A–H that each person was looking forward to.

Speaker 1 _____    A a ceremony
Speaker 2 _____    B a concert
Speaker 3 _____    C a course
Speaker 4 _____    D a game
Speaker 5 _____    E a museum
                   F a play
                   G a movie
                   H a trip

Now, choose from the list A–H for how each speaker felt at the end of the day.

Speaker 1 _____    A agitated
Speaker 2 _____    B disappointed
Speaker 3 _____    C emotional
Speaker 4 _____    D frustrated
Speaker 5 _____    E keen to repeat the experience
                   F relieved
                   G resentful of others
                   H thrilled by experience

## Use of English

**Strategy**
In the word-formation task, identify which part of speech is required to complete the gap and use your knowledge of suffixes to form the new noun, verb, adjective or adverb. In some cases, the new word may need a prefix as well. Look out for spelling changes when you add a suffix.

5 Read the Strategy and the text. Which part of speech is required to complete each gap? Then complete the text with the correct form of the word in brackets.

**Back to nature**

If your idea of a dream holiday is relaxing in a
$^1$_____ (luxury) villa in the Caribbean, you might be surprised by a new trend that is emerging in the UK. The $^2$_____ (popular) of remote wooden cabins in the country has increased dramatically in recent times in $^3$_____ (respond) to a demand from city dwellers for a place to get away from their highly $^4$_____ (stress) lives. Of course, the concept of a country retreat is not new. For centuries, families in countries in North America, Scandinavia and Eastern Europe have $^5$_____

(tradition) had a log cabin to escape to. But a lack of $^6$_____ (afford) land has prevented this practice becoming commonplace in the UK. For a small cabin to be attractive, the key is to $^7$_____ (maximum) space by having multi-purpose furniture and a small extra floor for the sleeping area. Not only is a cabin holiday more ecological than a trip to the Caribbean, but it is also less costly, permitting families to $^8$_____ (long) their stay by a week or so, due to not having to pay for international flights.

## Speaking

**Strategy**
In Part 2, use a variety of words and phrases for comparing and contrasting the various aspects of the photos to demonstrate your range of language.

6 Read the Strategy and decide which of the phrases below are comparing and contrasting. Compare the photos, which both show conflicts. Say what might have caused the conflict and how the people may be feeling.

alike  both  in common  instead  likewise  on the other hand  resemble  unlike  whereas  while

## Writing

**Strategy**
The same conventions apply to an email as to a letter, such as an opening salutation, clear paragraphing and closing phrasing.

7 Read the Strategy and task. Write a paragraph plan, an appropriate salutation, final sentence and closing salutation.

You have received an email from an English friend.

*As for my news, I've started working on Saturdays in my local supermarket. Actually, I'm not enjoying it very much, as one of my colleagues is always putting me down. It makes me feel really uncomfortable. Have you ever had a problem with someone you had to work with? If so, what did you do about it?*

8 Write the informal email (220–260 words) for the task in exercise 7.

# 7 Journeys

## A Road travel
*I can talk about roads and road users.*

**1** Complete the message-board discussion using the words below.

atlas  car  drivers  maintenance  stop  test  traffic

**Instant messenger**

**Jack1010:** Just wondering, is an automatic ¹_____ safer than a manual? Does anyone know? I'm just learning to drive. Thanks!

**EllieW:** Automatics are definitely safer for learner ²_____ because you've always got two hands on the wheel – for example, if you have to make an emergency ³_____.

**TheRat:** Be careful. If you take your driving ⁴_____ in an automatic, you can't drive manual cars.

**BarBar:** I totally disagree with EllieW. With a manual, you're more in control. Also, if you Google 'automatic v manual' and 'road-⁵_____ accidents' you'll find there's no evidence that automatics are safer.

**SpeedyX:** I don't know the answer, but I know my uncle used to put a road ⁶_____ on the accelerator of his automatic to give his foot a rest. ☺

**MrF1:** You don't need to know as much about vehicle ⁷_____ for an automatic as they don't have gears.

**BarBar:** Automatics do have gears.

**2** [🎧 2.11] Listen to six drivers talking about an experience on the road. Complete the sentences using six of the verbs below.

accelerate  brake  change gear  give way  indicate
overtake  pull over  reverse  stall  steer

1 Speaker 1 did not have time to _____, which annoyed other drivers.
2 Speaker 2 found it difficult to _____ and nearly crashed.
3 Speaker 3 needed to _____ suddenly and frightened his passenger.
4 Speaker 4 was told to _____ but was not sure why.
5 Speaker 5 didn't know whether or not to _____.
6 Speaker 6 could not _____ because of a mechanical fault.

**3** [🎧 2.11] Listen again. Match each speaker with the diagram (A–F) that shows where the event occurred. Complete the labels.

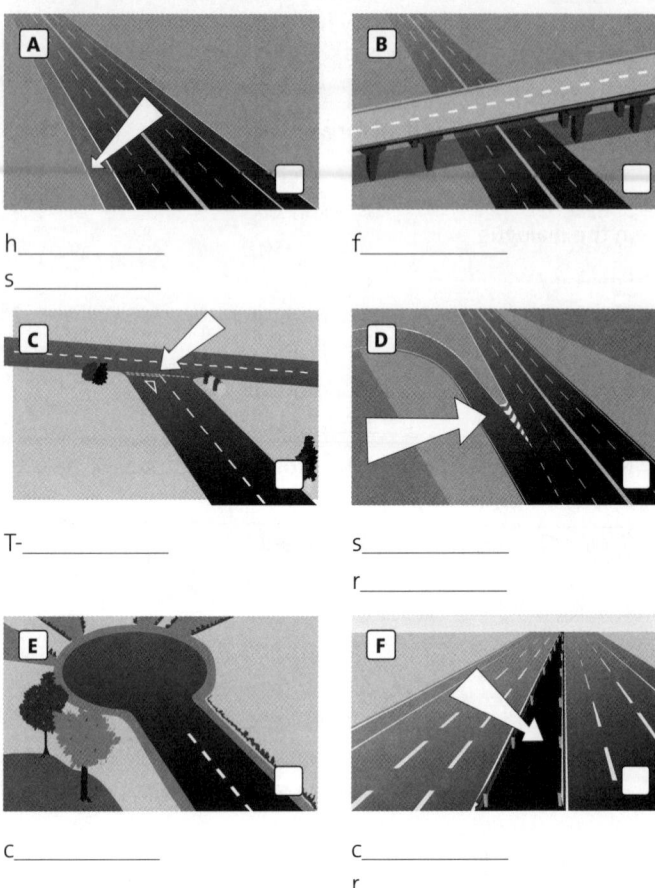

A  h_____
   s_____

B  f_____

C  T-_____

D  s_____
   r_____

E  c_____

F  c_____
   r_____

**4** Match the words for parts of a bike with the definitions below.

brake levers  chain  handlebars  pedals  pump  saddle
spokes  tyres

1 The _____ is the part you sit on.
2 The _____ are the things you press when you want to stop.
3 The _____ are the things you push with your feet.
4 The _____ are the metal things which strengthen the wheel.
5 The _____ are the things you hold when you cycle.
6 The _____ is the thing which makes the back wheel turn when you pedal.
7 The _____ are the rubber things on the outside of the wheels.
8 The _____ is for putting air in the wheels.

**1** Choose the best modal form (a or b) to complete each gap in the dialogue.

**Pat** Are you going? It's only ten o'clock.
**Jen** I know, but I ¹_____ an early night. I'm leaving for the airport at 6 a.m. tomorrow.
**Pat** Really? Where are you going?
**Jen** Indonesia. Surely I ²_____ you about my trip ...
**Pat** No, I had no idea! It sounds fantastic. You ³_____ so excited!
**Jen** Yes, I am.
**Pat** It's a shame Megan isn't here. She spent a few months in Indonesia. She ⁴_____ some useful tips.
**Jen** I'm sure she was here earlier. She ⁵_____.
**Pat** Oh yes, that's right. She ⁶_____ give her friend a lift home. She ⁷_____ back later though. Why don't you wait?
**Jen** No, I can't. Anyway, I'd ⁸_____ her when I'm there, if I have any questions.

| | | | |
|---|---|---|---|
| **1** a | must be getting | **b** | need to get |
| **2** a | must have told | **b** | should have told |
| **3** a | need to be | **b** | must be |
| **4** a | might have | **b** | needs to have |
| **5** a | must have left | **b** | should have left |
| **6** a | must | **b** | had to |
| **7** a | must be | **b** | should be |
| **8** a | be better off texting | **b** | better text |

**2** Complete the sentences with *didn't need to* or *needn't have* and the verb in brackets.

**1** In the end, we stayed with friends, so I _____ (spend) so much time looking at hotels last weekend!

**2** We _____ (change) trains – our train was direct all the way to Biarritz.

**3** We took bikes with us, so we _____ (hire) them when we were away.

**4** Thanks for all the gifts, although you _____ (buy) me so much!

**5** You _____ (come) by taxi – you could have walked here in ten minutes!

**6** The receptionist had our bill ready when we came downstairs – we _____ (ask) for it.

**3** Complete the second sentence so that it means the same as the first. Include one modal form from A and B below.

A can't have   may be   ~~might have~~   might not have   must have   shouldn't have

B ~~had to~~   had to   had to   having to   needed to   needed to

**1** Perhaps your friends were obliged to spend the night at the airport.
Your friends *might have had to spend the night* at the airport.

**2** It's wrong that it was necessary for you to leave your passport at reception.
You _____ your passport at reception.

**3** Perhaps it is necessary for him to work overtime today.
He _____ today.

**4** It's impossible that Bess was obliged to pay for her visa. They're free.
Bess _____ her visa. They're free.

**5** Without a doubt, it was necessary for your parents to walk home. There were no taxis.
Your parents _____ home. There were no taxis.

**6** Perhaps it was unnecessary for them to book a table in advance.
They _____ in advance.

**4** Write a sentence about something that:

**1** you'd better do before the end of the week.
_____
_____

**2** you should have done (but you didn't do it).
_____
_____

**3** you needn't have done (but you did it).
_____
_____

**4** might be doing soon.
_____
_____

# 7C Listening
## Crossing borders
*I can understand first-person accounts by migrants.*

**Revision:** Student's Book page 77

**1 Complete the sentences with the words below. There are two extra words.**

contaminated  delinquents  dinghy  disconsolate
doctorate  haversack  jetty  loudhailer  mortar
persecute

1 He was carrying a small _____ containing a few possessions.
2 They couldn't drink the water from the well because it was _____.
3 I learned to sail in a _____.
4 After her degree, she spent five years working on her _____.
5 By the time they arrived, the travellers were looking tired and _____.
6 The UN has condemned the country's dictatorship for continuing to _____ minorities.
7 Two boys were sitting on the _____, fishing.
8 The police officer was using a _____ to urge the protestors to remain peaceful.

**Listening Strategy**

To help you understand unknown words, ask yourself:

1 Is the general meaning of the word clear? For example: *'That's typical!' he retorted.* ('Retorted' is a speech verb.)
   *He wore a red cravat.* ('Cravat' is an item of clothing.)
2 Is the word part of a pair or list of more familiar words?
   *His clothes were old, dirty and dishevelled.* ('Dishevelled' must be related in meaning to 'old' and 'dirty'.)
3 Is the word followed by a result or explanation?
   *I felt so befuddled that I wasn't even sure why I was there.* ('Befuddled' must broadly mean 'confused'.)

**2** [2.12] **Read the Listening Strategy. Then listen to eight short extracts. Which word is missing from each extract? Circle the best word.**

1 challenging  repetitive  terrifying
2 cramped  damp  noisy
3 fashionable  faulty  over-priced
4 cake  coffee  newspaper
5 dark  comfortable  plastic
6 expensive  relaxing  sunny
7 awful  pleasant  surprising
8 animals  birds  insects

**3** [2.12] **Listen again. Which point from the Listening Strategy (1–3) helped you to work out each missing word?**

1 _____    3 _____    5 _____    7 _____
2 _____    4 _____    6 _____    8 _____

**4** [2.13] **Listen to five people talking about leaving the UK. In which country has each speaker decided to live?**

Speaker 1 _____    Speaker 4 _____
Speaker 2 _____    Speaker 5 _____
Speaker 3 _____

**5** [2.13] **Listen again. For questions 1 and 2, choose from the list (A–H). There are three extra sentences. Write your answers in the charts.**

1 What was each speaker's main reason for going to live in another country?
   A because the climate is healthier
   B to learn about another country's traditions
   C to pursue a course of studies
   D because of a valuable inheritance
   E to earn enough money to pay off debts
   F because no work was available at home
   G because of a family member's work
   H to escape from the stress of city life

| Speaker | 1 | 2 | 3 | 4 | 5 |
|---------|---|---|---|---|---|
|         |   |   |   |   |   |

2 What does each speaker miss about the UK?
   A spending time with friends
   B English television programmes
   C the British sense of humour
   D the British weather
   E the English countryside
   F the historic streets and buildings
   G traditional English breakfasts
   H the excitement of living in a big city

| Speaker | 1 | 2 | 3 | 4 | 5 |
|---------|---|---|---|---|---|
|         |   |   |   |   |   |

## Grammar
# Talking about ability
*I can talk about past, present and future ability.*

**1 Circle the correct answer. Choose both if both are correct.**

1 His Spanish is good but he _____ speak French.
  **a** isn't able to        **b** can't

2 I keep hearing a mosquito, but I _____ see it.
  **a** am not able to      **b** can't

3 My sister is a very shy person, although she _____ also be very funny at times.
  **a** can              **b** could

4 I had so little money with me that I _____ pay for my bus home.
  **a** could barely       **b** barely managed to

5 As the boat came closer, I grabbed the rope and _____ climb aboard.
  **a** could           **b** was able to

6 I got out of bed because I _____ smell burning.
  **a** could           **b** managed to

**2 Rewrite the sentences changing the <u>underlined</u> form of *be able to* to one of the verb forms below.**

can  could  could  couldn't  managed to

1 On the third attempt, I <u>was able to</u> enter my password correctly.
_____

2 It was dark, so I <u>wasn't able to</u> see his face clearly.
_____

3 Mozart <u>was able to</u> play the piano at a very young age.
_____

4 If I saved up, I <u>would be able to</u> buy a new phone.
_____

5 <u>I'll be able to</u> text you tomorrow night.
_____

**3 Complete the sentences with the verb forms below.**

be able to  being able to  to be able to

1 You should _____ see France from here.
2 I hate not _____ speak their language.
3 He's too old now _____ travel for free.
4 My grandfather remembers _____ park next to the runway at airports.
5 You must _____ get a phone signal here.

**4 Complete the text with the correct forms of the verbs below. Only use a form of *be able to* if no other verbs are possible.**

(not) be able to  can / can't  could / couldn't
managed to / didn't manage to

The Antarctic is a hostile environment to explore. Not only ¹_____ the temperature drop well below -50°C, but also fierce blizzards sometimes mean not ²_____ leave your tent for days on end. And yet the region has always fascinated explorers, many of whom go there hoping ³_____ reach the South Pole. The first person to reach it was the Norwegian explorer Roald Amundsen, who ⁴_____ get there in December 1911. A British expedition led by Robert Scott also ⁵_____ reach the Pole, but 33 days after Amundsen. Tragically, Scott and his men ⁶_____ complete the return journey, and died.

Improvements in transport and communications mean that these days anyone ⁷_____ visit the Antarctic, and several holiday companies offer excursions there. In the future, though, new laws ⁸_____ limit the number of visitors, in order to protect the natural environment and wildlife.

**5 Write a true sentence about:**

1 something you managed to do despite difficulties.
_____

2 somewhere you wish you could visit.
_____

3 something you hope to be able to do soon.
_____

4 something you've never been able to do.
_____

5 somebody who can do something you find surprising and / or impressive.
_____

# Verb patterns
*I can use various different verb patterns correctly.*

**1** **Match the examples below with the verb forms (a–h).**

being chased  broken  escaping  having decided
remember  to be made  to have happened  to promise

**a** infinitive _____
**b** passive infinitive _____
**c** gerund _____
**d** passive gerund _____
**e** base form _____
**f** past participle _____
**g** perfect gerund _____
**h** perfect infinitive _____

**2** **Complete the text with the verbs in brackets. Choose from the forms in exercise 1.**

**Henry Brown** was born into a family of slaves in Virginia, USA, in the the early part of the 19th century. Although he later described his master as very kind, Henry longed ¹_____ (live) as a free man. At this time in American history, certain states – generally those in the south – still allowed slaves ²_____ (keep). In the 'free states' of the north, slavery was against the law. Henry Brown knew that, if he managed ³_____ (get) to a free state, he would be free, so he decided ⁴_____ (devise) a plan. He had a special box ⁵_____ (make) and arranged for two friends ⁶_____ (post) the box to Pennsylvania.

On the day of his escape, he succeeded in ⁷_____ (send) home from work by deliberately burning his hand. He hid inside the box and had his friends ⁸_____ (hand) it over to the postal service. It was a long and uncomfortable journey – 27 hours in total – but he never considered ⁹_____ (give) up. Eventually the box arrived in Philadelphia, where members of the Anti-Slavery Society were waiting ¹⁰_____ (receive) it.

As a free man, Henry Brown spent several years ¹¹_____ (appear) at anti-slavery events, where he encouraged audiences ¹²_____ (support) abolition. After that he decided ¹³_____ (become) an entertainer and ended up ¹⁴_____ (tour) the USA and England as a successful stage magician.

**3** **Put the words in the correct order.**

**1** husband / insisted / selling / on / her
She _____
_____ the painting.

**2** had / animal / heard / given / being / of / never / an
I _____
_____ an award.

**3** poems / his / be / longed / for / to / published
My father always _____
_____ in a book.

**4** brother / resented / getting / her
She always _____
_____ better grades.

**5** having / work / confessed / son / to / made / his
He _____
_____ long hours for no pay.

**6** asking / waiter / can't / bring / face / the / to
I _____
_____ more water again.

**7** stop / shouted / his / at / to / chasing / dog
The man _____
_____ the sheep.

---

**VOCAB BOOST!**

When you come across new verbs that you want to learn, write down the verb patterns. Remember to:

- use brackets when part of the pattern is optional.
- make a note of any differences in meaning between different verb patterns.
  *help sb (to) do sth*
  *stop doing sth* (= not do it any more)
  *stop to do sth* (= pause so you can do it)

---

**4** **Read the *Vocab Boost!* box. Then look back at your answers to exercise 3 and write the verb patterns for the verbs below.**

**1** (insist) *insist on sb doing sth*
**2** (have heard) _____
**3** (long) _____
**4** (resent) _____
**5** (confess) _____
   (make) _____
**6** (can't face) _____
   (ask) _____
**7** (shout) _____
   (stop) _____

# Time traveller

*I can understand a text about whether time travel is possible or not.*

**Revision:** Student's Book page 80

### Reading Strategy

When a text is organised into paragraphs, the first one or two sentences of each paragraph often indicate what information it will contain. Use these paragraph openers to get a general understanding of what the text is about and to help you find your way around longer texts.

1  Read the Reading Strategy. Then read the first sentence or two of each paragraph (1–5). Which paragraph(s) is / are about:

  a  scientific theories of time travel? _____

  b  an event organised by a well-known scientist? _____

  c  an event organised by some students? _____

2  Read the text. Choose the best answer (a–d).

1  What was unusual about the way the party in 2009 was organised?
   a  Its location was given as co-ordinates rather than as a normal address.
   b  The invitations were sent out after the party had finished.
   c  The organiser did not want any guests to arrive.
   d  Refreshments were only provided after the guests had left.

2  The party convinced Hawking that travelling back in time:
   a  will never be mastered by humans.
   b  is not yet possible but will be one day.
   c  is a scientific fact.
   d  probably exists but cannot be proved.

3  The event at MIT was different from Hawking's party in that:
   a  far more invitations were issued.
   b  it was not openly publicised.
   c  the organisers did not expect anyone to attend.
   d  it was not only for people from the future.

4  Why did Mr Dorai suggest that time travellers should bring a solution to world poverty?
   a  To prove they are really from the future.
   b  Because poverty is a global problem.
   c  Because he hoped it would make him rich.
   d  To show people that the world is getting better.

5  The creation of 'wormholes' in space-time:
   a  is the only proven way to travel back in time.
   b  already allows travel into the future.
   c  is one possible way that time travel to the past might be achieved.
   d  is thought impossible by most scientists.

## TIME TRAVELLERS **WELCOME**

**1**  On 28 June 2009, the famous British physicist Professor Stephen Hawking held a party for time travellers. For several hours, surrounded by decorations and refreshments, Professor Hawking waited for other guests to arrive. Nobody came. The invitation to the party clearly stated the time and venue, even giving the GPS co-ordinates for the location. Unusually, though, no invitations were sent out until after the party had taken place.

**2**  The point of hosting the party in such a strange way was to demonstrate that time travel is almost certainly impossible. If time travellers existed, the fact that invitations to the party were only issued after the party had taken place would not have been a problem: the time travellers could simply have gone back in time in order to attend. The fact that this did not happen is an indication, in Professor Hawking's view, that travelling back in time is impossible – not only today but at any time in the future.

**3**  In fact, the idea of inviting time travellers to a special event did not originate with Professor Hawking. In 2005, some graduate students at the Massachusetts Institute of Technology, led by 22-year-old Amal Dorai, organised a similar event. They called it a 'convention for time travellers' and produced invitations on special long-lasting paper, which they placed inside random books in the library.

**4**  Unlike Professor Hawking's party, this event was not solely for time travellers; guests from the present era were also invited. An online invitation asked guests from the future to bring something with them that would convince people that they were genuine time travellers. Mr Dorai suggested that a cure for cancer or a solution to global poverty would be particularly appreciated. But he denied that, if no time travellers arrived, it would prove that time travel is impossible.

**5**  Although most physicists are sceptical about the possibility of travelling back in time, some do not rule it out completely. Einstein's theories of space-time seem to allow for the possible creation of a special kind of tunnel called a 'wormhole', which some people believe could provide a route backwards in time. Of course, travelling forwards in time is much easier; we are doing that constantly! And if we travelled away from Earth on a super-fast spacecraft and then returned, we would find that far less time had passed for us than for the people who had stayed on Earth. People who had been younger than us before we left would now be years older. This kind of travel into the future fits completely with Einstein's theories of space and time. Travelling into the past seems to be a great deal more challenging, if not impossible.

# 7G Speaking
## Collaborative task
*I can discuss and reach an agreement about holidays.*

**1 Match the two halves of these holiday activities. Then use one of them to label the photo.**

| | | | |
|---|---|---|---|
| 1 | admire | a | the slopes |
| 2 | get away | b | your feet up |
| 3 | hit | c | the local cuisine |
| 4 | lounge | d | the scenery |
| 5 | put | e | a film or show |
| 6 | sample | f | by the pool |
| 7 | take | g | from it all |
| 8 | take in | h | at water sports |
| 9 | try your hand | i | a dip in the sea |

He's _____.

**2 Explain in your own words what activities you would expect to do on these types of holiday:**

1 A Caribbean cruise: _____
_____

2 A spa holiday: _____
_____

3 A city break: _____
_____

**3 🎧 2.14 Listen to two students discussing plans for a holiday with friends after their exams. Tick (✓) the factors they mention. Which factor (a–f) do they agree is the most important?**

a the best type of accommodation _____

b the best location _____

c what activities are available _____

d travelling time to the destination _____

e overall cost of the holiday _____

f the likely weather at the destination _____

They agree that factor _____ is the most important.

**4 🎧 2.14 Read the Speaking Strategy. Then listen again and complete the questions the students ask.**

1 Why _____ of a villa?

2 Would _____ stay in the mountains?

3 Would _____ the holiday needs to be cheap?

4 What's _____ camping?

5 What _____ hotels?

6 Don't _____ cost is a really important factor?

**5 Which three questions from exercise 4 are closed rather than open?**

Questions _____, _____ and _____ are closed.

**6 Look at the task. Think about which factors would be most important and why. Make notes for each point.**

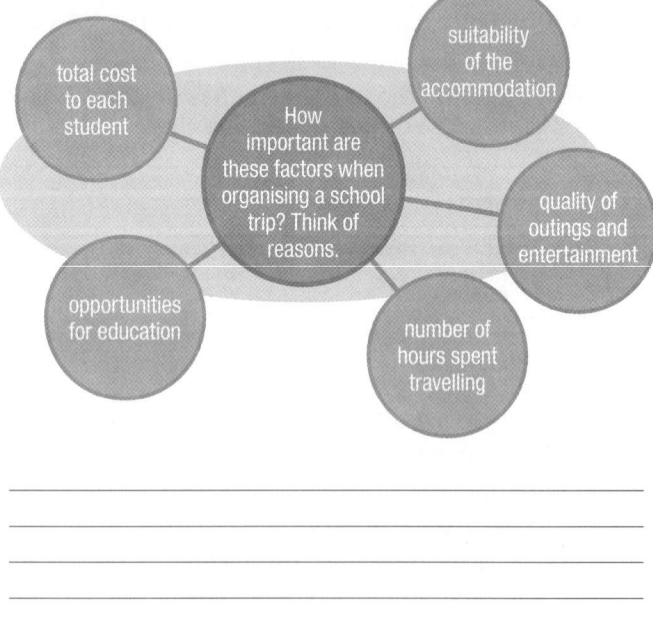

_____
_____
_____
_____
_____

**7 Now do the task using your notes from exercise 6.**

## Writing
# Letter of complaint
*I can write a letter of complaint.*

**1 Match the words below with the definitions.**

a mechanical fault   a pile-up   a puncture   a security alert
gridlock   industrial action   road works   turbulence

1 _____: a road-traffic accident involving a large number of vehicles
2 _____: disruption caused by a suspected bomb
3 _____: a hole in a vehicle's tyre
4 _____: a refusal to work by a group of employees
5 _____: repairs to the road network
6 _____: atmospheric conditions which cause aircraft to shake
7 _____: traffic congestion that is so bad that vehicles are unable to move at all
8 _____: a technical problem with a vehicle

**2 Read the task and the letter. Which two of the problems below did the writer face?**

cancellations   collision   delays   diversions   lost luggage
overcrowding

You recently experienced several problems with travel and accommodation while on an organised five-day hiking trip in the mountains. Write a letter of complaint to the holiday company explaining what went wrong and demanding action.

> **Writing Strategy**
> To make the language of a letter appropriately formal, we often use:
> - *should* + subject + base form instead of *if* + subject + present simple in first conditional sentences:
>   *Should you wish to complain, call this number.*
> - a possessive adjective instead of an object pronoun in verb patterns that include a gerund:
>   *I understand your wanting to complain.*
> - a variety of higher-level vocabulary instead of simple verbs like *go, try, do*, etc.
>   *We proceeded to the check-in area and attempted to find the correct desk.*

**3 Read the Writing Strategy. Then write examples from the essay of the three points above.**

_____
_____
_____

**4 Which paragraph of the letter (1–4) refers to:**

a problems with accommodation? _____
b reasons for writing the letter? _____
c what should happen next? _____
d travel problems? _____

Dear Sir or Madam,

I am writing to complain about the inadequate service I received from your travel company during a recent five-day trip to the Alps. Although I cannot fault the staff who accompanied us during the hikes, the provisions made by the company for travel and accommodation were completely unsatisfactory.

Having endured an early-morning flight to Zurich, we were extremely disappointed to learn that we would have to wait four hours for our free transfer to the hotel, so that passengers from later flights could share the same coach. During this time, we endeavoured to arrange our own transfer. However, the cost of this proved to be exorbitant, so we were obliged to wait.

The hotel we were eventually taken to was not the one advertised on your website and was, we felt, vastly inferior in terms of comfort and facilities. The rooms we were allocated did not offer adequate space for two people to share. The restaurant was also too small for the number of guests wishing to have breakfast in the mornings. When we complained, we were told that the package we had booked did not guarantee our being assigned to any particular hotel.

I trust that you will investigate this complaint fully and offer an appropriate form of compensation in due course. Should you wish to receive any further details of the holiday, please contact me by telephone.

Yours faithfully,

Mrs S Burton

You recently returned from a one-week language course in Ireland and were unhappy with the accommodation and excursions on offer. Write a letter of complaint to the holiday company explaining what went wrong and demanding action.

**5 Read the task. Then plan your letter using your answers to exercise 4 to help you.**

**6 Write your letter (220–260 words), using your plan from exercise 5.**

> **CHECK YOUR WORK**
> **Have you ...**
> ☐ checked your spelling and grammar?
> ☐ used appropriately formal language?
> ☐ written 220–260 words?

# 7 Review Unit 7

## Vocabulary

**1 Match the words below with the quotes.**

accelerate   automatic car   reflectors   road atlas   saddle
speed bumps

1 'It's really uncomfortable to sit on when you're cycling for a long time.' _____
2 'You're looking at the wrong page – we're nowhere near York at the moment.' _____
3 'Hey, slow down when you go over those!' _____
4 'You can go a bit faster – the speed limit is 70.' _____
5 'The best thing about this vehicle is that you don't have to change gears.' _____
6 'I should clean these, so people can see me more easily in the dark.' _____

Mark: ___ / 6

**2 Complete the sentences with suitable verbs.**

1 _____ a right turn at the end of this road.
2 The car went off the road and into a field, then it _____ to a halt.
3 You have to _____ way here, and wait for cars on the main road to pass.
4 Lisa _____ a glance at her taxi driver as he changed lanes without checking in his mirror.
5 Steam's coming from the engine, so let's _____ over onto the hard shoulder and see what the problem is.
6 The brakes _____ a shriek as the car suddenly stopped.
7 The car made a terrible sound when Toby clumsily _____ gear.

Mark: ___ / 7

## Word skills

**3 Complete the dialogue with the correct form of the verbs in brackets.**

**Simon** I expected ¹_____ (see) you at the concert, but you weren't there.
**Taylor** Yes, I'm really annoyed that I missed it. Mick's car broke down, so we were left ²_____ (sit) at the side of a road. We spent ages ³_____ (wait) for a bus to come, so by the time we managed ⁴_____ (arrive) at the venue, the gig had started.
**Simon** You should have texted me. I could have got them ⁵_____ (open) the doors for you.
**Taylor** I considered ⁶_____ (call) you, but I didn't want ⁷_____ (cause) you any trouble when you were busy doing the lighting.

Mark: ___ / 7

**4 Choose the correct words to complete the sentences.**

1 The **likely** / **so-called** 'time traveller' claimed to be a solider from the future. What nonsense!
2 **On the face of it** / **Likely**, this looks like an ordinary pen – but it actually contains a tiny listening device.
3 It's **ostensibly** / **alleged** that Christopher cheated in the exam, but he's denied it.
4 It's **supposed** / **apparent** that the man knew a lot about computers.
5 It's very **likely** / **supposed** that Sean is telling the truth.
6 We don't know how the magician managed to perform the **alleged** / **seemingly** impossible trick of disappearing in front of our eyes.

Mark: ___ / 6

**5 Complete the holiday adverts with the words below.**

admire   cruise   get away   hit   put   sample   sightseeing
take in   trekking

### Nine-night Caribbean ¹_____ on the *Ocean Princess*, departing Fort Lauderdale.

Visit the beautiful islands Puerto Rico, St Thomas, Antigua and Martinique on the *Ocean Princess*, with plenty of time in port to enjoy ²_____ tours of the islands or ³_____ the beach. On days spent entirely at sea, ⁴_____ your feet up and relax by the pool. Alternatively, ⁵_____ a film or a show – the *Ocean Princess* is famous for its on-board entertainment.

### Walk the Inca Way with Sacred Valley Holidays

⁶_____ from it all on our five-day ⁷_____ holiday on ancient Inca trails from Cuzco to the fabled city of Machu Picchu. ⁸_____ the beautiful scenery of the Urubamba Valley. Stay in local houses overnight and ⁹_____ the local cuisine.

Mark: ___ / 9

**6 Complete the words in the sentences.**

1 We had to put up with a three-hour d_____ on the motorway after an accident closed the road near Bradford.
2 The rail union has threatened i_____ a_____, with all staff stopping work.
3 After two days, the airline finally l_____ our lost luggage. But we were in London and it was in Oslo!
4 My bike's got a p_____ in the front the tyre.
5 We p_____ expensive tickets, but we were given uncomfortable seats with a poor view of the stage.
6 The museum was closed, and the guard outside d_____ to give us any information.

Mark: ___ / 6

# Review Unit 7

## Grammar

**7** Choose the correct words to complete the text.

| | | |
|---|---|---|
| 1 **a** should | **b** ought | **c** must |
| 2 **a** 'd better | **b** have to | **c** needn't |
| 3 **a** should have | **b** have to | **c** had to |
| 4 **a** needed to realise | **b** must have realised | **c** should have realised |
| 5 **a** oughtn't | **b** must | **c** needed to |
| 6 **a** had to | **b** should | **c** ought |
| 7 **a** needed to | **b** needn't have | **c** could have |
| 8 **a** would have had to | **b** needed to have | **c** ought to have |

Last summer we were in Paris, and we decided that we really $^1$_____ to visit the Palace of Versailles. We thought we $^2$_____ get there early to beat the crowds, so we $^3$_____ get up very early in the morning to catch the train. We $^4$_____ that even in the early morning, a world-famous attraction like the Palace of Versailles would have a huge queue to get in. My friends and I had to queue for nearly one and half hours before we finally got into the palace grounds!

Versailles Palace is beautiful, and you really $^5$_____ see it when you visit Paris – but you $^6$_____ do some research on the internet before you go. We didn't know that we $^7$_____ waited in the long queue because you can purchase 'jump the queue' priority tickets online. We $^8$_____ pay a bit more for those, but it would certainly have been worth it.

Mark: _____ / 8

**8** Complete the sentences with the correct form of the phrases below.

able / depart   be able / relax   be able / sing   can / be / easy
can / get   can / go   manage / prove   must / be able / reach

1 If I pass the exam, I _____ all summer.
2 Many scientists believe that there is actually more than one universe, but so far nobody _____ it.
3 We _____ any further because the road was closed.
4 The flight _____ because of bad weather, so we had to wait around in the airport all day.
5 Put medicines and any dangerous household chemicals in a locked cupboard – children _____ them.
6 Max _____ the invitation, or he would definitely be here.
7 I'd love _____ well, but unfortunately my voice is terrible.
8 I don't know how Børge Ousland managed to walk across the Arctic to Canada. It certainly _____.

Mark: _____ / 8

## Use of English

**9** Complete the text with one suitable word in each gap.

When we were on holiday in the USA last summer, and visiting Cookeville, Tennessee, some friends arranged $^1$_____ us to visit the nearby Cummins Falls.

The waterfall itself $^2$_____ be reached by road – you $^3$_____ park near a small visitor centre then hike down into a wooded gorge. After walking a few kilometres down a beautiful trail, you suddenly $^4$_____ to a halt as you catch your first glimpse of the spectacular falls. These tumble down a series of steps, which are so perfectly flat and parallel that they appear to have $^5$_____ deliberately cut, although they are completely natural.

The falls are a popular picnicking and swimming spot for locals, but you'd $^6$_____ be prepared for a shock if you decide to swim. Even in the height of summer, the cold water is likely to take your breath away at first. Unless you are an experienced and hardy local, you will probably be $^7$_____ to stay in the water for very long. I soon decided that I was better $^8$_____ sitting on a rock and enjoying the sun!

Mark: _____ / 8

Total: _____ / 65

## I can ...

Read the statements. Think about your progress and tick (✓) one of the boxes.

★ = I need more practice.   ★★★ = No problem!

★★ = I sometimes find this difficult.

| | ★ | ★★ | ★★★ |
|---|---|---|---|
| I can talk about roads and road users. | | | |
| I can use modal verbs correctly for advice and prohibition. | | | |
| I can understand first-person accounts by migrants. | | | |
| I can talk about past, present and future ability. | | | |
| I can use various different verb patterns correctly. | | | |
| I can understand a text about whether time travel is possible or not. | | | |
| I can discuss and reach an agreement about holidays. | | | |
| I can write a letter of complaint. | | | |

# 8 Secrets

## Vocabulary

## A Cover-up and conspiracy
*I can talk about cover-ups, privacy and journalism.*

**1 Match the words and phrases below to the definitions. Two phrases are not used.**

conspiracy theory   exposé   face allegations   hack into   libel
plot   secure a scoop   slander

1 the crime of saying untrue things about someone
_____

2 to illegally access someone's email, phone or electronic records _____

3 an article or TV programme which reveals surprising facts
_____

4 the crime of writing untrue things about someone
_____

5 a secret plan to do something _____

6 when you have to defend yourself against accusations that you've done wrong _____

**2 Choose the correct words to complete the text.**

| | | |
|---|---|---|
| 1 a plots | b scandal | c revelations |
| 2 a cover-up | b exposé | c public outcry |
| 3 a outcry | b smear | c scandal |
| 4 a obtain | b slander | c emerge |
| 5 a damage | b accuse | c secure |
| 6 a hamper | b smear campaign | c slander |
| 7 a accused | b libelled | c plotted |
| 8 a cover-up | b conspiracy | c revelation |
| 9 a secure | b obtain | c hamper |
| 10 a conspiracy theory | b public outcry | c cover-up |
| 11 a pay out | b damage | c emerge |
| 12 a libel | b damages | c allegations |
| 13 a issue | b secure | c settle |

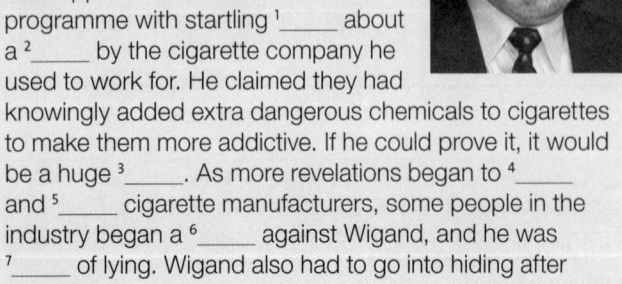

## Jeffrey Wigand fights the tobacco companies

**IN** 1996 biochemist Jeffrey Wigand appeared on an American TV programme with startling ¹_____ about a ²_____ by the cigarette company he used to work for. He claimed they had knowingly added extra dangerous chemicals to cigarettes to make them more addictive. If he could prove it, it would be a huge ³_____. As more revelations began to ⁴_____ and ⁵_____ cigarette manufacturers, some people in the industry began a ⁶_____ against Wigand, and he was ⁷_____ of lying. Wigand also had to go into hiding after receiving threats. It was a ⁸_____ to silence Wigand at any cost, and ⁹_____ any enquiry into his claims. But in the end, the ¹⁰_____ was so great that the US Congress investigated Wigand's claims – and cigarette companies had to ¹¹_____ billions in ¹²_____ in order to ¹³_____ lawsuits.

**3 Choose the correct words to complete the sentences.**

1 I certainly don't **comply with** / **condone** phone hacking.
2 We **concur** / **endorse** with you – you're right.
3 Sports people often **accede to** / **endorse** sports products and appear in advertisements for them.
4 All journalists at this newspaper have to **comply with** / **acquiese in** our new codes of conduct.
5 The Prime Minister has **concurred with** / **assented to** the demands for an investigation.
6 Why did you **accede to** / **acquiesce in** the cover-up when you knew it was illegal?

**4 🎧 2.15 Listen to someone talking about Edward Snowden. Are the sentences true or false?**

1 Edward Snowden was a journalist. _____
2 Snowden sold government secrets to the Russians. _____
3 Snowden has been accused of spying. _____
4 The Russian government has hampered American attempts to arrest him. _____

**5 🎧 2.15 Listen again and complete the sentences with 1–2 words.**

1 Snowden revealed how the NSA and other agencies were listening in on the _____ of millions of people.
2 The NSA were obtaining information about people's _____ opinions and private lives.
3 The revelations harmed America's international _____.
4 The Russian government doesn't _____ his actions, but it has allowed him to live in their country.
5 It hasn't acquiesced to US demands to _____ Snowden.
6 Some people think that Snowden has _____ efforts to catch terrorists, but others support his actions.

**6 Complete the sentences with suitable euphemisms.**

1 We had a _____ exchange of _____ – I accused him of theft and he called me a liar.
2 Dictators use false news stories and other _____ to convince their people that everything is going well.
3 We have to _____ 50 employees _____ because the company isn't doing very well at the moment.
4 A lot of _____ disadvantaged people live in Mumbai, but it's home to some very wealthy people too.
5 Grandad's hair is getting a little _____ on _____, but he doesn't want to wear a wig.
6 I've _____ on a few extra _____ over the Christmas period.

**Grammar**
# Emphatic forms
*I can use a variety of structures to add emphasis.*

**1** Rewrite the sentences with *it, what* or *all* to give more emphasis.

1 I just want you to be honest with me. (all)

_____

2 The police were puzzled by how the criminal managed to escape. (what)

_____

3 The only thing we need is more time. (all)

_____

4 Kelly loves Dan for his sense of humour. (it)

_____

5 We want more information from witnesses. (what)

_____

**2** Rewrite the sentences using the words and phrases below and emphatic forms.

goodness knows   on earth   trouble   truth   whatsoever

1 Who can tell why he gave up football, but he did.

_____

2 Jenny and Greg are both nice, but they don't get on.

_____

3 What are you doing in my room?

_____

4 To be honest, you really upset me – although I know you didn't mean to.

_____

5 I can't speak any Spanish.

_____

**3** Rewrite the sentences using *do / does / did* or reflexive pronouns for emphasis.

1 Students must write the stories for the competition, and not download anything from the internet.

_____

2 Please be on time tomorrow morning.

_____

3 You have to cook your own dinner tonight.

_____

4 Kelly really sings very well.

_____

5 Nobody helped me to prepare the presentation.

_____

**4** Choose the correct words to complete the mini-dialogues.

**Ruth**  I [1]**myself / did** like the song you guys performed, but whose song was it?

**Jenny**  We wrote the song [2]**ourselves / whatever**.

**Ruth**  Gosh, you [3]**do / yourself** have a lot of talent! Where [4]**on earth / whatsoever** do you get your ideas?

**Dad**  [5]**Goodness / Do** tell us when you're going to be home late, Carrie.

**Carrie**  [6]**What / All** I did was stay a bit longer. Why all the fuss?

**Dad**  [7]**The truth / It** is we were worried about you. [8]**Goodness / Whatever** knows – you read about terrible things in the paper these days.

**5** Complete the text. Write one word in each gap.

**ONLY** the worst prisoners were sent to Alcatraz – an 'inescapable' prison island in San Francisco Bay which boasted inmates like Al Capone and George 'Machine Gun' Kelly. [1]_____ made it impossible to escape Alcatraz was its location. It was tantalisingly close to San Francisco, but the [2]_____ was the sea currents that pulled swimmers out to sea, and to their deaths. Some prisoners [3]_____ try to escape from time to time, but they were all accounted for: caught, shot or drowned.

[4]_____ was Frank Lee Morris's arrival at Alcatraz in 1960 which changed things. [5]_____ Morris had known from an early age was a life of crime, and getting [6]_____ out of one prison after another. At Alcatraz he met Alan West and brothers John and Clarence Anglin. Together they made a plan, which involved secretly making [7]_____ digging tools, a crude life raft – and models of their heads! At night, they dug holes in their cell walls – then through the roof of their cell block. [8]_____ knows how they weren't caught!

[9]_____ was on 11 June 1962 that they attempted to escape. West couldn't get through the hole in his cell, and [10]_____ he could do was watch. The others [11]_____ break out, leaving dummy heads behind in bed so it looked like they were sleeping. They climbed out of their cell block, then across the roofs of Alcatraz.

[12]_____ happened after that remains a mystery to this day.

The [13]_____ is, 'Did the men make it?' How on [14]_____ could they get across the treacherous bay at night? And even if they [15]_____ reach the shore, where could they go afterwards, with no money or transport? Extensive searches revealed no sign of the men [16]_____. [17]_____ the police could do was hope for a tip-off from the public. It never came. Perhaps the men drowned that night, or perhaps they spent the rest of their lives as free men – the [18]_____ is that nobody knows.

# Spilling the beans

*I can understand people gossiping.*

**Revision:** Student's Book page 89

**1** **Complete the mini-dialogues with the words below.**

between   bite   breathe   further   gets out   hat
hearsay   latest   quote   rumour   sealed

**Matt**  Have you heard the ¹_____ gossip? Ryan's broken up with Kathy.

**Anya**  That's just ²_____ – it isn't true.

**Matt**  It is! Don't ³_____ me on this, but I actually heard Ryan telling his best mate it was over.

**Anya**  Really?

**Matt**  Yes, but keep that under your ⁴_____. I don't want people calling me a gossip.

**Anya**  It won't go any ⁵_____, honestly. I'll ⁶_____ my tongue.

**Anna**  ⁷_____ has it that Sam was caught shoplifting by the police. He was let off with a caution.

**Ravi**  Really? I wouldn't be surprised. ⁸_____ you and me, he's been acting really weirdly recently. I'll tell you something else about him if you keep a secret.

**Anna**  My lips are ⁹_____.

**Ravi**  Seriously – don't ¹⁰_____ a word of it. If word ¹¹_____, I'll be in big trouble. Anyway, last weekend, Sam ...

**Listening Strategy**

Notice how stress can affect the meaning of a sentence. Speakers stress certain words to indicate an alternative, make a contrast or to correct what someone has said.

'Have you been spreading rumours about me?'

'I haven't, but Kate has.'

'Did you walk round the hill?' 'No, we walked over it.'

**2** 🎧 **2.16** **Read the Listening Strategy. Then listen to the same question being repeated with different stress each time and number the statements.**

The speaker is asking ...

**A** who sent the text. _____

**B** if people were told by text or in another way. _____

**C** if everyone was told, or only some people. _____

**D** where Ian went with Pete's girlfriend. _____

**E** who went to the cinema with Pete's girlfriend. _____

**F** whose girlfriend Ian went out with _____

**3** 🎧 **2.17** **Listen to six more sentences, and underline the stressed words in each one.**

1 Mark is very talented, and he's nice.

2 I may go to the shops later – they're open 'til late tonight.

3 I got my first guitar when I was about twelve.

4 We don't think Clara was horrible to Rob at all.

5 Don't invite Liam to your party.

6 Never trust people who gossip a lot.

**4** 🎧 **2.18** **Listen to two conversations and choose the correct answers. There are two questions for each conversation.**

**Conversation 1:** you hear two people talking about someone's sports injury.

1 Mick claims ...

**A** Jessica injured herself by training too hard.

**B** the injury stopped her from getting into a team.

**C** Jessica is lying about her injury.

2 Mick and Aisha agree to ...

**A** tell a few people at school the rumours.

**B** ask Jessica's boyfriend about it.

**C** not discuss what Jessica's ex-boyfriend said with anyone else.

**Conversation 2:** you hear two people talking about someone's girlfriend.

3 Petra says that Angela ...

**A** isn't really very pretty.

**B** has just become a fashion model.

**C** isn't really who Scott says she is.

4 Petra says that Scott ...

**A** sometimes has difficulties at school.

**B** would like to go out with Angela.

**C** is respected by everyone at school.

**Grammar**

# *whatever, whoever, whenever, whichever, wherever* and *however*
*I can use* whatever, whoever, whenever, whichever, wherever *and* however.

**1** Match the parts of the sentences and complete them with *whatever, whenever, whoever* etc.

1 I always find something exciting to do in Berlin, ... _____
2 You can bring _____ ... _____
3 The Ministry of Culture will choose ... _____
4 Just let me know _____ ... _____
5 _____ you try and explain it, ... _____
6 _____ the children want to watch is fine, but ... _____
7 If you could have a house _____ you wanted, ... _____

a you like to the party: everybody's welcome!
b where would you live?
c _____ of the two designs is best for the new museum.
d they must be in bed by ten.
e you need assistance – I'm happy to help any time.
f _____ often I visit the city.
g it was still wrong to lie.

**2** Complete the text with *whatever, whenever, whoever* etc.

¹_____ you are and ²_____ your background, you've probably dreamt of being rich sometimes. It's fun to imagine that you could go on holiday ³_____ you felt like it, live ⁴_____ you choose, and buy ⁵_____ you want. But there are downsides to being wealthy too.

If you suddenly win a lot of money, you will experience a 'spike' of happiness. But ⁶_____ you do with your cash, you will soon get used to having it. For example, ⁷_____ luxury car you buy, it won't give you the same pleasure after you've used it for a while.

Guilt about being wealthy is another common problem. ⁸_____ hard you try to help others, you will probably still feel guilty ⁹_____ you see people who are poor. 'Help' is often just expected of you too, and this can mean being harassed by family and friends. ¹⁰_____ much money you choose to give away, someone will always want more.

Forming new friendships also becomes more difficult – because ¹¹_____ way you look at it, there are people out there who will try to use you. ¹²_____ comes along and wants to make friends, they should be regarded with suspicion until you know them better.

Being wealthy can be surprisingly tough, so perhaps we should be more careful what we wish for.

**3** Write the sentences using suitable tenses and adding *whatever, whenever, whoever* etc.

1 rich people / be able to / buy / they / want
*Rich people are able to buy whatever they want.*
2 we / visit / grandma / we can
_____
3 believe / that story / not be / very clever
_____
4 you / look great at tomorrow's event / of these two dresses / you / wear
_____
5 we / see posters for the concert / we / went
_____
6 it / be / a difficult decision / way you / look / at it
_____
7 some people / be / always successful / they / do
_____

**4** Rewrite the sentences, using *whatever, whenever, whoever* etc. Make any other necessary changes.

1 You can find anything you like to eat in Singapore.
_____
2 Phone me any time that you have a problem with your computer.
_____
3 Everyone I speak to is looking forward to the concert.
_____
4 It doesn't matter how hard I train – I'm still not fit enough to run a marathon.
_____
5 Everywhere you go in central London, cameras could be watching you.
_____
6 You can buy tickets for any of the seats that are free.
_____

**5** Complete the sentences. Use the correct form of the words below and *whatever, whenever, whoever* etc.

buy / you / prefer   ~~come / you / want~~   eat / you / like
go / you / want in the city   I / go / shopping
record / the criminal / say   you do / not touch it

1 The exhibition is open all day – *come whenever you want.*
2 Toby's always at the shopping mall on Saturdays. I see him _____.
3 Beijing has got a fantastic metro system, so it's easy _____.
4 They both look nice. Just _____.
5 That electric cable is dangerous. _____.
6 This is a police interview. We _____.
7 The food is free – _____.

# 8E

## Productive prefixes and suffixes

*I can use a range of useful prefixes and suffixes.*

**1** Complete the sentences with words formed from the words and prefixes and suffixes below.

-based -conscious -led mono- -phile -proof under-

Anglo bullet class exposed health rail student

1 The president wasn't hurt in the attack because the windows of his official car were _____.

2 You can take the _____ right around Sentosa Island. It's a great way to get between the sights.

3 _____ protests have erupted in Paris, paralysing the city centre.

4 Sally is _____ so she never eats junk food.

5 I'm a bit of an _____ – I love British culture.

6 The artist's work is very good, but she's _____ – few people have heard of her.

7 England in the 1800s was a strictly _____ society.

**2** Complete the article, adding suitable prefixes and suffixes to the words in brackets.

In August 2016, *Time Magazine* produced an article about how ¹_____ (space) is now full of trolls who are attacking people online. This is a growing problem, but it tends to be ²_____ (played) in the media – it isn't seen as being very ³_____ (news) unless it affects a famous person. As a result, the impact of trolls on social media is often ⁴_____ (estimated).

According to a 2014 survey by the ⁵_____ (US) Pew Research Center, 70% of 18–24-year-olds have been harassed online at some time. This harassment ranges from making cruel jokes to making threats, and ⁶_____ (loading) faked photos of people onto websites.

Many trolls engage in aggressive behaviour for what they call 'the Lulz' (laughs), or because they have a grudge against the victim. In some countries, opposition politicians and journalists are also regularly threatened by state-sponsored trolls. These are part of ⁷_____ (government) attempts to silence opposition.

⁸_____ (security) internet companies are making some ⁹_____ (praise) efforts to tackle the problem. They're ¹⁰_____ (grade) online safeguards and blocking the accounts of known trolls. But sadly, there's no ¹¹_____ (fool) way of keeping the internet totally ¹²_____ (troll).

**3** Rewrite the sentences using the correct form of the words below. Add prefixes or suffixes.

book (v) friend market road size tax

1 This washing powder is good for the environment.

_____

2 The plane was too full, so they paid two people to get off the flight.

_____

3 Our company has reduced its operations in China.

_____

4 You can buy everything in this airport shop without paying any money to the government.

_____

5 This car isn't safe enough to drive. It should be scrapped.

_____

6 Technology companies are driven by what people want – they invent lots of different things but only produce them if they will sell well.

_____

**VOCAB BOOST!**

Adding a prefix or suffix to a word often changes the word's part of speech. For example:

*size* (n/v), *sizeable* (adj), *downsize* (v)

*vandal* (n), *vandal-proof* (adj), *vandalise* (v)

**4** Read the *Vocab Boost!* box, then make new words with the prefixes and suffixes below.

-able -able -ance -ence inter- -ion mis- out-

1 read (v) _____ (adj)

2 take (v) _____ (n)

3 depend (v) _____ (n) _____ (adj)

4 act (v) _____ (n)

5 attend (v) _____ (n)

6 wit (n) _____ (v)

7 city (n) _____ (adj)

**5** Look at the word stems below. Try to form as many words as possible from them, using suffixes and / or prefixes.

A expect _____

_____

B drama _____

_____

C respect _____

_____

D real _____

_____

**Reading**
# Trade secrets
*I can understand texts about trade secrets.*

---

**Revision:** Student's Book page 93

**1 Complete the sentences with the correct form of the words below. There are three extra words.**

bear broker call in confirm reach remain research restore

1 They _____ the police after discovering the break-in.
2 We're _____ an article about the food business.
3 Lawyers _____ a deal between the two sides.
4 The identity of the attacker _____ a mystery.
5 We can't _____ or deny the story in the papers.

---

**Reading Strategy**
With multiple matching tasks consisting of several texts on the same topic, first identify the principal differences between the texts. This will help you to match sentences which contain more detailed information with the texts.

**2 Read the Reading Strategy. Then read the extracts and match them with the statements.**

Which text …

1 mentions unappreciated skills? _____
2 talks about the layout of a building? _____
3 mentions that people appreciate a conversation? _____
4 recommends that readers do some research? _____
5 mentions that two products are nearly the same? _____
6 says that something may not be as new as it appears? _____
7 refers to a scientific study? _____
8 mentions deliberately giving someone the wrong thing? _____

**A** Being a coffee-shop worker, or barista, is actually a harder job than it looks. It takes a while to learn the tricks of the trade. Did you know, for example, that when you order the biggest size in many coffee outlets, you don't get any extra coffee – only more hot water and milk. That marbled shape that baristas pour on top of your latte isn't just decoration either. If it has clear edges, it shows the barista that the milk was prepared correctly. Finally, it's worth being polite and waiting patiently for your morning shot if there's a queue. People who are rude and impatient may be given a decaf when they wanted caffeine – or vice versa – because you can't tell the difference.

**B** Supermarkets are usually cleverly designed, with the most expensive brands at eye-level, and the fruit and veg at the front – to give customers an impression of healthy, wholesome food when they enter. But the reality in some supermarkets is far from 'wholesome'. We forgive supermarkets for accidentally leaving the odd out-of-date product on the shelf, because it's clearly very difficult to keep track of thousands of different perishable goods. But did you know that some places indulge in 'food reconditioning'? This means that, for example, old pasta is ground up and repackaged as flour, and meat that has nearly expired is given a spicy marinade – then repackaged with a new 'use by' date. And unlike restaurants, supermarkets aren't immediately closed if they fail hygiene inspections. Amazingly, it's often up to the business themselves to clean up their act.

**C** If you think you're tired on a long-haul flight, spare a thought for your cabin crew. They've been on their feet for hours, and their body clocks are out of sync. When the cabin lights are dimmed at night, the crew actually like it when a passenger comes over and talks to them – it helps them to keep awake! Some passengers treat cabin crew as if they were glorified catering staff. In fact, they're highly trained people who may speak several languages and have skills ranging from building survival shelters to delivering a baby! Most passengers are well behaved, and the crew can usually spot trouble-makers when they first board. A bit of extra care usually pacifies these people. But it can be hard to preserve a smile when someone is going ballistic over their cold in-flight meal.

**D** Sure, hamburgers taste great – they're packed with salt, sugar and fat, which our brains are hard-wired to crave. But according to a 2013 report in a respected medical journal, only about 12% of that deliciously juicy-looking beef in your burger is really beef. The rest consists of fillers like soya protein, ground bone, and artificial flavourings. And those innocent-looking hamburger buns may well contain compounds like ammonium chloride – also used in explosives! Of course, there are plenty of good restaurants out there serving genuine home-made burgers made of real meat. But as customers, it pays to investigate for ourselves, and find the good places. It may come as a surprise to hear that many chefs never eat out!

# Discussion

*I can agree, disagree, give an opinion and justify it.*

**1** **Complete a student's ideas with the words below.**

add besides example not only opinion reason

> I'm of the same ¹_____ as Magdalena, who has made some really good points. ²_____ the arguments that we've just heard, I would ³_____ this one. The main ⁴_____ that I believe it is sometimes good to lie is that lies can be kinder than the truth. To give you just one ⁵_____, would it help to tell a friend that you hate her new hairstyle? ⁶_____ would this make her feel terrible, but also it would damage your friendship.

**2** **Complete the second sentence so it has a similar meaning to the first. Use 2–6 words, including the word in brackets.**

1 We'll never have the same opinion about this. (disagree)
  We'll have to _____ about this.
2 It may not always be true that lying is bad. (case)
  It's _____ lying is bad.
3 This is my main reason for having this opinion. (justification)
  This is my _____ thinking this.
4 You're completely right about that. (agree)
  I _____ 100%.
5 I totally support your point of view. (more)
  I couldn't _____ you.
6 I'd also say that nobody is 100% truthful. (add)
  I would _____ nobody is 100% truthful.

> **Speaking Strategy**
> In a discussion, listen carefully to the other participant(s) and, while they are speaking, work out your own opinion on the point under discussion. When it is your turn to speak, be prepared to pick up on points they have made, and either agree with them and reinforce them, or disagree with them and give your own opinion.

**3** **Read the Speaking Strategy. Then look at questions 1–3 and make notes about how you would answer them.**

1 Is it ever acceptable to disobey the law?
  _____
  _____
2 Some people think that people respect the law more as they grow older. Do you agree?
  _____
  _____
3 Do you think it is ever right not to report someone who is breaking the law?
  _____
  _____

**4** 🎧 **2.19** **Listen to two people discussing the questions in exercise 3. Which of the questions do they …**

1 agree about? _____
2 disagree about? _____

**5** 🎧 **2.19** **Listen again and tick (✓) the discourse markers that you hear.**

if anything ☐          even so ☐
as a matter of fact ☐   anyway ☐
besides ☐              incidentally ☐
to be honest ☐         by and large ☐

**6** **Choose the correct discourse markers to complete the sentences.**

1 I love the band. **As a matter of fact / Mind you**, I've just downloaded one of their albums.
2 Some people try to cheat in exams, but **incidentally / by and large** most students are honest.
3 I trust my friends. **To be honest / Even so**, I don't tell them all my secrets.
4 It was quite mean to play that practical joke on Matt. **Mind you / If anything**, it was very funny!
5 I don't know why Jenny is mad at me. **Mind you / If anything**, she's the one who should apologise.
6 It was wrong of you to do that. **Incidentally / Even so**, it's also against the law.

**7** **Read the statements below and think about whether you agree or disagree with them. Make notes giving reasons for your answers.**

Society would collapse if people disobeyed laws just because they didn't like them.
_____
_____

I don't think there's anything wrong with buying photocopied books or pirate DVDs.
_____
_____

It's never right to report a friend to the police, whatever they've done.
_____
_____

Laws are only binding if they are made with the consent of all the people.
_____
_____

**8** **Choose two of the questions above and practise answering them. Speak for about 30 seconds.**

**Writing**
# Discursive essay
*I can write a discursive essay using a variety of sources.*

**1** Read the task. Think of two more reasons why it might be good or bad to limit freedom of speech.

Your class has had a discussion about freedom of speech, and you have made the notes below:

1 divisive or violent views
2 government political control
3 free speech as a human right
4 _____
5 _____

Some opinions expressed in the discussion:
'Sexist and racist views clearly need to be restricted.'
'Governments can use censorship to control people.'
'People need to be protected from abuse.'

Write an essay discussing TWO of the points in your notes. Explain which point is more important in your view, giving reasons to support your answer. You may make use of the opinions expressed in the discussion, but you should use your own words as far as possible.

**2** Read the essay. Which points from the question and notes are not included?

Limiting freedom of speech is a controversial issue. Some people would argue that we should be able to say whatever we like, but others warn that people cannot be given unlimited freedom to express dangerous views.

In general, freedom of expression leads to a more tolerant society, where people value different opinions. However, it is argued that we have to impose some limits in order to protect people. This is <u>due to the fact that</u> some people have extreme and prejudiced views. These may <u>give rise to</u> violence. <u>Consequently</u>, we need to limit the freedom to express some opinions.

On the other hand, there are more controversial reasons why governments limit freedom of speech. All countries have state secrets such as the details of military operations. <u>As a result</u>, governments prosecute people who release sensitive information. But one of <u>the main consequences</u> of this is that governments can use national security as an excuse for hiding politically damaging information. Clearly it is totally undemocratic to limit people's freedom to discuss and criticise their government's activities.

To sum up, in general, freedom of expression is a good thing. However, I would argue that there have to be some limits to this freedom, due to the need to protect people and society from violent views.

**3** Use the underlined phrases from the text to complete the sentences.

1 The rise in crime is partly _____ the economic crisis has increased unemployment.
2 One of _____ of state censorship is that people are unable to make informed decisions.
3 The town was flooded _____ of the heavy rain.
4 Similarities between two exam essays can _____ accusations of copying.
5 The company wasn't successful. _____, it closed down.

> **Writing Strategy**
> When writing an essay, make sure you:
> 1 read the task carefully and include all the relevant information.
> 2 write in an appropriate style for the genre.
> 3 organise the text in an appropriate way, presenting ideas coherently, and linking sentences and paragraphs.
> 4 use a range of grammatical structures and vocabulary, and use them correctly.

**4** Read the Writing Strategy. Then read the task and plan your discursive essay. Make notes.

Your class has had a discussion about censoring art, music and literature, and you have made the notes below:
1 violent or shocking content
2 freedom of expression and creativity
3 offending some people
Some opinions expressed in the discussion:
'Many great works of art were offensive in their day.'
'People say that some lyrics encourage acts of violence.'
'Attacking religious figures or holy books should be off-limits because it offends a lot of people.'

Write an essay discussing TWO of the points in your notes. Explain which of the points is more important. You may make use of the opinions expressed in the discussion, but you should use your own words as far as possible.

**5** Write your essay (220–260 words) using your plan from exercise 4.

> **CHECK YOUR WORK**
> **Have you ...**
> ☐ organised the essay into clear paragraphs?
> ☐ introduced your essay topic?
> ☐ supported statements with suitable examples?
> ☐ given your opinion?

# 8 Review Unit 8

## Vocabulary

**1 Complete the words in the sentences.**

1 There was a huge public o_____ after the report about poor hygiene in hospitals was made public.

2 The FBI sometimes l_____ in on phone calls.

3 Please c_____ and answer all the questions.

4 The government attempted a c_____-up, but the truth came out in the end.

5 Many sports people e_____ sports-clothing companies like Nike and Asics by wearing their products.

6 A leading newspaper has i_____ an apology for publishing inaccurate information.

7 Ministers have a_____ to requests for an inquiry.

8 Our president is trying to h_____ an inquiry into his illegal activities.

9 Who a_____ him to see those top-secret documents? Someone must have given him permission.

10 The journalist won an award for her shocking e_____ of high-level corruption in the military.

Mark: / 10

**2 Match the sentence halves and complete them with the correct form of the words below.**

expect   misinformation   pre-owned
put on a few extra pounds   rest room

1 Don't believe everything you read on the internet – _____

2 Kelly had her baby boy two years ago and now ... _____

3 This car is good price because it was ... _____

4 Excuse me, can I use ... _____

5 You should go back to the gym. You've ... _____

a she _____ a girl.

b _____ since you stopped training.

c there's a lot of _____ out there.

d your _____, please?

e _____, but it's in good condition.

Mark: / 5

**3 Choose the correct words to complete the sentences.**

1 Don't **breathe / let on**, but Peter's leaving his job.

2 Have you heard the **latest / quote** about Matt and Jenny?

3 I don't believe the **word / rumour** about Paul. He's a nice person, and he wouldn't do that.

4 Keep this under your **lips / hat**, but I saw Yasmina at the gig with Robert – and they were very close.

5 I promise not to tell anyone. Bite my **tongue / lips**.

6 This mustn't go **between / any further**, but we're planning a surprise party for Jake.

Mark: / 6

## Word skills

**4 Complete the text with the correct form of the words in brackets. Use a prefix or suffix from below.**

-based  -conscious  cyber-  de-  down-  down-  -friendly
up-

INTERNET SECURITY GIANT Symantec have opened a brand-new $12-million high-tech centre to fight ¹_____ (crime) in Sydney, Australia. It's a bold move at a time when many IT companies are ²_____ (size). The ³_____ (US) company specialises in ⁴_____ (bug) computer systems for governments and ⁵_____ (security) industries like telecommunications. Worldwide, Symantec's software identifies an estimated 1 trillion electronic security threats per year. The company also produces ⁶_____ (user) anti-virus software for home computers, and security ⁷_____(date) for home users to ⁸_____ (load).

Mark: / 8

**5 Complete the sentences with words made from A and B below.**

A cyber   eco   fat   mono   over   techno   under

B book   exposed   free   friendly   lingual   phobe   space

1 This is a _____ dictionary, so both the words and explanations are in Arabic.

2 I'm an old man now, and a bit of a _____ – I've never learned to use a computer.

3 That cereal is _____, but it's got a lot of sugar in it.

4 We didn't expect the hotel to be _____ – when we arrived, there weren't enough rooms for all of our tour group.

5 These plastic bags are _____. They break down naturally in the environment.

6 Some virtual worlds in _____ are now so realistic that it's hard to tell them apart from the real world.

7 Ingrid Calame is a great artist, but her work is _____ – most people have never heard of her.

Mark: / 7

**6** Complete the statements with the words below.

agree to disagree   be honest   matter of fact   point
principal justification   the case

1 We have very different opinions on this, so I think we'll have to _____.
2 Kathy's just made another really good _____, but ...
3 Everyone tells white lies. As a _____, I had to tell one this morning.
4 The _____ for telling lies is that they can sometimes be kinder than the truth.
5 To _____, I don't think that what you said is correct.
6 It's often _____ that people really have to conceal the truth.

Mark: ___ / 6

## Grammar

**7** Complete the dialogue with the words below.

do   fact   herself   in the world   is   it's   question   what

**Mel**     What $^1$_____ is the matter, Pascale? You $^2$_____ look miserable.

**Pascale**   Mandy's split up with me. $^3$_____ I don't understand is why. The $^4$_____ is, she didn't even tell me $^5$_____ – she asked Jane to do it.

**Mel**     That $^6$_____ awful! Why not sit down and talk to her?

**Pascale**   I'd like to, but the $^7$_____ is how. She won't speak to me. I'm going to go round to hers later.

**Mel**     Well, $^8$_____ important not to do anything rash. How about I speak to her first?

Mark: ___ / 8

**8** Complete the sentences with *whatever, whoever, whichever, however, whenever* or *wherever*.

1 You must be very busy. _____ I see you – day or night – you're always in a hurry.
2 _____ we decide to do for my birthday, I'm sure we'll have a great time.
3 _____ has the winning ticket will get an all-expenses-paid holiday for two to Cancún.
4 _____ I saved that file on my computer, I just can't find it.
5 Both boxers are looking very tired, so _____ fighter has more stamina will probably win.
6 We have to finish this work, _____ boring it is to be inside when it's such a nice day.

Mark: ___ / 6

## Use of English

**9** Complete the text with the correct form of the word in brackets.

Gregg Bergersen, an American citizen $^1$_____ (author) to see secret documents at the Pentagon, was convicted of spying in 2015 after being secretly filmed in a dramatic $^2$_____ (cover) operation. Footage broadcast by CBS shows how hidden cameras filmed Bergensen $^3$_____ (where) he went in his car – and caught him accepting money from a foreign agent in return for information. (Bergensen later claimed he thought the agent came from a friendly power – but $^4$_____ (who) the agent is, it's still a crime!)

Bergersen was very careful to protect $^5$_____ (him) from internal surveillance. He didn't $^6$_____ (down) documents from the Pentagon's computer network – an activity which could easily be tracked. Instead he 'borrowed' paper files which were then copied by hand. Pentagon officials were keen to $^7$_____ (play) the Bergersen case, but since his arrest $^8$_____ (allege) have emerged of other American citizens selling secrets to do with naval and space technology. These $^9$_____ (reveal) show that home-grown espionage – by Americans against America – is a growing problem.

Mark: ___ / 9

Total: ___ / 65

## I can ...

Read the statements. Think about your progress and tick (✔) one of the boxes.

★ = I need more practice.          ★★★ = No problem!
★★ = I sometimes find this difficult.

| | ★ | ★★ | ★★★ |
|---|---|---|---|
| I can talk about cover-ups, privacy and journalism. | | | |
| I can use a variety of structures to add emphasis. | | | |
| I can understand people gossiping. | | | |
| I can use *whatever, whenever, whoever,* etc. | | | |
| I can use a range of useful prefixes and suffixes. | | | |
| I can understand texts about trade secrets. | | | |
| I can agree, disagree, give an opinion and justify it. | | | |
| I can write a discursive essay using a variety of sources. | | | |

# Exam Skills Trainer 4

## Reading

1 Read the Strategy above and question 1 in exercise 2. Follow the instructions in the Strategy to answer the question.

2 Read the article and questions 2–10. Match sections A–D with the questions.

Which hiding place...

1 failed to serve the function it was designed for? _____
2 was built to last well into the future? _____
3 is generally regarded as the best of its kind? _____
4 was missing from visual representations of the area? _____
5 must be reached by plane or ship? _____
6 has an uncertain future at present? _____
7 has a much greater potential than that which is currently being exploited? _____
8 was built paying meticulous attention to detail? _____
9 was procured with another function in mind? _____
10 is the site of unusual happenings which have not been explained? _____

### The Perfect Hiding Place

*Read about four of the world's most secret locations.*

**A  The Mountain**
Just a stone's throw from New York City lies a former iron-ore mine which has been converted into a heavily guarded storage facility known as The Mountain. Inside are the records of some of the largest and most influential companies in the USA. Purchased originally for growing mushrooms, the mine acquired its current function during the Cold War, when owner Herman Knaust realised its potential for protecting corporate information from nuclear attack and founded the company Iron Mountain Atomic Storage Inc. Apart from vital business records, The Mountain has housed art collections, valuable antiques and celebrity memorabilia in its 225 individually locked vaults, and today it is the premium storage location for the company now known as Iron Mountain Inc.

**B  Global Seed Vault**
In the depths of an icy mountain on Norway's remote Svalbard archipelago exists a resource of vital importance: the Global Seed Vault. Far from the dangers of world crises and natural disasters, the building will eventually contain the seeds of all the plants the Earth has ever seen. Currently holding 930,000 samples from every corner of the planet, the deposit is at less than a third of its maximum capacity. Its principle aim is to serve as a back-up if one of the world's 1,750 individual seed banks is damaged. A case in point is

the recent withdrawal of seeds from the Global Seed Vault to replace those lost during the transferral of an international agricultural research centre from Aleppo to Beirut as a result of the Syrian civil war.

**C  Burlington Bunker**
Below a disused quarry near Corsham in the south-west of England stretches a vast underground community that remained a closely guarded secret for over thirty years. The huge complex forms what was once intended to be the Central Government War Headquarters, more commonly known as the Burlington Bunker. Fearing nuclear war with the Soviet Union, the British government ordered its construction in 1955 and made provision for everything that would be needed to survive for three months: offices and bedrooms, a bakery, a hospital, and even a BBC broadcasting studio to communicate with survivors. Although the facility was never used, it was maintained until 1991 before being finally decommissioned in 2004 and put up for sale.

**D  Area 51**
Just over 160 km north of Las Vegas is an air base in the middle of the desert whose existence was not officially acknowledged until 2013. Known as Area 51, the facility is a top-secret US military installation which remained hidden for decades thanks to map-makers leaving it out and satellite imagery of the area being routinely deleted from government databases. It is understood that the base is the site at which the latest spy planes are developed and tested, giving rise to a number of reported sightings of UFOs over the years. These accounts have generally been attributed to the fact that witnesses were unaccustomed to seeing the lights of planes flying at such high altitudes as the ones being tested, but there are some who would strongly contest this justification.

## Listening

3 Read the Strategy above and the text in exercise 4. What information do you need to fill the gaps in questions 1–8?

4 🎧 2.20 You will hear a talk about the latest research into animal migration. For questions 1–8, complete the sentences with a word or short phrase.

**Remarkable journeys**
Humpback whales are the $^1$_____ that have the longest migration.
The leatherback turtle studied by scientists started its journey in $^2$_____.

# 4

# Exam Skills Trainer 4

The blue wildebeest's migration is prompted by a search for
³_____ to eat. The animal with the longest
terrestrial migration is the caribou, or ⁴_____. The
insect with the longest migration route appears to be a
⁵_____. The bar-headed goose flies south every year
to avoid the ⁶_____ in Mongolia.
Scientists have never measured a ⁷_____ flight
longer than the bar-tailed godwit's. The arctic tern's
migration is the longest because the birds visit the two
⁸_____ each year.

## Use of English

**Strategy**
In the multiple-choice cloze task, use your knowledge of
collocations, dependent prepositions and verb patterns to
eliminate the words that do not fit the gap. Then decide
which of the remaining words fit the gap semantically.

**5** Read the Strategy above. Then read the question and
options below. Which is the correct option? Why are the
other options wrong?

My grandparents are completely _____ to the idea of moving
house. In short, they refuse.

**a** against   **b** disagreed   **c** favourable   **d** opposed

**6** Complete the text. Write a, b, c or d.

### Lone woman cyclist reaches Iran

When journalist Rebecca Lowe announced she was planning
a twelve-month cycling trip to Iran, her friends and
family tried hard to ¹_____ her from going. They failed,
of course, and on 29 July 2015 Rebecca set off alone from
her London flat on what was to be a truly ²_____ journey.
Her main aim in making this daunting trip was to ³_____
a better understanding of the Middle East. She chose to
cycle believing her bike would ⁴_____ her to meet people
more easily. And she was right. Being a lone woman cyclist,
Rebecca ⁵_____ from all other visitors and attracted the right
sort of attention from locals. Nearly everyone she ⁶_____
offered her food, shelter and, what she was really after, an
insight into their lives. By the end of her journey, Rebecca
had ⁷_____ a grand total of 20 countries, including Turkey,
Lebanon and Sudan. She ⁸_____ her mission of reaching Iran
on 20 June 2016, when she arrived in Azadi Square.

**1 a** disapprove      **b** discourage
  **c** inhibit          **d** restrict
**2 a** evocative        **b** hazy
  **c** vivid            **d** unforgettable
**3 a** earn             **b** gain
  **c** make             **d** win
**4 a** allow            **b** authorize
  **c** let              **d** oblige

**5 a** put off          **b** stood out
  **c** stood up         **d** turned out
**6 a** fell out with    **b** friended
  **c** kept track of    **d** ran into
**7 a** circumnavigated  **b** conducted
  **c** roamed           **d** traversed
**8 a** accomplished     **b** achieved
  **c** attained         **d** realised

## Speaking

**Strategy**
In the discussion phase of the test, if you disagree with a
statement, you should do so politely, e.g. *I'm afraid I don't
agree*, rather than *That's wrong!*

**7** Read the Strategy. Add three more examples of phrases for
disagreeing politely.

**8** Politely disagree with the statements below using
phrases from exercise 7 and a full personal response.

If you have a secret, it's best not to confide in your best
friend.
Your employer should have access to all your personal
information.

## Writing

**Strategy**
Read the task carefully and choose the two points you feel
you could write most about. Make notes about each of the
points before you start writing, and think about how you
can develop them. You can use the opinions in the task if
you want to, but remember to paraphrase the actual words.

**9** Read the Strategy above and the task below. Make notes
about the two points you feel you could write most about.

Your class has had a discussion about how to improve road
safety. You have made the notes below:
Measures for improving road safety:
- reduce speed limits
- increase punishments for dangerous driving
- introduce obligatory safety courses

Some opinions expressed in the discussion:
'Drivers shouldn't be allowed to go so fast on motorways.'
'Dangerous drivers should be banned for life.'
'Drivers should take a safety course every five years.'
Write an essay discussing TWO of the measures in your
notes. You should explain which measure would improve
road safety the most, giving reasons to support your answer.

**10** Write the essay (220–260 words) for the task in exercise 9.

# 9 Endings

## A End of the world
*I can talk about potential threats to our planet.*

**1 Complete the definitions of global threats 1–8.**

**A** A nuclear _____ is a situation of mass destruction caused by the use of atomic weapons.

**B** A pole _____ is a change in the angle of the Earth's rotation.

**C** A global _____ is a disease that spreads all over the world.

**D** An asteroid _____ is an accident in which a large rock hits a planet.

**E** Robot _____ will occur if machines become superior to humans.

**F** An interplanetary _____ is an accident in which two planets crash into each other.

**G** A supervolcanic _____ is the explosion of a volcano of massive proportions.

**H** An alien _____ is when creatures from another world land on a planet and take over by force.

**2** 🎧 3.02 **Listen to five people discussing global threats. Match the threats in exercise 1 with the speakers 1–5.**

1 _____  2 _____  3 _____  4 _____  5 _____

**3** 🎧 3.02 **Listen again. Match speakers 1–5 with sentences A–H. There are three sentences you do not need.**

The speaker describes a threat which …

**A** might resemble an infamous event in history. _____

**B** would cause an increase in droughts and famines. _____

**C** would cross borders as if they didn't exist. _____

**D** would be a repetition of a similar event that supposedly destroyed the dominant species. _____

**E** would eject the Earth from the Solar System. _____

**F** may occur as a result of progress. _____

**G** could destroy the ozone layer. _____

**H** would cause severe respiratory problems. _____

**4 Complete the sentences with the correct form of the verbs and phrases below. Some of the answers are passive.**

detonate  hurtle  overthrow  slam into  spell disaster
unleash  wipe out  wreak havoc

1 Their car skidded and _____ a tree.

2 After losing control of his bike, he _____ down the hill into the bushes at the bottom.

3 The military held a coup in an attempt to _____ the government.

4 The bomb _____ using a remote-controlled device.

5 The hurricane _____ on the town, destroying everything in its path.

6 The announcement to close the hospital _____ a storm of protest.

7 The wet weather could _____ for farmers, whose crops are ripe for picking.

8 Whole settlements _____ by the earthquake.

**5 Complete the second sentence so that it means the same as the first. Write no more than six words and include the word in brackets.**

1 Abigail has very rich parents. (spoon)
She was born with _____.

2 You'll have to wait to find out what happens. (time)
Only _____.

3 When you're in an unfamiliar place, you should behave like the people around you. (Rome)
When _____.

4 People of the same sort are found together. (flock)
Birds _____.

5 Don't be sure of success – something may go wrong. (chickens)
Don't count _____.

6 If something bad is being said about something, it's usually true. (smoke)
There's _____.

**Grammar**
# Ellipsis and substitution
*I can use auxiliaries, modals,* so *and* not ... so *to avoid repetition.*

**1** 🎧 **3.03** **Read the dialogue and cross out the words that can be omitted. Then listen and check.**

| | |
|---|---|
| **Tamsin** | My great-grandma's 100 on Saturday. |
| **Millie** | Really? Are you having a party for her? |
| **Tamsin** | Yes, we are having a party for her. We're having it in our garden. |
| **Millie** | But I thought your great-grandma lived in a nursing home. |
| **Tamsin** | She does live in a nursing home, but she's coming out for the afternoon. |
| **Millie** | Can't she stay with you for longer? |
| **Tamsin** | She'd like to stay for longer, but the home won't let her stay for longer. Anyway, I wanted to ask you if you'd help me with her cake. |
| **Millie** | Of course I will help you with her cake! |

**2 Complete the dialogues with the phrases below.**

I didn't mean to   I'd love to   I do   I haven't   I intended to
I should   I used to   I will

1 **A** Who's got my phone charger?
   **B** _____. Maybe Freya's got it.
2 **A** Don't you like burgers?
   **B** _____, it's just that I don't fancy one now.
3 **A** Why are you shouting at me?
   **B** Sorry, _____. I'll take off my headphones.
4 **A** Can you turn down the music, please?
   **B** _____, as soon as this song finishes.
5 **A** Have you tidied your room?
   **B** Sorry, _____, but I forgot.
6 **A** Are you going to the gym tonight?
   **B** _____, but I can't be bothered.
7 **A** Do you want to join us for a bike ride tomorrow?
   **B** _____. What time?
8 **A** Do you play in a band?
   **B** _____, but we've just split up.

**3 Write a positive and negative response for each item, using the word in brackets.**

1 Do you think you'll pass all your exams? (guess)
   **A** _____
   **B** _____
2 Will you ever get married, do you think? (expect)
   **A** _____
   **B** _____
3 Will you enjoy university, do you think? (presume)
   **A** _____
   **B** _____
4 Are you going out tonight? (think)
   **A** _____
   **B** _____
5 Will you ever live abroad, do you think? (imagine)
   **A** _____
   **B** _____
6 Do you think you'll be going on holiday this summer? (suppose)
   **A** _____
   **B** _____

**4 Which three questions in exercise 3 have another possible response? Write the number of the question and the other possible response.**

_____  _____
_____  _____
_____  _____

**5** 🎧 **3.04** **Complete the dialogue. Write one word in each space. Then listen and check.**

**A** Did you get round to asking your grandparents about our history project?
**B** I'm afraid ¹_____. I meant ²_____, but I didn't see them last weekend. I had to help my brother move into his new flat, so I ³_____.
**A** Do you think they'll agree to be interviewed?
**B** I'm sure they ⁴_____. They love talking about the old days.
**A** Will they mind if we video them?
**B** There's a chance that they ⁵_____ at the start, but if they ⁶_____, we'll just have to talk them round.
**A** Will you be seeing them in the next couple of days?
**B** I presume ⁷_____. They usually come round for dinner on Tuesdays. I'll ask them then.
**A** Try not to forget. We haven't got much time left to do the interview.
**B** Don't worry, I ⁸_____.

# 9C

## Lost civilisations

*I can use context to understand a text on lost civilisations.*

**Revision:** Student's Book page 99

**1 Match 1–8 with a–h to make verb + noun collocations.**

| | |
|---|---|
| 1 enjoy _____ | **a** a role (in sth) |
| 2 fall _____ | **b** (sb) an indication |
| 3 give _____ | **c** a theory |
| 4 play _____ | **d** into decline |
| 5 put _____ | **e** (sth) into perspective |
| 6 spell _____ | **f** success |
| 7 trigger _____ | **g** the end (of / for sth) |
| 8 undermine _____ | **h** the demise (of sth) |

**2 Complete the sentences with the collocations in exercise 1. Use the correct form of the verb.**

1 European colonisation of the Americas *triggered the demise* of several important civilisations.
2 The Aztec Empire _____ until the arrival of Hernán Cortés.
3 The expeditions of Francisco Pizarro _____ for the Inca Empire.
4 Infectious diseases also _____ in the decimation of the population.
5 The discovery of Viking remains _____ that Columbus was the first to set foot in America.
6 Tales in the Sagas of Icelanders _____ that the Vikings went there before.
7 Leif Erikson's voyage across the Atlantic _____ the power of the Vikings.
8 The Viking settlement in Newfoundland soon _____ due to the inhospitable climate.

**Listening Strategy**

Read the rubric so that you are aware of the context of the task, and read the questions so that you are aware of the information you require. This will help you work out exactly what you need to retrieve from the recording, and show you when the answer is coming up.

**3 Read the Listening Strategy. Then look at the sentence below. What kind of information do you need to complete the sentence?**

Many tourists are drawn to Cambodia today by a _____ built by the Khmer civilisation.

**4 🎧 3.05 Listen and answer the questions.**

1 Which modern-day countries did the Khmer Empire cover?
2 When was the highpoint of the Khmer Empire?
3 In what ways were they inventive?
4 Who conquered the the Khmer Empire and when?
5 Why did the Khmer Empire fall into decline?

**5 🎧 3.06 You are going to hear a talk about two studies into the reasons for the decline of the Khmer Empire. What was the focus of each of the studies?**

1 the analysis of _____
2 the analysis of _____

**6 🎧 3.06 Listen again and complete the sentences with a word or a short phrase. First read the questions to be aware of the information you require.**

1 Until now, the fall of the Khmer Empire has often been attributed to land misuse or _____.
2 The only written references to the demise are observations made by _____ from China.
3 Brendan Buckley sought specimens for his research that were _____ – some were 1,000 years old.
4 The droughts probably caused a decline in health and _____ in the Empire.
5 Buckley suggests that _____ may have damaged the Khmer's water system.
6 Mary Beth Day's first sample was taken from the West Baray, one of the _____ in the Empire.
7 The result of Day's research was a millennium-long _____.
8 The results of both studies show that _____ are not enough to protect a civilisation.

**Grammar**
# Advanced uses of the infinitive
*I can use advanced uses of the infinitive.*

## 1 Correct the mistakes.

1 Navajo is one of the hardest to learn languages.
_____

2 That word is too formal for say in this context.
_____

3 Can you lend me a book for to read on holiday?
_____

4 My French isn't enough good to have a long chat.
_____

5 I'm the first person in my family going to university.
_____

6 I'm not as brave as to travel around India alone.
_____

## 2 Complete the sentences with a word from box A and the infinitive form of a verb from box B.

**A**
easiest  emails  enough  last  only  shy

**B**
answer  approach  discover  leave  make  understand

1 I was the _____ the room, so I turned off all the lights.

2 My brother's too _____ a speech in public.

3 Of the languages I know, I find Italian the _____.

4 I called the language school _____ all the classes were full.

5 I'm not confident _____ someone and start a conversation.

6 I've got a few _____, and then I'll turn off my laptop.

## 3 Complete the second sentence so that it means the same as the first. Write no more than six words and include the word in brackets.

1 I acquired a new passport, but I had it stolen the first time I used it. (only)
I acquired a new passport _____ the first time I used it.

2 Only one person signed up for the German exchange before me. (second)
I was _____ for the German exchange.

3 No place is better for learning a language than the country where it is spoken. (best)
_____ a language is in the country where it is spoken.

4 We can use the app I've downloaded if we need to ask for something. (to)
I've downloaded _____ if we need to ask for something.

5 They speak very fast, so I can't understand what they're saying. (too)
They speak _____ what they're saying.

6 The first episode of the series didn't make me want to watch the rest, as it wasn't very good. (so)
The first episode wasn't _____ want to watch the rest of the series.

## 4 USE OF ENGLISH Complete the text. Write one word in each gap.

### THE CORNISH REVIVAL

Kernewek, or Cornish, is one of the minority languages of the UK. Spoken only in Cornwall, a county in the south-western tip of England, the language was considered dead after the [1]_____ person to speak it fluently passed away in 1777. In the early 20th century, however, a revival of the language began, but there were very few written records [2]_____ go on. The [3]_____ attempt to provide standardised rules was made by Robert Morton Nance in his 1929 work *Cornish For All*. From then on, the revival gathered steam [4]_____ to come to a standstill in the 1980s due to an argument over the [5]_____ important decision to be made: which of the three or four dialects should be declared official? At one point it seemed that the differences of opinion might be [6]_____ great for a compromise to be reached. In 2008, however, a standard written form was agreed upon. Since then, Cornish has gained [7]_____ speakers for UNESCO to remove its classification of the language as 'extinct'. Today, some Cornish people are [8]_____ bold as to dream of living in their own independent country.

# Collocations with common verbs (*come*, *do*, *put* and *take*)

*I can use collocations with common verbs to discuss spoilers.*

**1 Choose the correct verb.**

1 Don't **come / do / put / take** it for granted that I'll help you – I may not have time.

2 The main character **came / did / put / took** to an untimely end when his car crashed into a tree.

3 It's time our school **came / did / put / took** a stop to the use of mobile phones in class.

4 My brother's **coming / doing / putting / taking** his utmost to find a part-time job.

5 Jenny's older brother seems to **come / do / put / take** pleasure in making her cry.

6 It **came / did / put / took** as a shock to Mia to discover that she'd failed most of her exams.

7 I really **came / did / put / took** my foot in it when I asked about his girlfriend – they've just split up!

8 It wouldn't **come / do / put / take** them any harm to walk to school once in a while.

**2 Complete the sentences with the correct form of *come*, *do*, *put* or *take* and one of the words or phrases below.**

charge   notice   (sb) under pressure   (sth) into practice
the trick   to mind   under fire   well

1 The police _____ last night for allowing the murderer to escape.

2 When I get hiccups, I find that drinking water out of the opposite side of a glass _____.

3 The fire chief _____ and ordered everyone out of the building.

4 I'm sure you'd _____ at university. Medicine is the type of thing you'd be good at.

5 Now that you can cook, you can _____ your new skills _____ and make the dinner.

6 Whenever I think of the summer, my local swimming pool _____.

7 Don't _____ any _____ of that phone call; I'm sure it was a hoax.

8 My coach is _____ to play our next match despite the fact that I'm injured.

**3 Rewrite the sentences replacing the <u>underlined</u> words with the correct form of six of the collocations in exercises 1 and 2.**

1 The concert <u>finished</u> to thunderous applause.

_____

2 The teachers want to <u>halt</u> bullying in our school.

_____

3 It <u>upset</u> Amy's parents to hear she was in hospital.

_____

4 The mistake <u>caused a lot of damage</u> to the company.

_____

5 Jamie had to study hard to <u>succeed</u> at school.

_____

6 I <u>always believed</u> that we'd never move house.

_____

> **VOCAB BOOST!**
>
> One of the most common verbs in English is *get*. Collocations with *get* are listed in a dictionary under the entries for the nouns and adjectives in the collocation. For example, *get your act together* is listed under *act* (*get your act together* = organise yourself in a more effective way).

**4 Read the *Vocab Boost!* box. Match the collocations below with the definitions 1–8.**

get a grip (on yourself)   get on sb's nerves   get nowhere
get sth off your chest   get sth straight   get the hang of sth
get the picture   get your own back on sb

1 understand a situation that sb is describing to you _____

2 annoy sb _____

3 make a situation clear _____

4 do sth to sb in return for harm they have done to you _____

5 talk about sth that has been worrying you in order to feel less anxious _____

6 control your emotions after being afraid, upset or angry _____

7 learn how to do sth _____

8 make no progress _____

**Revision:** Student's Book page 102

**1** Complete the sentences with the correct form of the phrasal verbs below.

be caught up in   break out of   bring up   come out
come up with   die down   hole up   track down

1 I wonder how the prisoner _____ jail.

2 I'm definitely seeing that movie when it _____.

3 His parents weren't around when he was young, so he _____ by his aunt.

4 She didn't start speaking until all the noise _____.

5 We were _____ in our basement during the tornado.

6 Police are using dogs to _____ the criminal.

7 That politician is in trouble – he _____ a corruption scandal.

8 Who _____ the solution to the problem?

**2** Read the article about disappointing film endings. Match the genres 1–3 with the films A–C.

1 comedy drama _____       3 crime thriller _____
2 war thriller _____

> **Reading Strategy**
> In a multiple matching task, the questions paraphrase the information given in the text. Read the question carefully and underline the key words and phrases. Then scan the text, watching out for paraphrases of the key words and phrases in the question.

**3** Read the Reading Strategy. Match questions 1–6 with paragraphs A–C.

Which paragraph mentions a movie in which ...

1 the story appears to be going nowhere? _____
2 the suspense increases with every moment? _____
3 one character is deceived by another? _____
4 the audience doesn't witness a vital moment? _____
5 the ending is narrated rather than represented visually? _____
6 viewers find themselves in the middle of the action in the opening scene? _____

# MOVIES THAT FAIL TO MOVE

**For critic Allen Palmer, a great movie does not need a happy ending, but one where the final scenes are emotionally satisfying. Below are three movies she feels do not fit the bill.**

**A NO COUNTRY FOR OLD MEN**

Despite the Coen brothers' four Academy Awards, I found the ending of this 2007 movie disappointing. The movie is a kind of cat-and-mouse tale, where Vietnam veteran Llewelyn Moss is the mouse, and hitman Anton Chigurh the cat. Finding a case containing two million pounds in a field in Texas, Moss flees with the money, and Chigurh is hired by its owners to recover it. Chigurh finishes off everyone standing between him and Moss, using his trademark coin flip to decide the victim's fate. The tension mounts as Chigurh nears his prey, but just when it appears that the two are set to clash, Moss is killed by someone else – off-screen. For me, the greatness of this movie lies in the journey, not the destination.

**B THE HURT LOCKER**

Kathryn Bigelow's 2008 movie is awesome – at least, for the first hour or so. When the lights go down, the audience is transported to the battle-scarred streets of Baghdad, where a bomb disposal squad is at work defusing an explosive device. At the start, the movie is a rollercoaster ride, with the tension rising and falling as the bombs are deactivated – or not. Later, however, it suddenly becomes clear that, although the bombs are getting bigger, the action is repeating itself. Towards the end, one soldier gets injured, another shows signs of mental stress and their leader goes home on leave until he can return to do the same all over again. What we seem to have here is the depiction of a conflict zone rather than the exploration of a plot line.

**C UP IN THE AIR**

Jason Reitman's 2009 satirical movie about corporate 'downsizer' Ryan Bingham is certainly a lot of fun at the start. Bingham – played by George Clooney – is employed by a Human Resources consultancy to travel the country firing people. Enter Alex, a beautiful executive in the same league as Bingham, and a new colleague, Natalie, whose innovative idea for remote firing via webcam threatens Bingham's very existence. The movie falls apart, however, when Bingham discovers that Alex isn't the woman he thought she was. From this point on, the audience is talked through the action rather than feeling it. We discover that Bingham gives Natalie a glowing reference to help her get a new job, but Alex gets no further mention. Bingham himself is last seen dropping his luggage in front of the destination board of an airport, which could mean anything, really.

# Collaborative task

*I can deal successfully with interruptions.*

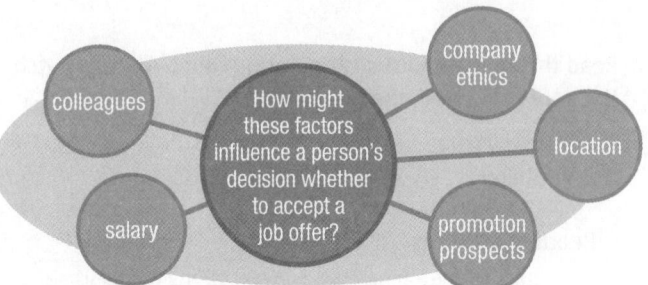

colleagues

company ethics

How might these factors influence a person's decision whether to accept a job offer?

location

salary

promotion prospects

**1** 3.07 **Read the task and listen to two students discussing it. Answer the questions.**

1 Which factors do the students talk about?

_____

2 Which of the two candidates tries to dominate the conversation? _____

3 How many times does the other candidate interrupt the dominating candidate? _____

**Speaking Strategy**

In a collaborative task, students are expected to share the interaction equally.

1 If the other student dominates the discussion, interrupt them politely to give your opinion.

2 If you are interrupted when you are speaking, you can choose to allow the interruption or to reject it politely.

3 If you reject the interruption, you need to go back to what you were saying.

**2 Read the Speaking Strategy. Match phrases 1–14 with categories A, B, C and D below. Write the numbers.**

A Interrupting _____ _____ _____ _____ _____

B Allowing an interruption _____ _____ _____

C Rejecting an interruption _____ _____ _____

D Continuing after an interruption _____ _____ _____

1 Yes, of course, go ahead. _____

2 Sorry for interrupting, but … _____

3 Continuing where I left off … _____

4 Before you go on, I'd just like to say … _____

5 Can I just stop you there for a moment? _____

6 Can I complete my train of thought? _____

7 Where was I? Oh yes, … _____

8 Do you mind if I finish? _____

9 If I could just come in here, I think … _____

10 Sure. What do you think? _____

11 Please let me continue. _____

12 As I was saying, I think … _____

13 Excuse me for butting in, but … _____

14 That's OK. What did you want to say? _____

**3** 3.07 **Listen again and tick (✓) the phrases 1–14 in exercise 2 you hear.**

Which two factors are the most important when deciding whether or not to accept a job offer?

**4** 3.08 **Read the question and listen to students doing the second part of the task. Which two factors do they choose?**

_____   _____

**5** 3.08 **Listen again. Who says the synonyms for *important* below? Write G (girl) or B (boy). There are some extra synonyms that are not used.**

critical _____     essential _____     significant _____

crucial _____     fundamental _____     vital _____

decisive _____     imperative _____

capacity

facilities

How important are these factors when choosing a venue to celebrate an end-of-year party?

location

price

menu

**6 Look at the task. Make notes about the importance of each option.**

_____
_____
_____
_____
_____

Which two factors are the least important when choosing a venue?

**7 Read the question above. Make a note of your choices and reasons.**

_____
_____
_____
_____

**8 Now do the task using your notes from exercises 6 and 7.**

# A report
*I can write a report.*

You have just finished a preparation course for being a lifeguard at a swimming pool. In the mornings you had classes, and in the afternoons you practised what you had learned in a swimming pool. The course director has asked you to write a report in which you should evaluate the programme, explain which part of it was most useful and recommend changes for future courses.

**1** Read the task above and the report. In the writer's opinion, which part of the course was the most useful?

## Ivybridge Sports
## Lifeguard Course

### Introduction
The aim of this report is to assess the effectiveness of the lifeguard course I recently participated in, identify the most valuable part of the course, and make some recommendations for improvements.

### Evaluation
On the ¹_____, I gained a great deal from the course. As well as learning different techniques for rescuing swimmers in difficulty, I acquired a thorough knowledge of health and safety legislation, and basic first-aid skills. The only ²_____ of the course was the price, which seems excessive considering most of the participants were students.

### Theory vs practice
In ³_____ of teaching, the morning classes definitely had the edge over the afternoon because the time was used more effectively. The morning classes were well planned and interesting, while the ones in the afternoon were much less well organised. This meant we spent much less time in the water, so we did not have the opportunity to practise as much as I would have liked. Therefore, I would say that I benefited more from the theory part of the course than the practical part.

### Recommendations
As a result of my experience, I would like to suggest the following:
• The classes should be more structured to allow for better use of the time available.
• Participants ought to spend more time practising life-saving skills in the water.
• Students should be given a discount on the fees to make the course more accessible to them.

If these recommendations are carried out, the lifeguard course at Ivybridge Sports is bound to improve.

**2** Read the report again and complete the phrases (1–3) for evaluating an experience / event and comparing and contrasting different aspects.

**3** Match the two halves of the sentences.

1 Broadly speaking, the programme _____
2 In general, the course lived _____
3 The afternoon classes were superb, unlike _____
4 Weighing up the different factors, _____

a I would say I benefited more from the mornings.
b leaves a lot to be desired.
c the morning classes, which were appalling.
d up to my expectations.

> **Writing Strategy**
> In a report you describe and evaluate an experience, and make recommendations for the future. You must use a formal impersonal style, and follow a clear structure, with a title and subheadings.
>
> • Paragraph 1 states the aim of the report by paraphrasing the three elements in the task.
> • Paragraphs 2–4 each explore one of the elements in the order they appear in the task.
>
> Read the task carefully to understand the context for the report and the three elements you need to explore.

**4** Read the Writing Strategy and the task. <u>Underline</u> the three elements in the task.

You have just finished a preparation course for being a helper at a summer camp. In the mornings you had theory classes, and in the afternoons you practised what you had learned with some children. The course director has asked you to write a report in which you should evaluate the programme, explain which part of it was most useful and recommend changes for future courses.

**5** Make notes about the three elements in the task.

1 _____
_____
2 _____
_____
3 _____
_____

**6** Write your report (220–260 words), using your notes from exercise 5.

> **CHECK YOUR WORK**
> **Have you ...**
> ☐ followed the structure in the Writing Strategy?
> ☐ included phrases for evaluating an experience / event and comparing and contrasting different aspects?
> ☐ checked the spelling and grammar?

# 9 Review Unit 9

## Vocabulary

**1 Match the global threats below to the quotes.**

alien invasion  asteroid  pandemic  pole shift  supervolcano

1 'The virus has already spread from West Africa to Europe. Today the first cases are being reported in Canada.'
2 'It's estimated to be about 300 metres wide and is expected to hit Earth somewhere in the southern hemisphere.'
3 'There are fears tonight that increased volcanic activity in the region could lead to the biggest eruption in history.'
4 'The change was massive and sudden. The Earth's new rotation is disrupting weather systems worldwide.'
5 'Strange flying objects have appeared in the sky over Lagos, Tokyo and Paris, causing widespread panic.'

Mark: ___ / 5

**2 Complete the words in the sentences.**

1 Luckily, the police were able to prevent a terrorist from d_____ the bomb outside the football stadium.
2 We've stopped the disease from spreading, but we haven't w_____ it o_____ completely yet.
3 A big solar storm could w_____ h_____ on Earth by destroying computer systems worldwide.
4 If countries pull out of the agreement, it could s_____ d_____ for our planet.
5 I don't think that intelligent computers will ever o_____ humans and take over Earth.
6 Asteroids have s_____ i_____ Earth many times.

Mark: ___ / 6

**3 Match the sentence halves and complete the sayings.**

1 Matt's lucky because his parents are rich. He ... _____
2 The band's very popular so concert tickets ... _____
3 You think you'll definitely win the competition, ... _____
4 It's better not to know how many viruses there are. Sometimes ... _____
5 The rumours are probably true. After all, ... _____
6 We don't know whether we can avert the worst effects of climate change. In the end, ... _____

a there's _____ without fire.
b will be sold on a _____, first served basis.
c _____ is bliss.
d was born with a _____ in his mouth.
e _____ will tell.
f but I wouldn't count _____ before they hatch.

Mark: ___ / 6

## 4 Choose the correct words to complete the text.

The great Roman cities of North Africa [1]**gave / enjoyed** huge wealth in their time. Today they stand abandoned. At one time it was felt that climate change [2]**triggered / put** the demise of Roman cities like Sabratha and Leptis Magna. Today, however, that theory has been [3]**given / undermined** by scientific data.

Natural events such as earthquakes undoubtedly [4]**enjoyed / played** a role in the destruction of some ancient North African cities, but we now believe that human actions are mostly to blame. Wars and invasions led to the destruction of irrigation systems. That was followed by widespread deforestation, which [5]**spelled / undermined** the end for agriculture. Visiting the semi-desert region today [6]**spells / gives** us an alarming indication of what will happen if we don't prevent deforestation in other parts of the world.

Mark: ___ / 6

## Word skills

**5 Complete the dialogue with the correct form of *come, do, put* or *take*.**

**Bradley** Who's [1]_____ charge of organising the college Arts Week this year?

**Meltem** I have – but I wish I hadn't! I'm [2]_____ my utmost to please everyone, but I'm [3]_____ under a lot of fire. Some students are even posting comments online, saying I'm not [4]_____ a good job.

**Bradley** Don't [5]_____ any notice of stupid comments like that.

**Meltem** I'm trying not to – but it's all [6]_____ as a bit of a shock to me.

Mark: ___ / 6

**6 Rewrite the sentences using the correct form of a phrasal verb formed from the verbs in brackets.**

1 Tom's grandparents looked after him as a child. (bring)

_____

2 Three prisoners have escaped a prison in Devon. (break)

_____

3 It'll take a while for these rumours to stop. (die)

_____

4 It wasn't easy to find you. (track)

_____

5 The criminal was hiding in a warehouse when the police found him. (hole)

_____

Mark: ___ / 5

# 9

## Review Unit 9

**7** Complete phrases A–H with 1–2 words. Then write them under the correct heading: interrupting, allowing an interruption, rejecting an interruption, continuing after an interruption.

**A** What did you _____ to say?

**B** Please _____ to continue.

**C** Can I just _____ you there?

**D** As I _____, I think ...

**E** Sure. What do you _____?

**F** _____ where I left off, ...

**G** Excuse me for _____ in, but ...

**H** Can I complete my _____ thought?

Mark: ___ / 8

## Grammar

**8** Rewrite the sentences, avoiding repetition by using ellipsis (E) or substitution (S).

**1** Have you done your homework yet, because I haven't done it? (E)

_____

**2** We don't want to leave, but we have to leave. (E)

_____

**3** I don't know if this will work but I hope it will work. (S)

_____

**4** We asked Tom to phone us, and he said he would phone but he hasn't phoned. (E)

_____

**5** I'd come to the party if I could come. But unfortunately I can't come. (E)

_____

**6** Our team could win the match, but I expect they won't win. (S)

_____

**7** You keep talking about wanting to learn to play the guitar, so I think you really should learn to play it. (E)

_____

**8** I don't know if Rachel is a professional artist, but I imagine that she is a professional. (S)

_____

Mark: ___ / 8

**9** Complete the sentences with the correct form of the words below.

anything nice / eat   easy / way / go   enough / hold
first person / make   me / lift   only / find   only student / pass

**1** We travelled all the way to Birmingham, _____ that the concert had been cancelled.

**2** Kathy was the _____ friends with me at college.

**3** You must be strong! That box is too heavy _____.

**4** The _____ to the station from here is along Stanton Road and over the canal bridge.

**5** I'm starving! Have we got _____ in the fridge?

**6** Rebecca was the _____ the test. It was far too difficult.

**7** The car isn't big _____ all these boxes, so we'll have to make two trips.

Mark: ___ / 7

## Use of English

**10** Complete the text. Write one word only in each gap.

Could Armageddon really strike some day and wipe [1] _____ most of mankind? Fifty-year-old Briton Peter Stanford certainly thinks [2] _____ – and he's doing everything he can [3] _____ prepare for it. Stanford is a 'prepper' – someone who is preparing for doomsday. Preppers consider all manner of events that could wreak havoc and [4] _____ disaster for the human race – and then they begin to make preparations to survive. Stanford already [5] _____ – his preparations include secret meeting places and a boat to stay at sea in for months.

Preppers may be readier than most of us for a global disaster, but will that guarantee their survival? I think [6] _____. After all, a lot will still depend on sheer luck. You might build yourself a nice shelter, [7] _____ to realise that it's right where a meteorite is projected to slam into Earth. Or when aliens go on the rampage, you may be so unlucky [8] _____ to find that someone else has discovered your hiding place – and isn't going to let you in!

Mark: ___ / 8

Total: ___ / 65

## *I can ...*

Read the statements. Think about your progress and tick (✓) one of the boxes.

★ = I need more practice.          ★★★ = No problem!

★★ = I sometimes find this difficult.

| | ★ | ★★ | ★★★ |
|---|---|---|---|
| I can talk about potential threats to our planet. | | | |
| I can use auxiliaries, modals, *so* and *not ... so* to avoid repetition. | | | |
| I can use context to understand a text on lost civilisations. | | | |
| I can use advanced uses of the infinitive. | | | |
| I can use collocations with common verbs. | | | |
| I can understand and react to an article about the endings of films. | | | |
| I can deal successfully with interruptions. | | | |
| I can write a report. | | | |

# 5 Exam Skills Trainer 5

## Reading

**Strategy**

Once you have chosen a paragraph, remember to check that it fits the text after the gap as well as the text before. Remember to focus on the development of the text, and not on the repetition of words.

1 Read the Strategy above and the gapped text in exercise 2. Read the paragraphs before and after gap 1 and missing paragraph D. Does paragraph D fit the gap? Why?/Why not?

2 Read the text. Match paragraphs A–G with gaps 1–6. There is one extra paragraph you do not need.

### How old is old?

As far as living organisms go, it would appear that trees are the ones that live the longest. But how do scientists determine the age of something that has been around for so much longer than they have?

1 _____
A more usual practice is to count the rings in a tree trunk, where one ring equals one year of growth. Tree-ring dating has several drawbacks, however: firstly, it only works for trees with an annual growth spurt, and secondly, it usually involves the tree being cut down.

2 _____
Those trees that have already been dated appear on the Old List, a register compiled by researchers in the USA. Notable entries are: a 2,222-year-old sacred fig tree in Sri Lanka; and a Patagonian Cypress tree in Chile, which is 3,627 years old. Extraordinary though these figures may seem, there are two trees that are even older than these.

3 _____
It is astonishing to think that both of these trees have witnessed the rise and fall of the Roman Empire. More amazing still is the fact that they were already established when the ancient Egyptians started building pyramids. But are they really the oldest single living things on the planet? That depends how you understand the word 'single'.

4 _____
Dating an organism of this kind is highly problematic, as the new plants grow in all directions and regenerate themselves as they go. Therefore, taking a section of one of the trunks will not tell you how old the whole tree is. Instead, scientists have used Pando's size to estimate its age, coming up with a figure somewhere 'between a few thousand and 80,000 years'.

5 _____
Scientists are almost certain that this is not the case for one simple reason: all known species can die, even species that appear not to age. However, certain factors do exist that appear to influence longevity, not only in the world of plants.

6 _____
For now, it seems, we will have to accept the Great Basin bristlecone pine as the oldest, precisely measured, organism on Earth, although Pando the quaking aspen and Antarctic glass sponges may well be older. Of course, there's also a chance that the oldest living organism has not yet been found.

A The quaking aspen is a remarkable tree which can multiply in a kind of clone-like way by having new plants sprout from the root system of the parent plant. One such tree, nicknamed Pando, has produced a forest of an estimated 50,000 trees in Fishlake National Park in Utah, USA.

B The least intrusive method is to consult records detailing which specimens are growing where, or look at maps showing significant ancient trees. Arboriculturalists also examine old paintings and artwork to see if their tree existed at a certain time.

C Take the Antarctic glass sponge, for example. Its freezing cold habitat causes it to grow extremely slowly. Scientists think that this slow growth contributes directly to its advanced age. With an estimated life span of 15,000 years, the Antarctic glass sponge is almost certainly the oldest living animal on the planet, although there is no scientific evidence to prove this title.

D A well-known method for measuring the age of a tree is dendrochronology, or tree-ring dating. This method has been used since the 1900s to establish how old a tree might be, and it is still the most common method used today.

E One is Methuselah, a Great Basin bristlecone pine growing in the White Mountains of California. Methuselah is an incredible 4,850 years old. But the tree that tops the list is an unnamed bristlecone pine from the same location. Aged 5,067, this tree has existed for over five millennia.

F The question is: if a tree can live to such a great age, are there any living organisms that are actually immortal?

G Fortunately, today's scientists have an instrument they can use to avoid this. It is called an increment borer, and is a kind of drill that allows them to extract a section of the trunk without killing the tree.

## Listening

**Strategy**

In multiple-choice tasks, you should choose the option for each question which best interprets the context.

3 🎧 3.09 Read the Strategy above. You will hear a radio interview about the future of the Olympic Games. For questions 1–6, choose the answer (A, B, C or D) which best interprets the context.

# 5 Exam Skills Trainer 5

1 What prompted the withdrawal of two cities from the 2024 Olympics bid?
  A Dissatisfaction with the selection process.
  B Objections from council members.
  C Opposition from the public.
  D The results of a vote.
2 When Los Angeles held the Games, the city
  A benefited directly from the event.
  B exceeded the financial plan considerably.
  C got into substantial debt with lenders.
  D invested unwisely on new installations.
3 According to Jeremy, there are very few visitors to the Olympic Park in Rio because
  A it is completely inaccessible.
  B it has been closed for a number of years.
  C it offers nothing for people to do.
  D it is way out of most people's price range.
4 Jeremy implies that past Olympic Games
  A weren't as well organised.
  B had a better atmosphere.
  C didn't have as many rules and regulations.
  D were much less commercialised.
5 Regarding the future of the Games, Jeremy thinks
  A its days are numbered.
  B it won't exist much longer in its current form.
  C it will always be held in the same place.
  D it may need to change some of the events.
6 In Jeremy's opinion
  A the Games should last for at least a month.
  B the medal winners should get more recognition.
  C the medal board should be shown more often.
  D the number of events should be limited.

## Use of English

> **Strategy**
> If the key word appears to have no connection with the first sentence, it may well be part of an idiom. Think of idioms you know that contain the key word, and choose the one that matches the meaning of the first sentence.

4 Read the Strategy and the sentence below. Which idioms do you know that contain the word TIME? Complete the second sentence with the correct 'time' idiom.

Kendra is always gossiping, so I don't really like her. **TIME**
I _____ Kendra because she's always gossiping.

5 For questions 1–6, complete the second sentence so that it has a similar meaning to the first sentence. Use between three and six words including the word given. Do not change the word given. Use the strategy in exercise 5 to help you.

1 Harry's great, but he forgets things very easily. **SIEVE**
  I'm very fond of Harry, but he _____.
2 Lucy doesn't agree with her cousin about politics. **EYE**
  Lucy and her cousin don't _____ about politics.
3 Hugh made a bad start on his first day at work. **FOOT**
  Hugh _____ on his first day at work.
4 I didn't enjoy that book you lent me. **GET**
  I _____ that book you lent me.
5 I promise I won't say a word. **LIPS**
  My _____, I promise.
6 She didn't start to speak until everyone was quiet. **DIED**
  She waited until the noise _____ before she started to speak.

## Speaking

> **Strategy**
> In the speaking test, you may not understand everything the examiner or the other candidate says. Use phrases to ask for repetition or clarification if necessary.

6 Read the Strategy. Complete the phrases below.
  1 I didn't _____ catch that. Would you _____ saying it again?
  2 Sorry, could you _____ that again? I just want to make _____ I understood the question.

7 Work in pairs. Do the task below. Use the ideas in the Strategy to ask for repetition if appropriate.

Which of these endings might be the most stressful?
- ending a relationship
- leaving school/university
- leaving home
- retiring from a job

## Writing

> **Strategy**
> When you write a report, you can use the facts from the task, but you will also need to make use of your own ideas and experiences.

8 Read the Strategy and the task below. Which of the facts from the task can you use and which of your own ideas and experiences?

You have just been on a school trip organised by your school. There have been a number of complaints about the trip. The head teacher has asked you to write a report in which you should evaluate the trip, outline the main problems and recommend changes for future trips.

9 Write the report (220–260 words) for the task in exercise 8.

# 1 Cumulative Review 1 (Units I–1)

## Listening

1 **(3.10)** Listen to a radio interview and choose the best answers (a–d).

1 What does Kauffman claim in his book?
  a It doesn't take as long as people think to become very good at something.
  b Twenty hours is enough time to learn any language fluently.
  c Everyone can quickly become reasonably competent at anything.
  d Learning any new skill takes no effort at all.

2 What does the speaker say about the 10,000-hour figure?
  a It's very inaccurate, and not well researched.
  b It's only true for some people.
  c It discourages people from trying to learn new things.
  d It doesn't match her experience of learning.

3 What is the first step in learning something new, according to Kauffman's book?
  a Breaking the skill down into smaller parts.
  b Discovering shortcuts to learning.
  c Learning how to memorise things fast.
  d Finding enough time to practise.

4 What does the speaker say is a major barrier to learning?
  a A lack of natural ability.
  b Inability to memorise or recall new information.
  c A lack of time to practise.
  d An inflexible attitude to learning.

5 What do Kaufmann and Gladwell both believe about learning?
  a The amount of time you spend learning something is totally unimportant.
  b There's no such thing as natural talent.
  c Talent isn't everything when it comes to learning.
  d People give up learning new skills too easily.

## Speaking

2 **Work in pairs. Take turns to ask and answer the questions.**
  • What subjects and skills do you enjoy and dislike learning? Why?
  • What do you find easy or difficult to remember? Why?
  • What skills do you have?
  • What new skills would you like to learn in the future? Why?
  • How do you like to spend your free time?
  • What do you think you will be doing in ten years' time?

## Reading

3 **Read the texts about vision and match them with questions 1–8. Each text can be matched with more than one question.**

Which text ...
1 mentions the brain creating something? _____
2 talks about qualified people being influenced? _____
3 mentions the link between language and perception? _____
4 mentions our inability to remember things? _____
5 discusses differences in colour perception? _____
6 suggests a reason for something by mentioning the natural world? _____
7 mentions seeing more when you pay attention? _____
8 suggests competitions are not as fair as they seem? _____

**A Do you see the same colour as me?**

The Candoshi native people of Peru have one word for orange and yellow, when most people in Peru would use separate Spanish words for these two colours. More surprisingly, they have the same colour word (*kavabana*) for colours from purple to blue to green, but another word (*kamachpa*) for what most Peruvians would call 'dark green'. It's clear that different groups of people tend to divide up colours differently, but do they actually see them in a different way?

Tests with the Himba people of Namibia suggest that we do see colours differently. In one experiment, a slightly different tone of green in a circle of green dots really stood out for the Himba people. This is interesting, bearing in mind it was almost impossible for Europeans to see the difference. In contrast, the Himba found a test where they had to find a light blue spot amongst light green ones very difficult. This may be owing to the fact that the Himba word for these two colours is the same. It seems that people around the world really do see things differently.

## B Seeing red

Whether or not a sports team will win their next match may partly depend on the colour of their shirts. Two British anthropologists at Durham University reached this startling conclusion by studying the results of boxing, wrestling and tae-kwondo matches from the 2004 Athens Olympics. Olympic officials randomly give blue or red clothes and equipment to competitors in these sports. However, the study found that in matches where the opponents were well matched in terms of skill, the competitor in red had won more often. It seems that colour was affecting the judgement of the referees. This is worrying, given that sports referees are highly qualified and must be impartial.

One explanation for this may be the role of red in nature, where the colour will usually indicate dominance and strength. Referees may tend to perceive players in red as being more capable – something that is crucial in sports where winning and losing often come down to points awarded by the judges. Interestingly, the study also suggested that competitors may feel more self-assured and confident when they are wearing red.

## C What do we see?

Stop anyone in the street and ask them about the things they've just walked past, like the colour of a car or what was in a shop window. The chances are they won't be able to recall these things – even if you try to jog their memory with questions.

Some scientists think the reason for this is that it would simply take too long for our minds to process everything that our eyes have seen. But, they say, we've all seen city streets before so we've built mental models of things like buildings and cars. When we walk along the street, they claim that we tend to rely on these models and don't actually 'experience' many of the real things around us.

According to this theory, we only really 'see' things when we pay attention to them – like avoiding a pedestrian who is about to walk into us. Even then, we are unlikely to perceive details like the person's hair or clothes – unless they're particularly unusual. But our mind does a great job of filling in the details, and consequently our world seems rich and detailed. In effect, we may all be living inside our own virtual models of the world: our own personal *Matrix*.

## Grammar and vocabulary

4 Choose the correct answers (a–d).

1  a are apt    b would always    c keep on    d tend to
2  a the brain    b a brain    c brain    d our brains
3  a place    b view    c mind    d case
4  a enduring    b abiding    c traumatic    d vague
5  a explains    b is    c works    d else
6  a human    b body    c mind    d volunteer
7  a evoke    b recall    c reminisce    d remind
8  a happened    b happening    c had happened    d would happen

## SEEING IN SLOW MOTION

People $^1$_____ report that time seems to slow down when we are in life-threatening situations. Objects seem to move in slow motion, and seconds seem to stretch as a person realises they are about to have an accident. So is $^2$_____ somehow able to work faster than normal during an emergency? This would give us more chance to make life-or-death decisions, but also slow down our perception of time.

In $^3$_____ of this common experience, neuroscientist David Eagelman conducted experiments where volunteers were asked to look at a fast-moving clock and try to read the numbers. They did this under normal conditions, and when they were in a $^4$_____ situation. (The latter involved dropping volunteers from a height of 70 feet attached to a bungee cord.) In both situations, the numbers moved too fast for the volunteers to read. Given this fact, Eagelman concluded that the brain wasn't working any faster than normal in stressful situations. But if that's not the reason for this commonly reported experience, then what $^5$_____?

One explanation might be that the $^6$_____ pays more attention to threats and dangers. This means that our brains process more information about them, so frightening events are associated with more detailed, vivid memories. When we remember the event later, we have more information to $^7$_____. This greater detail makes it feel like the event $^8$_____ in slow motion.

## Writing

5 Read the task then write an opinion essay of 220–260 words. Remember to plan your paragraphs before beginning to write.

We will soon have the technology to blot out or suppress painful or traumatic memories. But should we use this technology or not? Write an essay in which you discuss this question and give your opinion.

## Listening

1 [🎧 3.11] Listen to a speaker reviewing a book and complete the sentences with 1–2 words.

### *The Seven Basic Plots*, by Christopher Booker

1 Booker suggests that all stories are _____ on one of seven basic plots.

2 The speaker found the idea intriguing because as a teacher, she's used to _____.

3 In 'overcoming the monster' stories, the monster always appears _____ than the hero.

4 Often the plot contains a last-minute _____, after all appears lost.

5 The characters in 'rags to riches' stories don't _____ their poverty or bad circumstances.

6 In 'rags to riches' stories, the hero's _____ leads to their success in the end.

7 In 'voyage and return' stories, a character visits a place which is _____ from their ordinary world.

8 Plots may be similar because ancient stories are _____ in different cultures and times.

## Speaking

2 Work in pairs. Look at the photos and discuss the question.

What are the advantages and disadvantages of each of these presents? Which one would you prefer to receive?

## Reading

3 Read the text opposite about a famous person and her book and complete it with paragraphs A–G below. There is one extra paragraph that you do not need to use.

**A** Her chance came a few years later, when the Leakeys proposed that she lead a study of mountain gorillas living in Rwanda. This was quite a leap of faith for the Leakeys, when you consider that Dian Fossey had no qualifications in zoology.

**B** Challenging as those problems were, the biggest danger was the poachers – hunters who killed the gorillas to sell their body parts as chilling souvenirs. Fossey fought off the poachers, and refused to give in to their threats to kill her if she didn't leave.

**C** If I hadn't read the book, I wouldn't know anything about this remarkable woman, who gave her life to study and protect mountain gorillas. The book is a wonderful portrait both of the woman herself and of the animals that she devoted much of her short life to.

**D** *Gorillas in the Mist* is a touching and thought-provoking account of Fossey's life with the gorillas. Not only does it beautifully portray the gorillas, but it also highlights the grave dangers that they face. The book became a best-seller, and it led to a worldwide conservation campaign.

**E** Ultimately, so much of conservation work comes down to the efforts of people like Dian Fossey. Brave individuals who devote their lives to protecting wildlife and sometimes pay the ultimate price.

**F** It did take the mountain gorillas time to accept her, but eventually she was living with four gorilla families – an accepted member of their group. Fossey studied the animals for many years – earning a PhD for her work.

**G** No sooner had Fossey arrived in Africa in 1963 than she fell in love with the continent. There she met famous scientists Joan and Louis Leakey, who would later change her destiny. She also made friends with two wildlife photographers who were making a documentary about mountain gorillas. It was they who first took her to see these amazing creatures.

# 2

# Cumulative Review 2 (Units I–3)

**GORILLAS IN THE MIST**

A friend recently advised me to read *Gorillas in the Mist*, by Dian Fossey. I confess to having been reluctant at first because I don't generally enjoy autobiographies. But I'm glad that I took the time to read it.

**1** _____ Fossey had always loved animals as a child, but not until much later did she begin working in conservation. After graduating from university in 1953, Fossey worked with disabled children in Louisville, Kentucky. She lived on a farm in Louisville, looking after farm animals in her spare time and saving up money for the trip of lifetime – a journey through Africa.

**2** _____ Although she had only stayed in Africa for seven weeks, the experience changed her. The wildlife of Africa – and particularly the mountain gorillas – left a lasting impression on her. Africa was in her blood, and she was determined to go back.

**3** _____ Fossey returned to Africa in 1966, and in 1967, she founded the Karisoke Research Foundation, a camp on the slopes of a 14,000-foot volcano in Rwanda. There, she slowly learned how to approach the mountain gorillas – creatures that would have killed her had they felt threatened by her presence.

**4** _____ As well as her struggle to become accepted by the gorillas, Fossey constantly battled against the harsh realities of her day-to-day life. She was usually alone, and far from any help. And she was living in a high mountain forest nearly always blanketed by rain.

**5** _____ Fossey stayed on despite the threats, and by the mid-1980s, she had become the world's leading authority on the behaviour of gorillas. Then, tragically, in 1985 she was murdered – probably by poachers. Two years earlier, Dian Fossey had written her autobiography, *Gorillas in the Mist*. Ultimately this book ensured that her death was not in vain.

**6** _____ What is most striking about the book is Fossey's portrayal of the gorillas' complicated society and intricate social rules. Despite their fearsome reputation, mountain gorillas are clearly gentle creatures who care for one another.

The book was later made into a film, starring Sigourney Weaver. During film production, Weaver also spent time with the gorillas and, like Fossey, was deeply affected by them. Twenty years later, Sigourney Weaver visited the mountain gorillas again. She was happy to see that gorilla populations there are increasing. The future will be brighter for Rwanda's mountain gorillas – thanks to the sacrifice of Dian Fossey.

## Grammar and vocabulary

**4 Choose the correct words to complete the text.**

| | a | b | c | d |
|---|---|---|---|---|
| 1 | had sat | have sat | were sitting | were seated |
| 2 | wondered | mentioned | proposed | suggested |
| 3 | Why | Let's | Don't we | Why not |
| 4 | wasn't | isn't | wouldn't be | hadn't been |
| 5 | bigger and bigger | much more | by far | the biggest |
| 6 | So | Such | Much | Great |
| 7 | the most | like | by far | nearly |
| 8 | can you | you | are you | you don't |

In 1974, a group of young publishers and booksellers **1**_____ in a coffee shop in Kolkata, India, when someone **2**_____ the Frankfurt Book Fair. **3**_____ have a fair in Kolkata? they asked. Two years later, the first fair opened, with 56 bookstalls. It would probably have stayed as a small affair if it **4**_____ for the hard work of the booksellers and book lovers of Kolkata – but with their efforts, the fair grew **5**_____ over the years. **6**_____ was the demand for stalls at the fair that the venue had to move several times to accommodate everyone. Despite some setbacks, such as a huge fire in 1997 which destroyed thousands of books, the fair has become **7**_____ Asia's largest book festival, attracting a huge following. Nowhere in Asia today **8**_____ find so many publishers and books in one place.

## Writing

**5 Read the task below and write a review of 220–260 words. Remember to plan your paragraphs before you begin.**

Write a review of a book which you have recently read. What did you like and/or dislike about the book? (Think about the plot, characters, language and setting.) Give reasons why you would or wouldn't recommend the book.

# 3
# Cumulative Review 3 (Units I–5)

## Listening

1 **3.12** Listen to five people talking about problems with technology. For questions 1 and 2, choose from the list (A–H). There are three extra sentences.

1 What main problem does each speaker have?
  A They were denied access to information.
  B They found it very difficult to contact somebody.
  C Their house was damaged.
  D They lost something that they had enjoyed.
  E It took ages to download something.
  F A device which used to perform well has become less efficient.
  G They lost something that they had spent time on.
  H Doing something is taking up a lot of their time.

| Speaker | 1 | 2 | 3 | 4 | 5 |
|---------|---|---|---|---|---|
|         |   |   |   |   |   |

2 Why did each speaker feel annoyed?
  A They felt cheated.
  B They felt pressured to buy something.
  C They should have known how to do something.
  D It took them a lot of time to solve a problem.
  E They feel that technology is too difficult to grasp.
  F They feel that they have a right to something.
  G They feel pressured to do something.
  H Their work was often interrupted.

| Speaker | 1 | 2 | 3 | 4 | 5 |
|---------|---|---|---|---|---|
|         |   |   |   |   |   |

## Speaking

2 Work in pairs. Discuss the question. Think about topics such as the environment, entertainment and communications.

Has technology made life better or worse for most people in the last 50 years? Why?

## Reading

3 Read the text and choose the correct options (a–d).

1 What is true about the building in Chengdu mentioned by the author?
  a Like the Sydney Opera House, it's an entertainment complex.
  b The building has a symbolic value for the city.
  c It was designed to attract tourists.
  d It proves that Chengdu is now a megacity.
2 What does the text NOT say about the Industrial Revolution?
  a It led to migration from rural areas.
  b It didn't initially improve the lives of workers.
  c It made city planners immediately improve urban areas.
  d It led to the growth of new cities.
3 What does the writer say about city farms?
  a They are only possible in cities which have a lot of green space.
  b They already exist, but not in very big cities.
  c They will only be possible in cities with tall buildings.
  d They will lead to food shortages.

**RISE OF THE MEGACITIES**

In 2013, people in Chengdu, China, excitedly toured their city's latest attraction – a mammoth building twenty times bigger than the Sydney Opera House, with two 1,000-bed hotels, hundreds of shops, and an artificial beach complete with a Mediterranean village. Chengdu is one of the fastest-growing cities on the planet – just one of the many new megacities that are mushrooming worldwide. This showcase building was clearly intended to show the city's new wealth and power.

In 1800, only 3% of the world's population lived in urban areas. But in Europe, the Industrial Revolution was already underway, and new cities were growing up almost overnight. It was at this time that rural workers began migrating in large numbers in search of work and a better life in the cities. Most of those early migrants found little but poverty, overcrowding, pollution and disease. Urban life expectancy plummeted after the Industrial Revolution, until drastic improvements in city planning helped to put an end to some of the worst problems. By 1950, Tokyo had become the world's first 'megacity' – a city with a population of more than ten million. Today eleven cities are home to more than twice that number of people – and in the near future we will be seeing more.

4 The writer thinks that the growth of megacities ...
  a is definitely a good thing.
  b will mean that governments can't cope.
  c may well be unstoppable.
  d will be bad for mankind.
5 What message does the last paragraph contain?
  a The difference between a better or worse future depends a lot on what we do.
  b We need to halt the growth of megacities immediately.
  c We must invest more money in new technologies.
  d Wealthy countries will continue to act unfairly towards developing nations.

The streets of growing cities are often built on old farm land, so food for the city's sky-rocketing population has to come from further and further away. One solution may be to build farms inside the city – in small empty spaces between buildings, or even on rooftops. There are already such city farms in small cities like Havana and Vancouver, but the big challenge is to scale these up for megacities, where space is in even shorter supply. For this reason, some people envisage huge vertical farms in skyscrapers, where food can be grown on each floor.

Megacities like São Paulo and Los Angeles – where hundreds of new cars go onto the streets every week – are regularly paralysed by traffic congestion. Clearly, transport systems will need to be totally redesigned to cope with escalating urban populations. To this end, China will soon have developed an electric bus which can carry up to 1,000 people! And this megabus won't be taking up any space on the road – it's designed to be like a bridge on wheels, travelling over other traffic.

The growth of megacities is probably inevitable, but will it be a good or a bad thing? Optimists point to cities like Shanghai and Chengdu, which have transformed themselves and radically improved life for their populations. However, others point to megacities like Mumbai and Jakarta, where population growth far outpaces the ability of local governments to provide enough infrastructure. At the end of the day, wealthy governments need to do their bit to help improve the infrastructure of cities in developing nations. If they do this, megacities will become magnets of technology, education and culture, creating new opportunities for mankind. If they don't, untold millions will be forced to live in poverty-stricken, crime-ridden cities, competing desperately for dwindling resources.

## Grammar and vocabulary

4 **Choose the correct words to complete the text.**

| | a | b | c | d |
|---|---|---|---|---|
| 1 | using | were used | being used | that used |
| 2 | hadn't been | didn't yet | were not | couldn't have |
| 3 | most | few | more and more | far more |
| 4 | propose | recommend | inform | claim |
| 5 | as | like | being | as if |
| 6 | be making | are making | have made | be made |
| 7 | they are | it | could be | so |
| 8 | insist | argue | agree | urge |

## Should we be worried about ROBOTS?

The word 'robot' first appeared in Karel Čapek's 1920 play *RER*, which portrayed robots ¹_____ as factory workers before they rebelled and began to kill their human bosses. At the time, real robots ²_____ invented, but today they are a part of our lives. Robots are being used to do ³_____ jobs all the time, and they are useful in far more ways than Čapek could have dreamed. But what if he was right?

Today many scientists ⁴_____ that robots could one day be a grave danger to mankind. They point out that the computing power of devices is doubling every few years. Given this fact, it's seen ⁵_____ inevitable that one day machines will be able to think. But when that happens, will they be friendly or hostile towards us?

Armed military robots are already used on the battlefield – albeit under human control. But could robot soldiers ⁶_____ their own decisions one day, and could they also commit terrible atrocities? People like Elon Musk and Stephen Hawking certainly think ⁷_____ possible. They ⁸_____ us to find ways to control thinking machines before the first ones appear. If we don't, they warn, thinking machines could find ways to control us!

## Writing

5 **Read the essay task below and write an essay of 220–260 words. Remember to plan your paragraphs before you start writing.**

Some people argue that wind power is an important energy technology which helps to protect the environment. Others say that wind turbines are ugly structures which spoil the landscape. Write an essay which presents the advantages and disadvantages of using wind power.

## Listening

1 **(●) 3.13** Listen to a person describing a visit to the town of Selma, Alabama. Are the sentences true or false?

1 The speaker planned to visit Selma on his/her way to Dallas. _____

2 Elijah and his brothers took part in the 1965 protests in Selma. _____

3 At that time, African-Americans in Selma were supposed to have equal rights, but didn't. _____

4 Martin Luther King's campaign in Selma focused on education rights. _____

5 The authorities in Alabama used violence to prevent King's first protest march. _____

6 When people saw images of the protests on TV, most Americans approved of police tactics. _____

7 Things changed after someone was killed. _____

8 In the end, the march was banned by the federal government. _____

## Speaking

2 **Work in pairs and complete the task.**

Your school has asked you to plan a day trip for some visiting exchange students. What are the advantages and disadvantages of these ideas? Agree which one is the most appropriate.

- a visit to a museum, historical monument or castle
- a day at a shopping and entertainment centre
- a walk and picnic in the countryside
- a visit to a pretty nearby town or village
- an adventure sports day with canoeing and rock climbing

## Reading

3 **Read the text and answer the questions in your own words.**

1 How was the cave of crystals discovered?

_____

2 What can't the miner who died have known?

_____

3 Why is the human body unable to cope with the high heat and humidity in the caves?

_____

4 How did Paolo Forti's team overcome this problem?

_____

5 What work did the explorers do inside the caves?

_____

6 What does the writer think will happen in the future?

_____

# THE CAVE OF
# CRYSTALS

The Naica mine, near Chihuahua, Mexico, has been worked by generations of miners. Over the years, a maze of tunnels has slowly been excavated, some of which now reach hundreds of metres down under the ground. But until this century, nobody knew that a beautiful but deadly hidden world lay right next to the Naica mine.

In 2000, brothers Juan and Pedro Sanchez were digging for silver in the mine when they broke through a rock wall into a vast cave. The inside of the cave was a surreal world of huge crystals that dwarfed the men. The crystals, the biggest of which turned out to weigh 55 tonnes, grew at angles across the cave and glimmered in the light of their lamps.

The heat and humidity in the cave was so high that the men soon left – probably in the nick of time before being overcome by the lethal atmosphere. Two days later an iron door was installed – to stop anyone from going inside. However, one miner did enter the cave later. He might have hoped to take some pieces of crystal from the cave, but he can't have understood the dangers. When his body was later found, it had been slowly cooked by the intense heat and humidity.

Temperatures of over 65°C have been measured in the main cave, and the humidity is nearly 100%. As a result, it's impossible for the body to cool down. Unable to cope, the body diverts a lot of blood to the skin in a futile attempt to lose heat. Because of this, you lose consciousness as the brain is deprived of oxygen. Then you die.

In 2006, an international team of scientists led by Italian Paolo Forti conducted a series of expeditions to explore the cave, which people had by now called 'The Cave of Crystals'. Due to the intense heat and humidity, the scientists carried oxygen and wore specially designed clothes which had ice in them. Even with this equipment, exploring the caves nearly proved to be fatal.

## Grammar and vocabulary

**4** Choose the correct answers to complete the text.

1 **a** that posts   **b** posted   **c** to post   **d** which is posted
2 **a** it   **b** where   **c** their   **d** which
3 **a** may have   **b** can't have   **c** must have   **d** should have
4 **a** want   **b** had wanted   **c** was wanted   **d** would want
5 **a** to suggest   **b** I request   **c** begging   **d** they propose
6 **a** last   **b** end of the day   **c** end of it   **d** final
7 **a** worth   **b** necessary   **c** great   **d** important
8 **a** up   **b** in   **c** out   **d** off

It was difficult and dangerous for the explorers to climb over the crystals and make their way through the cave. What's more, they couldn't go slowly because the ice in their suits quickly melted. After that time, they became dangerously hot and had to retreat to specially cooled tents in the main mine.

Despite these difficulties, the scientists were able to map the main caves, take samples and analyse the chemistry which had led to this amazing environment. It turns out that the Cave of Crystals is actually three linked caves – one much bigger and hotter than the other two – and possibly there are more caves nearby. The crystals are made of a mineral called selenite. Over hundreds of thousands of years, the caves had been periodically flooded by water rich in the mineral gypsum. The heat produced by underground volcanic activity had turned this gypsum into glass-like crystals of selenite. The longest crystal found was nearly 12 metres in length, and it had probably been growing for about half a million years!

Paolo Forti's team mounted twelve short expeditions to the mine in 2006. Even so, the cave system hasn't yet been fully mapped. Since 2006, nobody has dared to go back there but no doubt one day explorers will. The Naica mine is still in use, but the door to the staggeringly beautiful and equally lethal Cave of Crystals remains firmly shut.

Student work and travel placements can be great for your English – and great fun too. *But do your research*, writes Fabrizzio Melegari.

I was excited when I saw an advert for a work and travel abroad scheme ¹_____ on my language school website. I went to the open day advertised, ²_____ was held at a local hotel. My application was processed on the spot, and they soon contacted me with two possible placements – one as a swimming coach in Durham, England, and the other in a restaurant in Tropic Utah, USA. I ³_____ checked the places out before replying, but I jumped at the chance of going to America.

It wasn't until I arrived that I realised that Tropic was a tiny settlement two hours from the nearest town – Cedar City. I was gutted. I ⁴_____ to have fun in the States, but here I was flipping burgers at a diner in the middle of nowhere. Initially I considered ⁵_____ the agency to change my placement. But at the ⁶_____ I'm glad I didn't. I made some good friends in Tropic, and had a surprisingly good time hanging out with them – even in a place where nothing ever happens. And nearby Dryce Canyon is beautiful, and really ⁷_____ seeing. So there was an upside to my experience. Having said that, I'd certainly recommend checking out any placement before signing ⁸_____ for it.

## Writing

**5** Read the question below and write an informal email in 220–260 words. Remember to plan your paragraphs before writing.

You've received an email from an English-speaking friend.

*I'm trying to get used to living in my new home – and new country – but it isn't easy. I miss my old friends, and my neighbourhood too. I know you're away from home all summer on a language course, so how are you feeling? Are you enjoying it or missing home? What do you think I should do?*

# Cumulative Review 5 (Units 1–9)

## Listening

1 **🎧 3.14** Listen and complete the sentences with a short word or phrase.

1 British illusionist Derren Brown didn't think that luck was a _____, but he wanted to test his theory.
2 Film-maker Dawn O'Porter helped him to create a _____ about a lucky statue in a small English town.
3 Most people said they'd heard about it because they didn't want to seem _____.
4 People began to visit the statue and they were _____ for good luck.
5 Slowly, the _____ of the town began to change.
6 Local butcher Wayne Stansfield strongly believed that he would always be _____.
7 Derren Brown's admission that the lucky dog was a hoax came _____ to people who had believed in it.
8 Amazingly, the town's _____ continued, even after they knew the truth.

## Speaking

2 **Work in pairs. Take turns to ask and answer the questions.**
- Do you think that some people are luckier than others? Why or why not?
- Have you ever been extremely lucky? What happened?
- Are you generally optimistic or pessimistic about the future? Why?
- What do you think are the most important dangers facing our planet? Why?
- What do you see yourself doing in twenty years' time?
- What important scientific breakthroughs do you think will happen in your lifetime?

## Reading

3 **Read texts A–C and match them with the statements.**

Which text mentions ...
1 something which can change people's behaviour?
2 criticism of a film by scientists?
3 a huge disaster which took place a long time ago?
4 something which may become more dangerous one day?
5 the fact that a film has exaggerated something?
6 the typical ending of a plot?
7 new evidence that a theory may be correct?
8 the low probability that something will happen soon?

### Global catastrophe is one of Hollywood's best-loved themes, but how realistic are disaster film scenarios? Read on for our reality check.

**A    A sudden climate change**

In the film *The Day after Tomorrow*, a weather circulation system over the Atlantic referred to by scientists as AMOC shuts down. This plunges Europe and North America into a sudden and severe ice age. The film was put down as rubbish by scientists at the time of its release in 2004, but a new study by the University of Southampton and the Max Planck Institute is making people reconsider.

Using sophisticated climate modelling programs, researchers calculated that climate change caused by carbon emissions could indeed cause AMOC to shut down – cooling the planet instead of warming it for a period of about 20 years. What is unrealistic in the film, however, is the speed and severity with which this happens. However badly climate change affects AMOC, it won't happen in the way depicted in the film.

FROM THE DIRECTOR OF INDEPENDENCE DAY

THE DAY AFTER TOMORROW

MAY 28    WHERE WILL YOU BE?

## B A zombie attack

Films such as *Resident Evil* and *The Walking Dead* portray embattled heroes fighting for their lives against a plague of killer zombies. Whatever Hollywood says, it's impossible for dead people to rise up from the grave. But could some future disease infect people and control their minds, turning them violent? Worryingly, some biologists think so.

Some mind-controlling diseases already exist, such as the parasite toxoplasmosis. This makes mice lose their fear of cats – the parasite needs the mouse to be eaten by the cat in order to complete its life cycle. Interestingly, human studies show that whoever becomes infected with toxoplasmosis tends to become bolder and take more risks.

Another virus already exists which causes people to become violent, and even bite others: rabies. Luckily, rabies is difficult to get, but viruses evolve over time and change. If one day rabies became as infectious as flu, it would be time to arm yourself and lock the doors!

## C A meteorite impact

Asteroid impacts are another favourite Hollywood theme – with blockbuster films featuring planet-killing rocks that hurtle towards Earth, only to meet their match in a heroic astronaut like Bruce Willis in *Armageddon* or Robert Duvall in *Deep Impact*. These tough-talking, good-looking heroes always manage to save us, only to die themselves after a suitably moving farewell.

The fact is that Earth has been hit by many big asteroids in the past – and will be again. A huge asteroid wiped out the dinosaurs 65 million years ago, causing worldwide destruction. So the big question is, when will this happen again?

What astronomers know is that there are millions of asteroids out there. A really big one could hit us at almost any time – but statistically it isn't likely for thousands of years. By that time scientists hope to have figured out a way to deal with them – either destroying the asteroid or changing its orbit so it flies harmlessly past Earth.

## Grammar and vocabulary

4 Choose the correct answers to complete the text.

| | | | | |
|---|---|---|---|---|
| 1 | a That | b That | c What | d It |
| 2 | a they are | b such | c them | d so |
| 3 | a it | b which | c for | d what |
| 4 | a is named | b to be named | c named | d they named |
| 5 | a we | b to | c to be | d as |
| 6 | a will be | b must have | c had | d are |
| 7 | a Whenever | b Whichever | c However | d Whatever |
| 8 | a it | b all | c so | d that |

## USE OF ENGLISH

Is it possible that there are intelligent aliens somewhere out there, on a distant planet far from Earth? [1]_____ we've learned about the universe in the last few decades certainly suggests [2]_____ The question is, will any of them ever visit Earth? And what would happen if they did?

SETI is a scientific organisation [3]_____ searches for intelligent alien life. A division of SETI [4]_____ the Post Detection Task Force has plans in place for what to do in the event of alien contact. These basically involve contacting the United Nations and scientific agencies, sharing data, and working out how to respond. The military would be the last [5]_____ involved. The thinking behind this is simple: any aliens who actually manage to cross light-years of interstellar space and get here [6]_____ developed technology that is far more advanced than ours. [7]_____ weapons they have will be incomparably better than ours, so attempting to fight them would be futile.

At the end of the day, [8]_____ we can hope is that any aliens who do visit us will turn out to be friendly – more like the gentle creatures in the film *Arrival* than the killers of *Independence Day*.

## Writing

5 Read the task. Then write a report of 220–260 words. Remember to plan your paragraphs before writing.

You have been asked to write a report about how ready your school is to deal with an emergency such as a fire, flood or earthquake. In your report, you should examine what facilities and equipment your school has (e.g. emergency stairs, fire extinguishers, etc.) and how well staff and students have been prepared for an emergency (e.g. first-aid-trained staff, emergency drills, etc.). Evaluate your school's preparations and make recommendations to improve them.

## Discursive Essay / CAE Part 1 Essay

Your class has watched a TV documentary about the negative effects of CCTV surveillance on society.
You have made the notes below:

**Effects of surveillance:**

- the loss of privacy and freedom
- the decline in 'real' policing
- the lack of crime reduction

**Some opinions expressed in the documentary:**

- 'You cannot escape the cameras even if you are doing nothing wrong.'
- 'The authorities use CCTV cameras as an excuse for reducing the number of police officers on the streets.'
- 'Cameras are intended to reduce crime but there is little evidence that they are effective.'

**Write an essay (220–260 words) discussing two of the effects of surveillance. You should explain which effect is more important, giving reasons in support of your answer.**

Over the past few years, especially after recent terrorist attacks, public safety has become an important issue. It is undoubtedly true that the use of video surveillance (CCTV) has increased, but it is also true to say that this is not without drawbacks. This essay will take a closer look at two of the main disadvantages of video surveillance.

The purpose of security measures is not only to keep people safe but also to instil confidence in the general public. In this respect, CCTV is a poor substitute for good neighbourhood policing. Indeed, there is even some evidence to suggest that the presence of CCTV cameras makes people feel less secure, because they associate the cameras with high-crime areas. And yet, for financial reasons, police numbers continue to be cut, while CCTV surveillance increases.

There is another problem with the spread of CCTV surveillance which concerns our rights as citizens. We are surrounded by cameras throughout our everyday lives, even when our activities are entirely law-abiding. This represents a significant infringement of our civil liberties. Cameras which are installed to prevent crime can also be used to monitor our behaviour in other ways.

While the appeal of using video surveillance as a security measure is understandable, the potential dangers are, in my opinion, too great. The risk to civil liberties is the more important of the two issues discussed in this essay, because widespread surveillance threatens our way of life and our privacy. Individual freedoms and rights which took centuries to achieve should not be sacrificed so easily.

- Make sure your essay covers all the information requested in the task. Remember to organise the information into separate paragraphs.

- In the first paragraph (the introduction) establish the topic for your essay, alluding briefly to any recent events or trends that are relevant. Outline the structure of your essay to help the reader follow your argument.

- Remember that you will be assessed on the range of language you use as well as its correct use, so do not limit yourself to simple vocabulary and structures.

- Try to develop your points wherever possible, using appropriate linking words to introduce the additional information.

- Your essay can include opinions from the task, but try to express them in your own words. (This sentence rephrases the first opinion in the task.)

- In the final paragraph (the conclusion) sum up your opinion. If the task requires it, include a clear statement of which point you consider more important and why.

# Writing Bank

## Discursive Essay / CAE Part 1 Essay

Your class has had a discussion about the possible uses of space travel in the near future. You have made the notes below:

**Possible uses:**
- finding new planets to inhabit
- space tourism
- searching for natural resources

**Some opinions expressed in the discussion:**
- 'Earth will become less habitable because of climate change.'
- 'As space travel gets cheaper, it will become a popular leisure activity.'
- 'Other planets and moons could definitely provide a rich source of precious metals.'

Write an essay (220–260 words) discussing two of the uses of space travel. You should explain which use is more important, giving reasons in support of your answer.

It is more than half a century since humans first ventured into space, and we now appear to be on the verge of a new era in space travel, as private companies develop new kinds of re-usable space craft. In this essay, I will discuss two different aspects of this imminent revolution in space travel.

- In your introduction, it may be a good idea to place the topic in its historical context.

Space tourism is already becoming a reality and a handful of extremely wealthy individuals have paid to experience the adventure of space flight. As new technologies are developed, this opportunity is sure to become more affordable. Naturally, safety will be a concern initially, but with time, space craft will become as safe as aeroplanes and it is possible to envisage an era when adventure holidays on the Moon are commonplace.

- If you are writing about the future, use a range of appropriate grammatical forms, including *will*, modal verbs and set phrases like '*be bound / sure / certain to*'.

Aside from tourism, other uses for space travel will certainly emerge over the coming decades. At some point in the future, it may become necessary for humans to leave Earth, owing to climate change, nuclear war or simply over-population, and to live in space or colonise another planet. The first steps towards this are already being taken, as NASA prepares for a manned mission to Mars. Moreover, studies are continually being undertaken to assess how humans might cope with life in a space colony.

- Make sure your essay is written in an appropriately formal style. This is likely to include passive forms. Avoid colloquial language.

- Try to display a good knowledge of topic-related vocabulary.

Enthralling as the possibility of holidays in space may be, the quest for other habitable planets is undoubtedly more important as it concerns the very survival of the human race. It seems certain that, at some point, our species will expand beyond Earth. Whether this happens by choice or through necessity remains to be seen.

- Your essay will achieve a higher mark if you use a variety of sentence structures, including subordinate clauses where appropriate.

- When writing about future possibilities, you may wish to conclude with a rhetorical question or open-ended remark.

# W Writing Bank

## Review

Your college magazine would like students to submit film reviews for the next issue. They would like these reviews to focus in particular on whether films would appeal to older teenagers. You decide to write a review of two films you have seen, one of which is very appealing to older teenagers and the other much less so. Write your review (220–260 words) in an appropriate style.

In 2017, two films were released which attempted to capture the older teenage market: *The Mummy*, starring Tom Cruise and Russell Crowe, and *It*, based on a Stephen King book familiar to many older teenagers. Universal Studios, who produced *The Mummy*, have announced that it will be the first in a series of films known as *Dark Universe*, while a second instalment of *It* is already being planned.

- In the introduction, mention the titles and a few other key facts about the film or films you are reviewing.

The film *It* tells the story of an evil clown who kills children in a small American town. A group of teenagers, known as 'The Losers' Club' because they are all victims of bullying, come together to fight the demon. The film is brilliantly directed, with the cinematography and lighting adding to the terror. There are moments of comedy too, which lighten what is admittedly a slightly over-long film.

- In the following paragraphs, describe the film(s): include a plot summary and mention some of the strengths and weaknesses.

In *The Mummy*, an ancient princess awakens from her tomb beneath the desert. As the victim of betrayal centuries earlier, she now seeks to inflict a terrible revenge on the modern world. The film has an all-star cast and is a true Hollywood blockbuster. Although the storyline is rather far-fetched, many older teenagers will enjoy the mix of action, adventure and fantasy.

- A film review should include some film-specific vocabulary: *plot*, *cast*, *cinematography*, *lighting*, and so on.

While I found both films enjoyable, I would recommend *It* rather than *The Mummy* for older teenagers, partly because of the age of the protagonists, but also because of the gripping storyline and excellent acting. Stephen King himself considers the film *It* a triumph and I am confident that most older teenagers would share his opinion.

- Use appropriate adjectives, either positive or negative, to describe aspects of the films: *gripping, far-fetched, (un)convincing, fast-/slow-paced*, and so on.

- Keep in mind the specific audience for your review that the task mentions. It may be a good idea to mention this explicitly in your conclusion.

# Writing Bank

## Report

As part of a temporary summer job, you recently accompanied a group of teenage students from your country on a two-week study holiday in England. Your manager has asked you to write a report evaluating the trip from both your own and the students' perspectives and suggesting improvements for next year's trip.

Write your report (220–260 words) in an appropriate style.

## Report on the two-week study holiday in England

### Introduction

The aim of this report is to evaluate the trip from the students' point of view, as well as from my own perspective as an employee. It is based primarily on my own opinions but also reflects conversations with several students during the two-week stay.

### Overall assessment

The trip went smoothly and provided the students with an enjoyable opportunity to improve their English and broaden their knowledge of the culture. I felt able to offer support and advice to the students where necessary and no major problems were encountered. The small team of employees collaborated effectively.

### Specific strengths and weaknesses

The host families provided friendly and comfortable accommodation, though several students would have preferred a more central location. Although the English tuition was felt to be of a high standard, several students felt that their progress was hampered by being in large, mixed-ability groups. As far as the organised activities were concerned, students enjoyed some excursions more than others, and were generally frustrated by the lack of time available for shopping and relaxation.

### Recommendations

There are several changes that I would suggest for next year's trip to England.
- Ensure that host families are located as close to town centres as possible.
- Reduce the size of the groups for English tuition.
- Eliminate the least popular excursions to allow more free time for students.

These adjustments would ensure an even better experience for the students and for the employees who accompany them.

- It is appropriate to give your report a title. For clarity, you may also wish to add a sub-heading to the start of each paragraph.

- In the first paragraph, give the aims and objectives of your report and explain where you are drawing your information from.

- Decide how best to divide up the information in your report and organise your paragraphs accordingly. Remember that a simple, logical structure is easier to follow.

- In a report, it is often better to soften negative comments with more words than necessary (periphrasis) or by not being direct (euphemism).

- Finish with clear recommendations if the task requires you to make them. Use bullet points, if you wish.

## F Functions Bank

### Introducing reasons and explanations

given (+ noun phrase) / given that (+ clause) (1G)

what with (+ noun phrase) (1G)

seeing as / that (+ clause) (1G)

in view of (+ noun phrase) (1G)

owing to (+ noun phrase) (1G)

bearing in mind (+ noun phrase) / bearing in mind (that) (+ clause) (1G)

### Marking a change of topic

As far as (hobbies) are concerned, ... (1G)

When it comes to (hobbies), ... (1G)

As for (hobbies), ... (1G)

As regards (hobbies), ... (1G)

Regarding (hobbies), ... (1G)

### Comparing and contrasting photos

The most obvious similarity between the photos is ... (2G)

The photos are similar in that ... (2G)

What the photos have in common is ... (2G)

The clearest difference between the photos is ... (2G)

In contrast to photo 1, photo 2 depicts ... (2G)

Photo 1 shows ... . On the other hand, photo 2 shows ... (2G)

In photo 1 ... , while / whereas in photo 2 ... (2G)

### Expressing, justifying and adding opinions

Off the top of my head, I'd say ... (2G)

I tend to think that, ... (2G)

There's a part of me that thinks ... (2G)

All things considered, ... (2G)

It would seem to me that ... (2G)

I'm of the opinion that ... (2G)

I think it's true to say that ... (2G)

It would be wrong to argue that ... (2G)

As I see it, ... (2G)

The principle justification for this point of view is ... (8G)

The main reason for believing this is (that) ... (8G)

The reason I say that is ... (8G)

To give you just one example, ... (8G)

And I would add that ... (8G)

As well as that, I'd say ... (8G)

And besides the argument we've just heard, ... (8G)

It's also the case that ... (8G)

Not only that, but ... (8G)

### Talking about advantages and disadvantages

the main (dis)advantage of ... is ... (3G)

one major benefit / drawback of ... is ... (3G)

the upside / downside of ... is ... (3G)

weighing up the pros and cons ... , I'd say ... (3G)

... has some additional benefits / drawbacks, such as ... (3G)

... has the added bonus of ... (3G)

the advantages outweigh the disadvantages (3G)

... for me, it's a plus / minus. (3G)

For me, the main benefit / drawback would be ... (7G)

Personally, ... would be a real plus / minus. (7G)

I think ... would be a bonus. (7G)

The upside / downside would be ... (7G)

There are pros and cons. (7G)

### Disagreeing politely and acknowledging without agreeing

I can't help thinking that ... (3G)

That's one way of looking at it, I suppose, but ... (3G)

Maybe, but I just wonder if ... (3G)

It isn't always the case (that ...) (8G)

I think we'll have to agree to disagree. (8G)

I'm not so sure about that. (8G)

That's not necessarily true. (8G)

That's a fair point, but I still think ... (4G)

True, but what it really comes down to is ... (4G)

Maybe so , but what it really boils down to is ... (4G)

Perhaps, although in my view ... (4G)

I see what you mean, but at the end of the day, ... (4G)

That may be the case, but for me, it's more about ...

I take your point, but at the same time, ... (4G)

That could well be true, but even so, I think ... (4G)

### Agreeing and asking if your partner agrees

Would you be happier if ... ? (3G)

You wouldn't disagree with that, would you? (3G)

Would you go along with that? (3G)

I couldn't agree more. (8G)

I'm of the same opinion. (8G)

That's a really good point. (8G)

I was going to make the same point myself. (8G)

I would concur with that. (8G)

I'm with you 100% on that. (8G)

# F

# Functions Bank

### Conceding a point and concluding a discussion

Good point. I hadn't thought of that. (3G)

Fair enough. I can accept that. (3G)

Yes, I suppose you're right. (3G)

So, have we come to a decision? (3G)

Which one are we going for, then? (3G)

Let's wrap this up, shall we? (3G)

### A proposal: stating the purpose

The main aim of this proposal is to ... (3H)

This proposal is intended to ... (3H)

In this proposal, I will present ... (3H)

### Background information

Comments made during focus groups show that ... (3H)

Feedback from ... suggests that ... (3H)

Following a survey of ... it was revealed that ... (3H)

### Making recommendations and suggestions

There ought to be ... (3H)

I recommend that ... (3H)

... need / should (+ passive infinitive) (3H)

### Final recommendation

Unless these ideas are implemented, it is unlikely ... (3H)

The results of ... suggest that ... would be the best option. (3H)

If these recommendations are carried out, ... (3H)

### Introducing, speculating and listing arguments

For me, ... (1C)

To my mind ... (1C)

As far as I'm concerned ... (1C)

I wonder, in fact, if ... (5G)

No doubt ... (5G)

In all probability, ... (5G)

I daresay ... (5G)

The chances are ... (5G)

I imagine that ... (5G)

My best guess would be that ... (5G)

It's highly unlikely that ... (5G)

My initial impression is that ... (5G)

His expression suggests that ... (5G)

It's not entirely clear if / how / what, etc. (5G)

It is often / sometimes argued that ... (5H)

Some people maintain / hold / believe that ... (5H)

There is a strong case for ... (5H)

One argument in favour of / against ... (5H)

Another compelling argument / reason for ... is ... (5H)

### The reasoning is as follows. To begin / start with, ... (5H)

In the first / second place , ... (5H)

Last but not least , ... (5H)

### Fillers and paraphrasing

Well, ...   Let's see, ...   Let me think, ... (5G)

What else? ...   You know, ...   Actually, ... (5G)

if you see what I mean ...   You see, ...   I suppose (5G)

What I mean is, ...   It's a kind of ...   You use it to ... (5G)

it looks a bit like a ...   it's similar to a ...   How do you say? (5G)

I'm not sure what it is in English ...   those things that you ... (5G)

### Introducing similar and opposing points

Similarly, ...   Likewise, ...   In the same way, ... (5H)

By the same token , ...   Equally, ... (5H)

By contrast , ...   Alternatively, ...   All the same, ... (5H)

On the other hand, ...   Having said that, ... (5H)

Putting the same idea in a different way, ... (5H)

In other words, ...   To put it (more) ... (5H)

Simply, ...   In a nutshell, ... (5H)

### Adding further information

Besides, ...   What's more, ...   As well as that, ... (6G)

### Announcing the subject in advance

As for ...,   As far as ...   is concerned, ... (6G)

Regarding ..., (6G)

### Clarifying

I mean, that is to say, ...   in other words, ... (6G)

### Concession

It's true, ...   Certainly , ...   Of course, ... (6G)

### Counter-argument

All the same , ...   Even so, ...   Still, ... (6G)

### Explaining the reason for something

As a result , ...   Because of this, ...   Consequently, ... (6G)

### Generalising

On the whole, ...   By and large, ...   Broadly speaking, ... (6G)

### Structuring

To start with , ...   For one thing, ...   For another thing, ... (6G)

### Showing empathy

I don't know about you, but I ... (6H)

If it's any consolation, you aren't the only one who ... (6H)

I see where you're coming from with ... (6H)

I'm sure everything will turn out all right in the end. (6H)

If it helps, ... (6H)

I know what you mean about ... (6H)

# F

# Functions Bank

## Eliciting a response

What do you think of the idea that ... ? (7G)

What's your view of ... ? (7G)

Don't you agree that ... ? (7G)

Would it be fair to say that ... ? (7G)

Why do / don't you like the idea of ... ? (7G)

Would you prefer to ... ? (7G)

What do you like / dislike about ... ? (7G)

## Causes and consequences

This situation / state of affairs has been brought about by ... (8H)

This is due to ... / This is the result of ... (8H)

One reason for ... is ... (8H)

The situation / problem has been exacerbated by ... (8H)

The principle cause of ... is ... (8H)

This has given rise to ... (8H)

One of the main consequences of ... is ... (8H)

This has resulted in ... (8H)

Consequently, ... / As a result, ... / Hence, ... (8H)

## Dealing with interruptions

Can I just stop you there for a moment? (9G)

Sorry for interrupting, but ... (9G)

Excuse me for butting in, but ... (9G)

Before you go on, I'd just like to say ... (9G)

If I could just come in here, I think ... (9G)

Sure. What do you think? (9G)

That's OK. What did you want to say? (9G)

Yes, of course, go ahead. (9G)

Please let me continue. (9G)

Can I complete my train of thought? (9G)

Do you mind if I finish? (9G)

As I was saying , I think ... (9G)

Continuing where I left off ... (9G)

Where was I? Oh yes, ... (9G)

## Evaluating an experience / event

Broadly speaking, ... leaves a lot to be desired (9H)

The downside of my placement was ... (9H)

In general, ... lived up to my expectations. (9H)

On the whole , I gained a great deal / very little from ... (9H)

In terms of ... , ... definitely has / had the edge over ... (9H)

The ... was superb, unlike the ... , which was appalling. (9H)

Weighing up the different factors, I would say ... (9H)

# Wordlist

## Unit 1

| | | |
|---|---|---|
| a trip down memory lane | /ə ˌtrɪp ˌdaʊn ˌmeməri ˈleɪn/ | |
| abrasive (adj) | /əˈbreɪsɪv/ | |
| account for (phr v) | /əˈkaʊnt fə(r)/ | |
| biochemist (n) | /ˌbaɪəʊˈkemɪst/ | |
| biochemistry (n) | /ˌbaɪəʊˈkemɪstri/ | |
| biological (adj) | /ˌbaɪəˈlɒdʒɪkl/ | |
| biologically (adv) | /ˌbaɪəˈlɒdʒɪkli/ | |
| biologist (n) | /baɪˈɒlədʒɪst/ | |
| biology (n) | /baɪˈɒlədʒi/ | |
| biotechnology (n) | /ˌbaɪəʊtekˈnɒlədʒi/ | |
| blend in (phr v) | /ˌblend ˈɪn/ | |
| blot out (v) | /ˌblɒt ˈaʊt/ | |
| breakdown (n) | /ˈbreɪkdaʊn/ | |
| breakthrough (n) | /ˈbreɪkθruː/ | |
| broad-minded (adj) | /ˌbrɔːd ˈmaɪndɪd/ | |
| busybody (n) | /ˈbɪzibɒdi/ | |
| catch on (phr v) | /ˌkætʃ ˈɒn/ | |
| chemical warfare (n) | /ˌkemɪkl ˈwɔːfeə(r)/ | |
| chemical weapons (n) | /ˌkemɪkl ˈwepən/ | |
| chemist (n) | /ˈkemɪst/ | |
| chemistry (n) | /ˈkemɪstri/ | |
| come across (phr v) | /ˈkʌm əˌkrɒs/ | |
| come down to (phr v) | /ˌkʌm ˈdaʊn tə/ | |
| cynical (adj) | /ˈsɪnɪkl/ | |
| designer babies (n) | /dɪˌzaɪnə ˈbeɪbiz/ | |
| down to earth (adj) | /ˌdaʊn tuː ˈɜːθ/ | |
| drop-out (n) | /ˈdrɒp ˌaʊt/ | |
| ecologically (adv) | /iˈkɒlədʒi/ | |
| ecologist (n) | /iˈkɒlədʒɪst/ | |
| eco-friendly (adj) | /ˌiːkəʊ ˈfrendli/ | |
| ecosystem (n) | /ˈiːkəʊsɪstəm/ | |
| ecotourism (n) | /ˈiːkəʊtʊərɪzəm/ | |
| ecotourist (n) | /ˈiːkəʊtʊərɪst/ | |
| end up (phr v) | /ˈend ˌʌp/ | |
| eradicate a disease | /ɪˌrædɪkeɪt ə dɪˈziːz/ | |
| ethically unacceptable | /ˌeθɪkli ˌʌnəkˈseptəbl/ | |
| evocative (adj) | /ɪˈvɒkətɪv/ | |
| evoke (v) | /ɪˈvəʊk/ | |
| extrovert (n) | /ˈekstrəvɜːt/ | |
| fit in (phr v) | /ˌfɪt ˈɪn/ | |
| gene (n) | /dʒiːn/ | |
| gene therapy (n) | /ˈdʒiːn ˌθerəpi/ | |
| genetic (adj) | /dʒəˈnetɪk/ | |
| geneticist (n) | /dʒəˈnetɪsɪst/ | |
| genetics (n) | /dʒəˈnetɪks/ | |
| genetically (adv) | /dʒəˈnetɪkli/ | |
| genetically modified | /dʒəˌnetɪkli ˈmɒdɪfaɪd/ | |
| get away with (phr v) | /ˌget əˈweɪ ˌwɪð/ | |
| go down (phr v) | /ˌgəʊ ˈdaʊn/ | |
| go for (phr v) | /ˈgəʊ fə(r)/ | |
| gullible (adj) | /ˈgʌləbl/ | |

| | | |
|---|---|---|
| hand over (phr v) | /ˌhænd ˈəʊvə(r)/ | |
| hereditary diseases (n) | /həˈredɪtri dɪˌziːzɪz/ | |
| introvert (n) | /ˈɪntrəvɜːt/ | |
| lasting (adj) | /ˈlɑːstɪŋ/ | |
| life and soul (of a party) | /ˌlaɪf ən ˌsəʊl (əv ə ˈpɑːti)/ | |
| look into (phr v) | /ˈlʊk ˌɪntə/ | |
| look up to (phr v) | /ˌlʊk ˈʌp tə/ | |
| make up (phr v) | /ˌmeɪk ˈʌp/ | |
| microbiologist (n) | /ˌmaɪkrəʊbaɪˈɒlədʒɪst/ | |
| microbiology (n) | /ˌmaɪkrəʊbaɪˈɒlədʒi/ | |
| mind (n) | /maɪnd/ | |
| narrow-minded (adj) | /ˌnærəʊ ˈmaɪndɪd/ | |
| nostalgia (n) | /nɒˈstældʒə/ | |
| pass (it) on (phr v) | /ˌpɑːs (ˌɪt) ˈɒn/ | |
| placid (adj) | /ˈplæsɪd/ | |
| play God | /ˌpleɪ ˈgɒd/ | |
| play up (phr v) | /ˌpleɪ ˈʌp/ | |
| punctual (adj) | /ˈpʌŋktʃuəl/ | |
| put up with (phr v) | /ˌpʊt ˈʌp ˌwɪð/ | |
| quick-tempered (adj) | /ˌkwɪk ˈtempəd/ | |
| recall (v) | /rɪˈkɔːl/ | |
| recollections (n) | /ˌrekəˈlekʃnz/ | |
| remind (v) | /rɪˈmaɪnd/ | |
| reminisce (v) | /ˌremɪˈnɪs/ | |
| reserved (adj) | /rɪˈzɜːvd/ | |
| runaway (n) | /ˈrʌnəweɪ/ | |
| self-assured (adj) | /ˌself əˈʃʊəd/ | |
| self-effacing (adj) | /ˌself ɪˈfeɪsɪŋ/ | |
| set in your ways | /ˌset ˌɪn ˌjɔː ˈweɪz/ | |
| setback (n) | /ˈsetbæk/ | |
| shrewd (adj) | /ʃruːd/ | |
| shrinking violet | /ˌʃrɪŋkɪŋ ˈvaɪələt/ | |
| sign up (phr v) | /ˌsaɪn ˈʌp/ | |
| someone's bark is worse than their bite | /ˌsʌmwʌnz ˈbɑːk ɪz ˌwɜːs ðən ˌðeə ˈbaɪt/ | |
| spontaneous (adj) | /spɒnˈteɪniəs/ | |
| stand-off (n) | /ˈstænd ˌɒf/ | |
| stand out (phr v) | /ˌstænd ˈaʊt/ | |
| stand up for (phr v) | /ˌstænd ˈʌp fə(r)/ | |
| suppress (v) | /səˈpres/ | |
| take after (phr v) | /ˈteɪk ˌɑːftə(r)/ | |
| think you are God's gift | /ˌθɪŋk juə ˈgɒdz ˌgɪft/ | |
| to come flooding back | /tə ˌkʌm ˌflʌdɪŋ ˈbæk/ | |
| to have a memory like a sieve | /tə ˌhæv ə ˌmeməri ˌlaɪk ə ˈsɪv/ | |
| to jog your memory | /tə ˌdʒɒg ˌjɔː ˈmeməri/ | |
| to know something by heart | /tə ˌnəʊ ˌsʌmθɪŋ ˌbaɪ ˈhɑːt/ | |
| to rack your brains | /tə ˈræk ˌjɔː ˌbreɪnz/ | |
| to ring a bell | /tə ˌrɪŋ ə ˈbel/ | |
| to take you back to | /tə ˈteɪk ju ˌbæk tə/ | |
| turnaround (n) | /ˈtɜːnəraʊnd/ | |
| unecological (adj) | /ˌʌnˌiːkəˈlɒdʒɪkl/ | |
| upbringing (n) | /ˈʌpbrɪŋɪŋ/ | |

# W Wordlist

| | | |
|---|---|---|
| trustworthy (adj) | /ˈtrʌstwɜːði/ | _____ |
| turn down (phr v) | /ˌtɜːn ˈdaʊn/ | _____ |
| turn out (phr v) | /ˌtɜːn ˈaʊt/ | _____ |
| unforgettable (adj) | /ˌʌnfəˈgetəbl/ | _____ |
| walk out on (phr v) | /ˌwɔːk ˈaʊt ˌɒn/ | _____ |
| warm to (phr v) | /ˈwɔːm tə/ | _____ |
| wear your heart on your sleeve | /ˌweə ˌjɔː ˌhɑːt ˌɒn jɔː ˈsliːv/ | _____ |

## Unit 2

| | | |
|---|---|---|
| a bit of a bookworm | /ə ˌbɪt əv ə ˈbʊkwɜːm/ | _____ |
| a breakdown | /ə ˈbreɪkdaʊn/ | _____ |
| a fast pace | /ə ˌfɑːst ˈpeɪs/ | _____ |
| a happy ending | /ə ˌhæpi ˈendɪŋ/ | _____ |
| a real page turner | /ə ˌrɪəl ˈpeɪdʒ ˌtɜːnə(r)/ | _____ |
| action (n) | /ˈækʃn/ | _____ |
| alliteration (n) | /əˌlɪtəˈreɪʃn/ | _____ |
| an intriguing plot | /ən ɪnˌtriːgɪŋ ˈplɒt/ | _____ |
| analogy (n) | /əˈnælədʒi/ | _____ |
| assonance (n) | /ˈæsənəns/ | _____ |
| award-winning (adj) | /əˈwɔːd ˌwɪnɪŋ/ | _____ |
| be of assistance | /ˌbiː əv əˈsɪstəns/ | _____ |
| be surprised at | /ˌbi səˈpraɪzd ət/ | _____ |
| beautifully drawn | /ˈbjuːtɪfli ˌdrɔːn/ | _____ |
| bent on | /ˈbent ˌɒn/ | _____ |
| best-selling (adj) | /ˈbest ˌselɪŋ/ | _____ |
| big-budget (adj) | /ˈbɪg ˌbʌdʒɪt/ | _____ |
| break down (phr v) | /ˌbreɪk ˈdaʊn/ | _____ |
| break up (n) | /ˈbreɪk ˌʌp/ | _____ |
| breaking news | /ˈbreɪkɪŋ ˌnjuːz/ | _____ |
| breathtaking (adj) | /ˈbreθ ˌteɪkɪŋ/ | _____ |
| central (adj) | /ˈsentrəl/ | _____ |
| chambers (n) | /ˈtʃeɪmbəz/ | _____ |
| characters you can identify with | /ˌkærəktəz ju kən aɪˈdentɪfaɪ ˌwɪð/ | _____ |
| check in (desk) (n) | /ˈtʃek ˌɪn (ˌdesk)/ | _____ |
| chilling (adj) | /ˈtʃɪlɪŋ/ | _____ |
| clichéd (adj) | /ˈkliːʃeɪd/ | _____ |
| colour (n) | /ˈkʌlə(r)/ | _____ |
| comic book (n) | /ˈkɒmɪk ˌbʊk/ | _____ |
| compelling (adj) | /kəmˈpelɪŋ/ | _____ |
| complex (adj) | /ˈkɒmpleks/ | _____ |
| crack down | /ˈkræk ˌdaʊn/ | _____ |
| creep (v) | /kriːp/ | _____ |
| cut a long story short | /ˌkʌt ə ˌlɒŋ ˌstɔːri ˈʃɔːt/ | _____ |
| dig around for | /ˈdɪg əˌraʊnd fə(r)/ | _____ |
| disappointing (adj) | /ˌdɪsəˈpɔɪntɪŋ/ | _____ |
| determined (adj) | /dɪˈtɜːmɪnd/ | _____ |
| earnestness (adj) | /ˈɜːnɪstnəs/ | _____ |
| easy-going (adj) | /ˌiːzi ˈgəʊɪŋ/ | _____ |
| English-speaking (adj) | /ˈɪŋglɪʃ ˌspiːkɪŋ/ | _____ |
| ethics (n) | /ˈeθɪks/ | _____ |
| euphemism (n) | /ˈjuːfəmɪzəm/ | _____ |
| evocative descriptions | /ɪˈvɒkətɪv dɪˌskrɪpʃnz/ | _____ |

| | | |
|---|---|---|
| fable (n) | /ˈfeɪbl/ | _____ |
| fairy tale (n) | /ˈfeəri ˌteɪl/ | _____ |
| fantasy (n) | /ˈfæntəsi/ | _____ |
| far-fetched (adj) | /ˌfɑː ˈfetʃt/ | _____ |
| fast-moving (adj) | /ˈfɑːst ˌmuːvɪŋ/ | _____ |
| fast-paced (adj) | /ˈfɑːst ˌpeɪst/ | _____ |
| fear (v) | /fɪə(r)/ | _____ |
| feelings (n) | /ˈfiːlɪŋz/ | _____ |
| folk tale (n) | /ˈfəʊk ˌteɪl/ | _____ |
| garments (n) | /ˈgɑːmənts/ | _____ |
| get into it | /ˌget ˈɪntuː ɪt/ | _____ |
| good bedtime reading | /ˌgʊd ˌbedtaɪm ˈriːdɪŋ/ | _____ |
| graphic novel (n) | /ˌgræfɪk ˈnɒvl/ | _____ |
| grave (adj) | /greɪv/ | _____ |
| gripping (adj) | /ˈgrɪpɪŋ/ | _____ |
| ground-breaking (adj) | /ˈgraʊnd ˌbreɪkɪŋ/ | _____ |
| gruesome (adj) | /ˈgruːsəm/ | _____ |
| gutsy (adj) | /ˈgʌtsi/ | _____ |
| gutter press | /ˈgʌtə ˌpres/ | _____ |
| hand-made (adj) | /ˌhænd ˈmeɪd/ | _____ |
| heavy going | /ˌhevi ˈgəʊɪŋ/ | _____ |
| high-road (n) | /ˈhaɪ ˌrəʊd/ | _____ |
| hinge on (phr v) | /ˈhɪndʒ ˌɒn/ | _____ |
| hue (n) | /hjuː/ | _____ |
| humorous (adj) | /ˈhjuːmərəs/ | _____ |
| humour (n) | /ˈhjuːmə(r)/ | _____ |
| hyperbole (n) | /haɪˈpɜːbəli/ | _____ |
| immediately (adv) | /ɪˈmiːdiətli/ | _____ |
| incognito (adj) | /ˌɪnkɒgˈniːtəʊ/ | _____ |
| infiltrate (v) | /ˈɪnfɪltreɪt/ | _____ |
| judge a book by its cover | /ˌdʒʌdʒ ə ˌbʊk ˌbaɪ ɪts ˈkʌvə(r)/ | _____ |
| last-minute goal | /ˌlɑːst ˌmɪnɪt ˈgəʊl/ | _____ |
| lead-free (adj) | /ˈled ˌfriː/ | _____ |
| life-threatening (adj) | /ˈlaɪf ˌθretnɪŋ/ | _____ |
| lift-off | /ˈlɪft ˌɒf/ | _____ |
| light-hearted (adj) | /ˌlaɪt ˈhɑːtɪd/ | _____ |
| lightweight (adj) | /ˈlaɪtweɪt/ | _____ |
| love interest | /ˈlʌv ˌɪntrəst/ | _____ |
| low-budget (adj) | /ˈləʊ ˌbʌdʒɪt/ | _____ |
| macabre (adj) | /məˈkɑːbrə/ | _____ |
| make up (phr v) | /ˌmeɪk ˈʌp/ | _____ |
| make-up (n) | /ˈmeɪk ˌʌp/ | _____ |
| many-sided | /ˈmeni ˌsaɪdɪd/ | _____ |
| media coverage | /ˈmiːdiə ˌkʌvərɪdʒ/ | _____ |
| mediocre (adj) | /ˌmiːdiˈəʊkə(r)/ | _____ |
| meet with (phr v) | /ˈmiːt ˌwɪð/ | _____ |
| metaphor (n) | /ˈmetəfə(r), -fɔː(r)/ | _____ |
| middle-aged (adj) | /ˌmɪdl ˈeɪdʒd/ | _____ |
| mystery and suspense | /ˌmɪstri ən səˈspens/ | _____ |
| myth (n) | /mɪθ/ | _____ |
| nail-biting (adj) | /ˈneɪl ˌbaɪtɪŋ/ | _____ |
| narrative (n) | /ˈnærətɪv/ | _____ |
| natural dialogue | /ˌnætʃrəl ˈdaɪəlɒg/ | _____ |

# Wordlist

| | | |
|---|---|---|
| never-ending (adj) | /ˈnevər ˌendɪŋ/ | _____ |
| news channel | /ˈnjuːz ˌtʃænl/ | _____ |
| novel (n) | /ˈnɒvl/ | _____ |
| on the instant | /ˌɒn ði ˈɪnstənt/ | _____ |
| onomatopoeia (n) | /ˌɒnəˌmætəˈpiːə/ | _____ |
| open (v) | /ˈəʊpən/ | _____ |
| opinion poll (n) | /əˈpɪnjən ˌpəʊl/ | _____ |
| personification (n) | /pəˌsɒnɪfɪˈkeɪʃn/ | _____ |
| play (n) | /pleɪ/ | _____ |
| please (v) | /pliːz/ | _____ |
| poetry (n) | /ˈpəʊətri/ | _____ |
| poignant (adj) | /ˈpɔɪnjənt/ | _____ |
| point of view (n) | /ˌpɔɪnt əv ˈvjuː/ | _____ |
| portrayal (n) | /pɔːˈtreɪəl/ | _____ |
| powerful (adj) | /ˈpaʊəfl/ | _____ |
| predictable (adj) | /prɪˈdɪktəbl/ | _____ |
| press conference (n) | /ˈpres ˌkɒnfərəns/ | _____ |
| press freedom | /ˌpres ˈfriːdəm/ | _____ |
| pressure group (n) | /ˈpreʃə ˌgruːp/ | _____ |
| read between the lines | /ˌriːd bɪˌtwiːn ðə ˈlaɪnz/ | _____ |
| realistic, believable characters | /ˌriːəˌlɪstɪk bɪˌliːvəbl ˈkærəktəz/ | _____ |
| receive (v) | /rɪˈsiːv/ | _____ |
| recommend (v) | /ˌrekəˈmend/ | _____ |
| red herring | /ˌred ˈherɪŋ/ | _____ |
| revelations (n) | /ˌrevəˈleɪʃnz/ | _____ |
| rip off (phr v) | /ˌrɪp ˈɒf/ | _____ |
| rip-off (n) | /ˈrɪp ˌɒf/ | _____ |
| rooms (n) | /ruːmz/ | _____ |
| scandal (n) | /ˈskændl/ | _____ |
| sensational (adj) | /senˈseɪʃnl/ | _____ |
| sensations (n) | /senˈseɪʃnz/ | _____ |
| sentimental (adj) | /ˌsentɪˈmentl/ | _____ |
| seriousness (n) | /ˈsɪəriəsnəs/ | _____ |
| set (v) | /set/ | _____ |
| shallow (adj) | /ˈʃæləʊ/ | _____ |
| short story (n) | /ˌʃɔːt ˈstɔːri/ | _____ |
| simile (n) | /ˈsɪməli/ | _____ |
| singular (adj) | /ˈsɪŋgjələ(r)/ | _____ |
| slow-moving (adj) | /ˈsləʊ ˌmuːvɪŋ/ | _____ |
| spectacular (adj) | /spekˈtækjələ(r)/ | _____ |
| steal after (phr v) | /ˌstiːl ˈɑːftə(r)/ | _____ |
| strange (adj) | /streɪndʒ/ | _____ |
| strong-willed (adj) | /ˌstrɒŋ ˈwɪld/ | _____ |
| take away (phr v) | /ˌteɪk əˈweɪ/ | _____ |
| take-away (n) | /ˈteɪk əˌweɪ/ | _____ |
| tax-free (adj) | /ˌtæks ˈfriː/ | _____ |
| tedious (adj) | /ˈtiːdiəs/ | _____ |
| thought-provoking (adj) | /ˈθɔːt prəˌvəʊkɪŋ/ | _____ |
| three-hour movie | /ˈθriː ˌaʊə ˌmuːvi/ | _____ |
| tip off (phr v) | /ˌtɪp ˈɒf/ | _____ |
| tip-off (n) | /ˈtɪp ˌɒf/ | _____ |
| touching (adj) | /ˈtʌtʃɪŋ/ | _____ |
| turn towards (phr v) | /ˈtɜːn təˌwɔːdz/ | _____ |

| | | |
|---|---|---|
| twists and turns | /ˌtwɪsts ən ˈtɜːnz/ | _____ |
| two-dimensional (adj) | /ˌtuː daɪˈmenʃənl/ | _____ |
| (un)convincing (adj) | /(ˌʌn)kənˈvɪnsɪŋ/ | _____ |
| unfold (v) | /ʌnˈfəʊld/ | _____ |
| user-friendly (adj) | /ˌjuːzə ˈfrendli/ | _____ |
| warm-hearted (adj) | /ˌwɔːm ˈhɑːtɪd/ | _____ |
| warm up (phr v) | /ˌwɔːm ˈʌp/ | _____ |
| warm-up (n) | /ˈwɔːm ˌʌp/ | _____ |
| welcome (v) | /ˈwelkəm/ | _____ |
| well-dressed (adj) | /ˌwel ˈdrest/ | _____ |
| well-rounded (adj) | /ˌwel ˈraʊndɪd/ | _____ |
| wish to (v) | /ˈwɪʃ tə/ | _____ |
| wonder at (v) | /ˈwʌndər ət/ | _____ |
| world famous (adj) | /ˌwɜːld ˈfeɪməs/ | _____ |
| worldwide (adj) | /ˈwɜːldwaɪd/ | _____ |
| written in the third person | /ˌrɪtn ɪn ðə ˌθɜːd ˈpɜːsn/ | _____ |
| 20-storey (adj) | /ˈtwenti ˌstɔːri/ | _____ |
| 800-page novel | /ˌeɪt ˌhʌndrəd ˌpeɪdʒ ˈnɒvl/ | _____ |

## Unit 3

| | | |
|---|---|---|
| a face like thunder | /ə ˌfeɪs ˌlaɪk ˈθʌndə(r)/ | _____ |
| act like sheep | /ˌækt ˌlaɪk ˈʃiːp/ | _____ |
| aggrieved (adj) | /əˈgriːvd/ | _____ |
| as blind as a bat | /əz ˌblaɪnd əz ə ˈbæt/ | _____ |
| as cool as a cucumber | /əz ˌkuːl əz ə ˈkjuːkʌmbə(r)/ | _____ |
| as deaf as a post | /əz ˌdef əz ə ˈpəʊst/ | _____ |
| as dry as a bone | /əz ˌdraɪ əz ə ˈbəʊn/ | _____ |
| as quiet as a mouse | /əz ˌkwaɪət əz ə ˈmaʊs/ | _____ |
| as light as a feather | /əz ˌlaɪt əz ə ˈfeðə(r)/ | _____ |
| attract investors (v) + (n) | /əˌtrækt ɪnˈvestəz/ | _____ |
| baffled (adj) | /ˈbæfld/ | _____ |
| be doomed (v) | /ˌbi ˈduːmd/ | _____ |
| be inseparable (v) | /ˌbi ɪnˈseprəbl/ | _____ |
| be like chalk and cheese | /ˌbi laɪk ˌtʃɔːk ən ˈtʃiːz/ | _____ |
| be on the same wavelength | /ˌbi ˌɒn ðə ˌseɪm ˈweɪvleŋθ/ | _____ |
| bond with somebody over something (phr v) | /ˈbɒnd ˌwɪð ˌsʌmbədi ˌəʊvə ˌsʌmθɪŋ/ | _____ |
| boost confidence (v) + (n) | /ˌbuːst ˈkɒnfɪdəns/ | _____ |
| break into a market (v) + (n) | /ˈbreɪk ˌɪntu ə ˌmɑːkɪt/ | _____ |
| break somebody's heart | /ˌbreɪk ˌsʌmbədiz ˈhɑːt/ | _____ |
| captivating (adj) | /ˈkæptɪveɪtɪŋ/ | _____ |
| close a deal (v) + (n) | /ˌkləʊz ə ˈdiːl/ | _____ |
| compatibility (n) | /kəmˌpætəˈbɪləti/ | _____ |
| confidence (n) | /ˈkɒnfɪdəns/ | _____ |
| co-operation (n) | /kəʊˌɒpəˈreɪʃn/ | _____ |
| cry like a baby | /ˌkraɪ ˌlaɪk ə ˈbeɪbi/ | _____ |
| cut costs (v) + (n) | /ˌkʌt ˈkɒsts/ | _____ |
| daunting (adj) | /ˈdɔːntɪŋ/ | _____ |
| devastated (adj) | /ˈdevəsteɪtɪd/ | _____ |

# Wordlist

| | | |
|---|---|---|
| drift apart (phr v) | /ˌdrɪft ə'pɑːt/ | _____ |
| drive (n) | /draɪv/ | _____ |
| drop out (phr v) | /ˌdrɒp 'aʊt/ | _____ |
| drop somebody (v) | /'drɒp ˌsʌmbədi/ | _____ |
| dump somebody (v) | /'dʌmp ˌsʌmbədi/ | _____ |
| eat like a horse | /ˌiːt ˌlaɪk ə 'hɔːs/ | _____ |
| ecstatic (adj) | /ɪk'stætɪk/ | _____ |
| elated (adj) | /i'leɪtɪd/ | _____ |
| fall out with somebody (phr v) | /ˌfɔːl 'aʊt wɪð ˌsʌmbədi/ | _____ |
| fight like cats and dogs | /ˌfaɪt ˌlaɪk ˌkæts ən 'dɒgz/ | _____ |
| fit like a glove | /ˌfɪt ˌlaɪk ə 'glʌv/ | _____ |
| flexibility (n) | /ˌfleksə'bɪləti/ | _____ |
| frenetic (adj) | /frə'netɪk/ | _____ |
| friend somebody (v) | /'frend ˌsʌmbədi/ | _____ |
| get acquainted with somebody | /ˌget ə'kweɪntɪd wɪð ˌsʌmbədi/ | _____ |
| get on like a house on fire | /ˌget ˌɒn ˌlaɪk ə 'haʊs ɒn ˌfaɪə(r)/ | _____ |
| get talking to somebody | /ˌget 'tɔːkɪŋ tə ˌsʌmbədi/ | _____ |
| go back a long way | /ˌgəʊ ˌbæk ə ˌlɒŋ 'weɪ/ | _____ |
| gobsmacked (adj) | /'gɒbsmækt/ | _____ |
| get off on the wrong foot | /ˌget ˌɒf ɒn ðə ˌrɒŋ 'fʊt/ | _____ |
| gutted (adj) | /'gʌtɪd/ | _____ |
| have a soft spot for | /ˌhæv ə 'sɒft ˌspɒt fə(r)/ | _____ |
| have (your) ups and downs | /ˌhæv (jɔːr) ˌʌps ən 'daʊnz/ | _____ |
| head over heels in love with | /ˌhed ˌəʊvə ˌhiːlz ɪn 'lʌv ˌwɪð/ | _____ |
| hire employees (v) + (n) | /ˌhaɪər ɪm'plɔɪiːz/ | _____ |
| hit it off | /ˌhɪt ɪt 'ɒf/ | _____ |
| honoured (adj) | /'ɒnəd/ | _____ |
| impervious (adj) | /ɪm'pɜːviəs/ | _____ |
| keep a friendship going | /ˌkiːp ə ˌfrendʃɪp 'gəʊɪŋ/ | _____ |
| keep track of somebody | /ˌkiːp 'træk əv ˌsʌmbədi/ | _____ |
| know somebody inside out | /ˌnəʊ ˌsʌmbədi ˌɪnsaɪd 'aʊt/ | _____ |
| launch a product (v) + (n) | /ˌlɔːntʃ ə 'prɒdʌkt/ | _____ |
| life is like an open book | /ˌlaɪf ˌɪz ˌlaɪk ən ˌəʊpən 'bʊk/ | _____ |
| like two peas in a pod | /ˌlaɪk ˌtuː ˌpiːz ɪn ə 'pɒd/ | _____ |
| meet a deadline (v) + (n) | /ˌmiːt ə 'dedlaɪn/ | _____ |
| miniscule (adj) | /'mɪnəskjuːl/ | _____ |
| not see eye to eye | /ˌnɒt ˌsiː ˌaɪ tuː 'aɪ/ | _____ |
| on the rocks | /ˌɒn ðə 'rɒks/ | _____ |
| outraged (adj) | /'aʊtreɪdʒd/ | _____ |
| passion (n) | /'pæʃn/ | _____ |
| patch things up | /ˌpætʃ ˌθɪŋz 'ʌp/ | _____ |
| perplexed (adj) | /pə'plekst/ | _____ |
| perturbed (adj) | /pə'tɜːbd/ | _____ |
| place an order (v) + (n) | /ˌpleɪs ən 'ɔːdə(r)/ | _____ |
| plain sailing | /'pleɪn ˌseɪlɪŋ/ | _____ |
| privileged (adj) | /'prɪvəlɪdʒd/ | _____ |
| profound (adj) | /prə'faʊnd/ | _____ |
| pulled out (phr v) | /ˌpʊld 'aʊt/ | _____ |

| | | |
|---|---|---|
| punctuality (n) | /ˌpʌŋktʃu'æləti/ | _____ |
| respect (n) | /rɪ'spekt/ | _____ |
| rigid (n) | /'rɪdʒɪd/ | _____ |
| run into somebody | /'rʌn ˌɪntə ˌsʌmbədi/ | _____ |
| see a lot of somebody | /ˌsiː ə 'lɒt əv ˌsʌmbədi/ | _____ |
| sharing the same passion for | /ˌʃeərɪŋ ðə 'seɪm ˌpæʃn fə(r)/ | _____ |
| sign a contract (v) + (n) | /ˌsaɪn ə 'kɒntrækt/ | _____ |
| sleep like a log | /ˌsliːp ˌlaɪk ə 'lɒg/ | _____ |
| startling (n) | /'stɑːtlɪŋ/ | _____ |
| stay in touch with somebody | /ˌsteɪ ɪn 'tʌtʃ wɪð ˌsʌmbədi/ | _____ |
| stick together through thick and thin | /ˌstɪk təˌgeðə ˌθruː ˌθɪk ən 'θɪn/ | _____ |
| strike up a friendship with somebody (phr v) | /ˌstraɪk ˌʌp ə 'frendʃɪp wɪð ˌsʌmbədi/ | _____ |
| stunned (adj) | /stʌnd/ | _____ |
| sweep somebody off their feet | /ˌswiːp ˌsʌmbədi ˌɒf ðeə 'fiːt/ | _____ |
| take off (phr v) | /ˌteɪk 'ɒf/ | _____ |
| talk about somebody behind their back | /ˌtɔːk əˌbaʊt ˌsʌmbədi bɪˌhaɪnd ðeə 'bæk/ | _____ |
| talk somebody into something (phr v) | /ˌtɔːk ˌsʌmbədi 'ɪntə ˌsʌmθɪŋ/ | _____ |
| tie the knot | /ˌtaɪ ðə 'nɒt/ | _____ |
| toy with the idea of | /'tɔɪ wɪð ðiː aɪˌdɪər əv/ | _____ |
| troubled (adj) | /'trʌbld/ | _____ |
| trust (n) | /trʌst/ | _____ |
| unconcerned (adj) | /ˌʌnkən'sɜːnd/ | _____ |
| unfriend somebody (v) | /ˌʌn'frend ˌsʌmbədi/ | _____ |
| witness a milestone | /ˌwɪtnəs ə 'maɪlstəʊn/ | _____ |
| work like a dream | /ˌwɜːk ˌlaɪk ə 'driːm/ | _____ |
| wreck a friendship (v) + (n) | /ˌrek ə 'frendʃɪp/ | _____ |

## Unit 4

| | | |
|---|---|---|
| aches and pains | /ˌeɪks ən 'peɪnz/ | _____ |
| adapt / adaptation (v/n) | /ə'dæpt, ˌædæp'teɪʃn/ | _____ |
| address (v) | /ə'dres/ | _____ |
| adjust / adjustment (v/n) | /ə'dʒʌst, ə'dʒʌstmənt/ | _____ |
| advise (v) | /əd'vaɪz/ | _____ |
| alter / alteration (v/n) | /'ɔːltə(r), ɔːltə'reɪʃn/ | _____ |
| amend / amendment (v/n) | /ə'mend, ə'mendmənt/ | _____ |
| armed conflicts (n) | /ˌɑːmd 'kɒnflɪkts/ | _____ |
| blurt (v) | /blɜːt/ | _____ |
| caution (v) | /'kɔːʃn/ | _____ |
| chant (v) | /tʃɑːnt/ | _____ |
| conceive (v) | /kən'siːv/ | _____ |
| conjecture (v) | /kən'dʒektʃə(r)/ | _____ |
| convert / conversion (v/n) | /kən'vɜːt, kən'vɜːʃn/ | _____ |
| cosmetic (adj) | /kɒz'metɪk/ | _____ |
| crash (v) | /kræʃ/ | _____ |
| dead and buried | /ˌded ən 'berid/ | _____ |

# Wordlist

| | | |
|---|---|---|
| discard (v) | /dɪsˈkɑːd/ | |
| distribute (v) | /dɪˈstrɪbjuːt/ | |
| dos and don'ts | /ˌduːz ən ˈdəʊnts/ | |
| dramatic (adj) | /drəˈmætɪk/ | |
| drastic (adj) | /ˈdræstɪk/ | |
| dwindle (v) | /ˈdwɪndl/ | |
| elicit (v) | /iˈlɪsɪt/ | |
| ensure (v) | /ɪnˈʃʊə(r)/ | |
| entreat (v) | /ɪnˈtriːt/ | |
| epidemics (n) | /ˌepɪˈdemɪks/ | |
| escalate (v) | /ˈeskəleɪt/ | |
| evolve / evolution (v/n) | /iˈvɒlv, ˌiːvəˈluːʃn/ | |
| fair and square | /ˌfeər ən ˈskweə(r)/ | |
| famine (n) | /ˈfæmɪn/ | |
| flatline (v) | /ˈflætlaɪn/ | |
| fluctuate (v) | /ˈflʌktʃueɪt/ | |
| fundamental (adj) | /ˌfʌndəˈmentl/ | |
| global capitalism (n) | /ˌgləʊbl ˈkæpɪtəlɪzəm/ | |
| high and dry | /ˌhaɪ ən ˈdraɪ/ | |
| highlight (v) | /ˈhaɪlaɪt/ | |
| hiss (v) | /hɪs/ | |
| keep pace with | /ˌkiːp ˈpeɪs ˌwɪð/ | |
| lag behind (v) | /ˌlæg bɪˈhaɪnd/ | |
| level off (v) | /ˌlevl ˈɒf/ | |
| life expectancy (n) | /ˈlaɪf ɪkˌspektənsi/ | |
| live and learn | /ˌlɪv ən ˈlɜːn/ | |
| make or break | /ˌmeɪk ɔː ˈbreɪk/ | |
| marginal (adj) | /ˈmɑːdʒɪnl/ | |
| marked (adj) | /mɑːkt/ | |
| minimal (adj) | /ˈmɪnɪməl/ | |
| modify / modification (v/n) | /ˈmɒdɪfaɪ, ˌmɒdɪfɪˈkeɪʃn/ | |
| momentous (adj) | /məˈmentəs/ | |
| mount (v) | /maʊnt/ | |
| mouth (v) | /maʊθ/ | |
| mushroom (v) | /ˈmʌʃrʊm/ | |
| mutate / mutation (v/n) | /mjuːˈteɪt, mjuːˈteɪʃn/ | |
| nag (v) | /næg/ | |
| neat and tidy | /ˌniːt ən ˈtaɪdi/ | |
| nose-dive (v) | /ˈnəʊz ˌdaɪv/ | |
| outpace (v) | /ˌaʊtˈpeɪs/ | |
| outstrip (v) | /ˌaʊtˈstrɪp/ | |
| overtake (v) | /ˌəʊvəˈteɪk/ | |
| pick and choose | /ˌpɪk ən ˈtʃuːz/ | |
| plateau (v) | /ˈplætəʊ/ | |
| plummet (v) | /ˈplʌmɪt/ | |
| plunge (v) | /plʌndʒ/ | |
| population growth (n) | /ˌpɒpjuˈleɪʃn ˌgrəʊθ/ | |
| poverty (n) | /ˈpɒvəti/ | |
| probe (v) | /prəʊb/ | |
| prove (v) | /pruːv/ | |
| radical (adj) | /ˈrædɪkl/ | |
| refugees (n) | /ˌrefjuˈdʒiːz/ | |
| remain constant | /rɪˌmeɪn ˈkɒnstənt/ | |

| | | |
|---|---|---|
| retort (v) | /rɪˈtɔːt/ | |
| revise / revision (v/n) | /rɪˈvaɪz, rɪˈvɪʒn/ | |
| rough and ready | /ˌrʌf ən ˈredi/ | |
| rumour (n) | /ˈruːmə(r)/ | |
| safe and sound | /ˌseɪf ən ˈsaʊnd/ | |
| scold (v) | /skəʊld/ | |
| seek (v) | /siːk/ | |
| short and sweet | /ˌʃɔːt ən ˈswiːt/ | |
| sick and tired | /ˈsɪk ən ˌtaɪəd/ | |
| skyrocket (v) | /ˈskaɪrɒkɪt/ | |
| snap (v) | /snæp/ | |
| snivel (v) | /ˈsnɪvl/ | |
| soar (v) | /sɔː(r)/ | |
| squeal (v) | /skwiːl/ | |
| submit (v) | /səbˈmɪt/ | |
| subtle (adj) | /ˈsʌtl/ | |
| surge (v) | /sɜːdʒ/ | |
| surpass (v) | /səˈpɑːs/ | |
| sweeping (adj) | /ˈswiːpɪŋ/ | |
| tease (v) | /tiːz/ | |
| terrorism (n) | /ˈterərɪzəm/ | |
| through and through | /ˌθruː ən ˈθruː/ | |
| transform / transformation (v/n) | /trænsˈfɔːm, ˌtrænsfəˈmeɪʃn/ | |
| tumble (v) | /ˈtʌmbl/ | |
| vary / variation (v/n) | /ˈveəri, ˌveəriˈeɪʃn/ | |
| wear and tear | /ˌweər ən ˈteə(r)/ | |
| whine (v) | /waɪn/ | |
| yell (v) | /jel/ | |
| yield (v) | /jiːld/ | |

## Unit 5

| | | |
|---|---|---|
| a danger to | /ə ˈdeɪndʒə tə/ | |
| absolutely freezing | /ˌæbsəluːtli ˈfriːzɪŋ/ | |
| admit (v) | /ədˈmɪt/ | |
| allies (n) | /ˈælaɪz/ | |
| announce (v) | /əˈnaʊns/ | |
| appeal for | /əˈpiːl fə(r)/ | |
| appeal to | /əˈpiːl tə/ | |
| argue (v) | /ˈɑːgjuː/ | |
| asymmetric warfare (n) | /eɪsəˌmetrɪk ˈwɔːfeə(r)/ | |
| atrocities (n) | /əˈtrɒsətiz/ | |
| available to someone | /əˈveɪləbl tə ˌsʌmwʌn/ | |
| bitterly regret | /ˌbɪtəli rɪˈgret/ | |
| boast (v) | /bəʊst/ | |
| border (n) | /ˈbɔːdə(r)/ | |
| break the stalemate | /ˌbreɪk ðə ˈsteɪlmeɪt/ | |
| carry out a suicide attack | /ˌkæri ˌaʊt ə ˈsuːɪsaɪd əˌtæk/ | |
| civilian government (n) | /səˈvɪliən ˌgʌvənmənt/ | |
| claim (v) | /kleɪm/ | |
| claim victory | /ˌkleɪm ˈvɪktəri/ | |
| coalition (n) | /ˌkəʊəˈlɪʃn/ | |
| complain (v) | /kəmˈpleɪn/ | |

| | | |
|---|---|---|
| compulsively gripping | /kəmˌpʌlsɪvli ˈɡrɪpɪŋ/ | |
| concede (v) | /kənˈsiːd/ | |
| confirm (v) | /kənˈfɜːm/ | |
| declare war | /dɪˌkleə ˈwɔː(r)/ | |
| deeply touched | /ˌdiːpli ˈtʌtʃt/ | |
| defend someone against | /dɪˈfend ˌsʌmwʌn əˌɡenst/ | |
| deny (v) | /dɪˈnaɪ/ | |
| differ from | /ˈdɪfə frəm/ | |
| differ with | /ˈdɪfə wɪð/ | |
| disapprove of | /ˌdɪsəˈpruːv əv/ | |
| dismiss (v) | /dɪsˈmɪs/ | |
| disregard for | /ˌdɪsrɪˈɡɑːd fə(r)/ | |
| doubt (v) | /daʊt/ | |
| enquire (v) | /ɪnˈkwaɪə(r)/ | |
| excuse someone for | /ɪkˈskjuːz ˌsʌmwʌn fə/ | |
| ferociously steep | /fəˈrəʊʃəsli ˌstiːp/ | |
| form of | /ˈfɔːm əv/ | |
| guerrilla raids (n) | /ɡəˈrɪlə ˌreɪdz/ | |
| have/lose sympathy for | /ˌhæv, ˌluːz ˈsɪmpəθi fə(r)/ | |
| highly probable | /ˌhaɪli ˈprɒbəbl/ | |
| highly successful | /ˌhaɪli səkˈsesfl/ | |
| improve on | /ɪmˈpruːv ˌɒn/ | |
| improvement (in) | /ɪmˈpruːvmənt (ɪn)/ | |
| inflict casualties | /ɪnˌflɪkt ˈkæʒuəltiz/ | |
| inform (v) | /ɪnˈfɔːm/ | |
| injustice of | /ɪnˈdʒʌstɪs əv/ | |
| insist (v) | /ɪnˈsɪst/ | |
| insurgency (n) | /ɪnˈsɜːdʒənsi/ | |
| intent on | /ɪnˈtent ɒn/ | |
| invasion (n) | /ɪnˈveɪʒn/ | |
| issue an ultimatum | /ˌɪʃuː ən ˌʌltɪˈmeɪtəm/ | |
| justfied in | /ˈdʒʌstɪfaɪd ɪn/ | |
| leader (n) | /ˈliːdə(r)/ | |
| limit to | /ˈlɪmɪt tə/ | |
| lose one's life | /ˌluːz wʌnz ˈlaɪf/ | |
| make a breakthrough | /ˌmeɪk ə ˈbreɪkθruː/ | |
| make up (phr v) | /ˌmeɪk ˈʌp/ | |
| means of | /ˈmiːnz əv/ | |
| mention (v) | /ˈmenʃn/ | |
| object (to) (v) | /əbˈdʒekt (tə)/ | |
| observe (v) | /əbˈzɜːv/ | |
| occupation (n) | /ˌɒkjuˈpeɪʃn/ | |
| occupy a country / an area | /ˈɒkjupaɪ ə ˌkʌntri, ən ˌeəriə/ | |
| opposed to | /əˈpəʊzd tə/ | |
| preferable to | /ˈprefrəbl tə/ | |
| propose (v) | /prəˈpəʊz/ | |
| protest (v) | /prəˈtest/ | |
| protest against | /ˈprəʊtest əˌɡenst/ | |
| put up resistance | /ˌpʊt ˌʌp rɪˈzɪstəns/ | |
| question (v) | /ˈkwestʃən/ | |
| refuse a request | /rɪˌfjuːz ə rɪˈkwest/ | |
| regret (v) | /rɪˈɡret/ | |

| | | |
|---|---|---|
| remark (v) | /rɪˈmɑːk/ | |
| resent (v) | /rɪˈzent/ | |
| resort to | /rɪˈzɔːt tə/ | |
| responsible for | /rɪˈspɒnsəbl fə(r)/ | |
| restrict to | /rɪˈstrɪkt tə/ | |
| result in | /rɪˈzʌlt ɪn/ | |
| reveal (v) | /rɪˈviːl/ | |
| ridiculously expensive | /rɪˈdɪkjələsli ɪkˌspensɪv/ | |
| security (n) | /sɪˈkjʊərəti/ | |
| seize power | /ˌsiːz ˈpaʊə(r)/ | |
| special forces (n) | /ˈspeʃl ˌfɔːsɪz/ | |
| stage a protest | /ˌsteɪdʒ ə ˈprəʊtest/ | |
| stage an ambush | /ˌsteɪdʒ ən ˈæmbʊʃ/ | |
| station troops (in) | /ˈsteɪʃn ˌtruːps (ɪn)/ | |
| strongly suggest | /ˈstrɒŋli səˌdʒest/ | |
| suffer losses | /ˌsʌfə ˈlɒsɪz/ | |
| supply arms (to) | /səˌplaɪ ˈɑːmz (tə)/ | |
| terrorist-training camps (n) | /ˈterərɪst ˈtreɪnɪŋ ˌkæmps/ | |
| terrorists (n) | /ˈterərɪsts/ | |
| threat of | /ˈθret əv/ | |
| threat to | /ˈθret tə/ | |
| threaten (v) | /ˈθretn/ | |
| troops (n) | /truːps/ | |
| unrelentingly dangerous | /ˌʌnrɪˌlentɪŋli ˈdeɪndʒərəs/ | |
| warn (v) | /wɔːn/ | |
| warn someone about | /ˈwɔːn ˌsʌmwʌn əˌbaʊt/ | |
| warn someone against | /ˌwɔːn ˌsʌmwʌn əˈɡenst/ | |
| withdraw someone's forces | /wɪðˈdrɔː ˌsʌmwʌnz ˌfɔːsɪz/ | |

## Unit 6

| | | |
|---|---|---|
| a race against time | /ə ˌreɪs əˌɡenst ˈtaɪm/ | |
| accomplish / achieve / attain / fulfil / meet / reach an objective (v) + (n) | /əˌkʌmplɪʃ, əˌtʃiːv, əˌteɪn, fʊlˌfɪl, ˌmiːt, ˌriːtʃ ən əbˈdʒektɪv/ | |
| accomplish / complete a mission (v) + (n) | /əˌkʌmplɪʃ, kəmˌpliːt ə ˈmɪʃn/ | |
| achieve / attain / reach a goal (v) + (n) | /əˌtʃiːv, əˌteɪn, ˌriːtʃ ə ˈɡəʊl/ | |
| achieve / fulfil an aim (v) + (n) | /əˌtʃiːv, fʊlˌfɪl ən ˈeɪm/ | |
| achieve / fulfil / meet an aspiration (v) + (n) | /əˌtʃiːv, fʊlˌfɪl, ˌmiːt ən ˌæspəˈreɪʃn/ | |
| achieve / fulfil / realise a dream (v) + (n) | /əˌtʃiːv, fʊlˌfɪl, ˌriːəlaɪz ə ˈdriːm/ | |
| achieve / fulfil / realise an ambition (v) + (n) | /əˌtʃiːv, fʊlˌfɪl, ˌriːəlaɪz ən æmˈbɪʃn/ | |
| achieve / meet / reach a target (v) + (n) | /əˌtʃiːv, ˌmiːt, ˌriːtʃ ə ˈtɑːɡɪt/ | |
| actor / actress (n) | /ˈæktə, ˈæktrəs/ | |
| air steward / air stewardess (n) | /ˈeə ˌstjuːəd, ˈeə ˌstjuːəˌdes/ | |
| alone (adj) | /əˈləʊn/ | |
| anxiety (n) | /æŋˈzaɪəti/ | |
| attitude (n) | /ˈætɪtjuːd/ | |

# W Wordlist

| | | |
|---|---|---|
| barman / barmaid (n) | /ˈbɑːmən, ˈbɑːmeɪd/ | |
| becoming (adj) | /bɪˈkʌmɪŋ/ | |
| blend (n) | /blend/ | |
| businessman / businesswoman (n) | /ˈbɪznəsmæn, ˈbɪznəswʊmən/ | |
| chaperone (v) | /ˈʃæpərəʊn/ | |
| cleaning lady (n) | /ˈkliːnɪŋ ˌleɪdi/ | |
| condemn (v) | /kənˈdem/ | |
| consternation (n) | /ˌkɒnstəˈneɪʃn/ | |
| converge (v) | /kənˈvɜːdʒ/ | |
| cowardly (adj) | /ˈkaʊədli/ | |
| critical (adj) | /ˈkrɪtɪkl/ | |
| crystallise (v) | /ˈkrɪstəlaɪz/ | |
| demeanour (n) | /dɪˈmiːnə(r)/ | |
| dire (adj) | /ˈdaɪə(r)/ | |
| disappointed (adj) | /ˌdɪsəˈpɔɪntɪd/ | |
| dismal (adj) | /ˈdɪzməl/ | |
| dismay (v) | /dɪsˈmeɪ/ | |
| distinguished (adj) | /dɪˈstɪŋgwɪʃt/ | |
| dreary (adj) | /ˈdrɪəri/ | |
| escort (v) | /ɪˈskɔːt/ | |
| fainthearted (adj) | /ˌfeɪntˈhɑːtɪd/ | |
| fall out (phr v) | /ˌfɔːl ˈaʊt/ | |
| fearless (adj) | /ˈfɪələs/ | |
| fitting (adj) | /ˈfɪtɪŋ/ | |
| foreshadow (v) | /fɔːˈʃædəʊ/ | |
| get on (phr v) | /ˌget ˈɒn/ | |
| get over (phr v) | /ˌget ˈəʊvə(r)/ | |
| get up (phr v) | /ˌget ˈʌp/ | |
| ghost (n) | /gəʊst/ | |
| go off (phr v) | /ˌgəʊ ˈɒf/ | |
| great (adj) | /greɪt/ | |
| hair-raising (adj) | /ˈheə ˌreɪzɪŋ/ | |
| have no time for | /ˌhæv ˈnəʊ ˌtaɪm fə(r)/ | |
| have the time of your life | /ˌhæv ðə ˌtaɪm əv jɔː ˈlaɪf/ | |
| ideas (n) | /aɪˈdɪəz/ | |
| improper (adj) | /ɪmˈprɒpə(r)/ | |
| in the nick of time | /ˌɪn ðə ˌnɪk əv ˈtaɪm/ | |
| in time | /ˌɪn ˈtaɪm/ | |
| insignificant (adj) | /ˌɪnsɪgˈnɪfɪkənt/ | |
| intolerant (adj) | /ɪnˈtɒlərənt/ | |
| leave out (phr v) | /ˌliːv ˈaʊt/ | |
| liberal (adj) | /ˈlɪbərəl/ | |
| living on borrowed time | /ˌlɪvɪŋ ɒn ˌbɒrəʊd ˈtaɪm/ | |
| make up (phr v) | /ˌmeɪk ˈʌp/ | |
| make up for lost time | /ˌmeɪk ʌp fə ˌlɒst ˈtaɪm/ | |
| mankind (n) | /mænˈkaɪnd/ | |
| negligible (adj) | /ˈneglɪdʒəbl/ | |
| notion (n) | /ˈnəʊʃn/ | |
| obscure (v) | /əbˈskjʊə(r)/ | |
| policeman / policewoman (n) | /pəˈliːsmən, pəˈliːswʊmən/ | |
| postman (n) | /ˈpəʊstmən/ | |

| | | |
|---|---|---|
| put on (phr v) | /ˈpʊt ˌɒn/ | |
| put out (phr v) | /ˈpʊt ˌaʊt/ | |
| quiet (adj) | /ˈkwaɪət/ | |
| resonate (v) | /ˈrezəneɪt/ | |
| revive (v) | /rɪˈvaɪv/ | |
| right place at the right time | /ˌraɪt ˌpleɪs ət ðə ˌraɪt ˈtaɪm/ | |
| salesman (n) | /ˈseɪlzmən/ | |
| settle down (phr v) | /ˌsetl ˈdaʊn/ | |
| spectre (n) | /ˈspektə(r)/ | |
| spokesman / spokeswoman (n) | /ˈspəʊksmən, ˈspəʊkswʊmən/ | |
| subdued (adj) | /səbˈdjuːd/ | |
| switch off (phr v) | /ˌswɪtʃ ˈɒf/ | |
| take in (phr v) | /ˌteɪk ˈɪn/ | |
| take off (phr v) | /ˌteɪk ˈɒf/ | |
| thrilling (adj) | /ˈθrɪlɪŋ/ | |
| unaccompanied (adj) | /ˌʌnəˈkʌmpənid/ | |
| unbiased (adj) | /ʌnˈbaɪəst/ | |
| unknown (adj) | /ˌʌnˈnəʊn/ | |
| unsuitable (adj) | /ʌnˈsuːtəbl/ | |
| valiant (adj) | /ˈvæliənt/ | |
| waiter / waitress (n) | /ˈweɪtə(r), ˈweɪtrəs/ | |
| wife / husband (n) | /waɪf, ˈhʌzbənd/ | |

## Unit 7

| | | |
|---|---|---|
| accelerate (v) | /əkˈseləreɪt/ | |
| admire the scenery (phr v) | /ədˌmaɪə ðə ˈsiːnəri/ | |
| alleged (adj) | /əˈledʒd/ | |
| any day now | /ˌeni ˌdeɪ ˈnaʊ/ | |
| apparent (adj) | /əˈpærənt/ | |
| at the end of the day | /ət ðiː ˌend əv ðə ˈdeɪ/ | |
| automatic car (n) | /ˌɔːtəˌmætɪk ˈkɑː(r)/ | |
| back seat (n) | /ˌbæk ˈsiːt/ | |
| beach holiday (n) | /ˈbiːtʃ ˌhɒlədeɪ/ | |
| brake (v) | /breɪk/ | |
| brake levers (n) | /ˈbreɪk ˌliːvəz/ | |
| break something up (phr v) | /ˌbreɪk ˌsʌmθɪŋ ˈʌp/ | |
| call a halt to something | /ˌkɔːl ə ˈhɔːlt tə ˌsʌmθɪŋ/ | |
| cancellations (n) | /ˌkænsəˈleɪʃnz/ | |
| Caribbean cruise (n) | /ˌkærɪˌbiːən ˈkruːz/ | |
| central reservation (n) | /ˌsentrəl ˌrezəˈveɪʃn/ | |
| chain (n) | /tʃeɪn/ | |
| change gear (v) | /ˌtʃeɪndʒ ˈgɪə(r)/ | |
| city break (n) | /ˈsɪti ˌbreɪk/ | |
| collision (n) | /kəˈlɪʒn/ | |
| congestion (n) | /kənˈdʒestʃən/ | |
| come to a halt | /ˌkʌm tuː ə ˈhɔːlt/ | |
| crossroads (n) | /ˈkrɒsrəʊdz/ | |
| cul-de-sac (n) | /ˈkʌl də ˌsæk/ | |
| day in day out | /ˌdeɪ ˌɪn ˌdeɪ ˈaʊt/ | |
| delays (n) | /dɪˈleɪz/ | |

# Wordlist

| | | | | | |
|---|---|---|---|---|---|
| diversion (n) | /daɪˈvɜːʃn/ | | road-traffic accident (n) | /ˌrəʊd ˈtræfɪk ˌæksɪdənt/ | |
| driving test (n) | /ˈdraɪvɪŋ ˌtest/ | | road trip (n) | /ˈrəʊd ˌtrɪp/ | |
| drop in on somebody (phr v) | /ˌdrɒp ˈɪn ɒn ˌsʌmbədi/ | | road users | /ˈrəʊd ˌjuːzəz/ | |
| drop somebody off (phr v) | /ˌdrɒp ˌsʌmbədi ˈɒf/ | | road works | /ˈrəʊd ˌwɜːks/ | |
| | | | saddle (n) | /ˈsædl/ | |
| dual carriageway (n) | /ˌdjuːəl ˈkærɪdʒweɪ/ | | safari (n) | /səˈfɑːri/ | |
| emergency stop (n) | /iˌmɜːdʒənsi ˈstɒp/ | | sample the local cuisine | /ˌsɑːmpl ðə ˌləʊkl kwɪˈziːn/ | |
| first aid (n) | /ˌfɜːst ˈeɪd/ | | | | |
| flyover (n) | /ˈflaɪəʊvə(r)/ | | security alert | /sɪˈkjʊərəti əˌlɜːt/ | |
| from day one | /frəm ˌdeɪ ˈwʌn/ | | see somebody off (phr v) | /ˌsiː ˌsʌmbədi ˈɒf/ | |
| gears (n) | /ɡɪəz/ | | seemingly (adv) | /ˈsiːmɪŋli/ | |
| get away (phr v) | /ˌɡet əˈweɪ/ | | shoot a glance at somebody or something | /ˌʃuːt ə ˈɡlɑːns ət ˌsʌmbədi ɔː ˌsʌmθɪŋ/ | |
| get away from it all (phr v) | /ˌɡet əˈweɪ frəm ˌɪt ˌɔːl/ | | | | |
| give a shriek | /ˌɡɪv ə ˈʃriːk/ | | side street (n) | /ˈsaɪd ˌstriːt/ | |
| give way | /ˌɡɪv ˈweɪ/ | | sightseeing tour (n) | /ˈsaɪtsiːɪŋ ˌtʊə(r)/ | |
| gridlock (n) | /ˈɡrɪdlɒk/ | | skiing trip (n) | /ˈskiːɪŋ ˌtrɪp/ | |
| handlebars (n) | /ˈhændlbɑːz/ | | slip road (n) | /ˈslɪp ˌrəʊd/ | |
| hard shoulder (n) | /ˌhɑːd ˈʃəʊldə(r)/ | | so-called (adj) | /ˈsəʊ ˌkɔːld/ | |
| have another attempt | /ˌhæv əˌnʌðər əˈtempt/ | | spa holiday (n) | /ˈspɑː ˌhɒlədeɪ/ | |
| hit the slopes (phr v) | /ˌhɪt ðə ˈsləʊps/ | | speed bumps (n) | /ˈspiːd ˌbʌmps/ | |
| in this day and age | /ɪn ˌðɪs ˌdeɪ ən ˌeɪdʒ/ | | spokes (n) | /spəʊks/ | |
| indicate (v) | /ˈɪndɪkeɪt/ | | stall (v) | /stɔːl/ | |
| industrial action (n) | /ɪnˌdʌstriəl ˈækʃn/ | | stand (n) | /stænd/ | |
| kerb (n) | /kɜːb/ | | steer (v) | /stɪə(r)/ | |
| lay-by (n) | /ˈleɪ ˌbaɪ/ | | T-junction (n) | /ˈtiː ˌdʒʌŋkʃn/ | |
| learner drivers (n) | /ˈlɜːnə ˌdraɪvəz/ | | supposed (adj) | /səˈpəʊzd/ | |
| level crossing (n) | /ˌlevl ˈkrɒsɪŋ/ | | tailbacks (n) | /ˈteɪlbæks/ | |
| likely (adj) | /ˈlaɪkli/ | | take a dip in the sea (phr v) | /ˌteɪk ə ˌdɪp ˌɪn ðə ˈsiː/ | |
| lost luggage (phr) | /ˌlɒst ˈlʌɡɪdʒ/ | | | | |
| lounge by the pool (phr v) | /ˌlaʊndʒ ˌbaɪ ðə ˈpuːl/ | | take in a film or show (phr v) | /ˌteɪk ɪn ə ˈfɪlm ɔː ˈʃəʊ/ | |
| | | | the other day | /ðiː ˈʌðə ˌdeɪ/ | |
| make a left turn | /ˌmeɪk ə ˈleft ˌtɜːn/ | | time to call it a day | /ˌtaɪm tə ˌkɔːl ɪt ə ˈdeɪ/ | |
| mechanical fault | /məˈkænɪkl ˌfɔːlt/ | | trekking holiday (n) | /ˈtrekɪŋ ˌhɒlədeɪ/ | |
| on the face of it | /ɒn ðə ˈfeɪs əv ˌɪt/ | | try your hand at water sports (phr v) | /ˌtraɪ jɔː ˌhænd ət ˈwɔːtə ˌspɔːts/ | |
| ostensibly (adv) | /ɒˈstensəbli/ | | | | |
| overcrowding (n) | /ˌəʊvəˈkraʊdɪŋ/ | | turbulence (n) | /ˈtɜːbjələns/ | |
| overtake (v) | /ˌəʊvəˈteɪk/ | | tyres (n) | /ˈtaɪəz/ | |
| pass through (a place) (phr v) | /ˌpɑːs ˈθruː (ə ˌpleɪs)/ | | valve (n) | /vælv/ | |
| | | | vehicle maintenance (n) | /ˌviːəkl ˈmeɪntənəns/ | |
| pedals (n) | /ˈpedlz/ | | villa holiday (n) | /ˈvɪlə ˌhɒlədeɪ/ | |
| (a) pile-up (n) | /(ə) ˈpaɪl ˌʌp/ | | | | |
| pull out (phr v) | /ˌpʊl ˈaʊt/ | | | | |
| pull over (phr v) | /ˌpʊl ˈəʊvə(r)/ | | | | |
| pump (n) | /pʌmp/ | | a frank exchange of views | /ə ˌfræŋk ɪksˌtʃeɪndʒ əv ˈvjuːz/ | |
| puncture (n) | /ˈpʌŋktʃə(r)/ | | | | |
| purport (v) | /pəˈpɔːt/ | | accede to (v) | /əkˈsiːd tə/ | |
| put somebody up (phr v) | /ˌpʊt ˌsʌmbədi ˈʌp/ | | acquiesce in (v) | /ˌækwiˈes ɪn/ | |
| put your feet up (phr v) | /ˌpʊt ˌjɔː ˈfiːt ˌʌp/ | | Anglophile/phobe (n) | /ˈæŋɡləʊfaɪl, -fəʊb/ | |
| reflector (n) | /rɪˈflektə(r)/ | | assent to (v) | /əˈsent tə/ | |
| reverse (v) | /rɪˈvɜːs/ | | authorise (v) | /ˈɔːθəraɪz/ | |
| road atlas (n) | /ˈrəʊd ˌætləs/ | | banoffee (n) | /bəˈnɒfi/ | |
| road safety (n) | /ˌrəʊd ˈseɪfti/ | | be accused of libel | /ˌbiː əˌkjuːzd əv ˈlaɪbl/ | |
| | | | be expecting | /ˌbiː ɪkˈspektɪŋ/ | |
| | | | bear a resemblance to | /ˌbeər ə rɪˈzembləns tə/ | |

## Unit 8

# Wordlist

| | | |
|---|---|---|
| between you and me | /bɪ,twiːn ,juː ən ˈmiː/ | |
| biopic (n) | /ˈbaɪəʊpɪk/ | |
| bite your tongue | /,baɪt ,jɔː ˈtʌŋ/ | |
| blog (n) | /blɒg/ | |
| Brexit (n) | /ˈbreksɪt/ | |
| broker a deal | /,brəʊkər ə ˈdiːl/ | |
| brunch (n) | /brʌntʃ/ | |
| bullet-proof (adj) | /ˈbʊlɪt ,pruːf/ | |
| call in the police | /,kɔːl ,ɪn ðə pəˈliːs/ | |
| champagne socialist (n) | /,ʃæmpeɪn ˈsəʊʃəlɪst/ | |
| chillax (v) | /tʃɪˈlæks/ | |
| class-based (adj) | /ˈklɑːs ,beɪst/ | |
| climb the greasy pole | /,klaɪm ðə ,griːsi ˈpəʊl/ | |
| comply with (v) | /kəmˈplaɪ ,wɪð/ | |
| concur with (v) | /kənˈkɜː ,wɪð/ | |
| condone (v) | /kənˈdəʊn/ | |
| confirm a story | /kən,fɜːm ə ˈstɔːri/ | |
| conspiracy (n) | /kənˈspɪrəsi/ | |
| conspiracy theory (n) | /kənˈspɪrəsi ,θɪəri/ | |
| cover-up (n) | /ˈkʌvər ,ʌp/ | |
| cover up (v) | /,kʌvər ˈʌp/ | |
| cybercafé (n) | /ˈsaɪbəkæfeɪ/ | |
| cyberspace (n) | /ˈsaɪbəspeɪs/ | |
| damage someone's reputation | /,dæmɪʤ ,sʌmwʌnz ,repjuˈteɪʃn/ | |
| debug (v) | /,diːˈbʌg/ | |
| deforest (v) | /,diːˈfɒrɪst/ | |
| download (v) | /,daʊnˈləʊd/ | |
| downsize (v) | /ˈdaʊnsaɪz/ | |
| eco-terrorism (n) | /ˈiːkəʊterərɪzəm/ | |
| economically disadvantaged | /,iːkə,nɒmɪkli ,dɪsədˈvɑːntɪʤd/ | |
| endorse (v) | /ɪnˈdɔːs/ | |
| ethnic cleansing | /,eθnɪk ˈklenzɪŋ/ | |
| exposé (n) | /ekˈspəʊzeɪ/ | |
| face allegations of / that | /ˈfeɪs ,æləˈgeɪʃnz əv, ðət/ | |
| fanzine (n) | /ˈfænziːn/ | |
| fat-free (adj) | /,fæt ˈfriː/ | |
| future-proof (adj) | /ˈfjuːtʃə ,pruːf/ | |
| get on your soapbox | /,get ,ɒn jɔː ˈsəʊpbɒks/ | |
| getting thin on top | /,getɪŋ ,θɪn ɒn ˈtɒp/ | |
| glamping (n) | /ˈglæmpɪŋ/ | |
| hack into someone's voicemail | /,hæk ,ɪntə ,sʌmwʌnz ˈvɔɪsmeɪl/ | |
| hamper an inquiry | /,hæmpər ən ɪnˈkwaɪəri/ | |
| have friends in high places | /,hæv ,frendz ɪn ,haɪ ˈpleɪsɪz/ | |
| health-conscious (adj) | /ˈhelθ ,kɒnʃəs/ | |
| hear the latest | /,hɪə ðə ˈleɪtɪst/ | |
| if word gets out | /,ɪf ,wɜːd ,gets ˈaʊt/ | |
| issue a public apology | /,ɪʃuː ə ,pʌblɪk əˈpɒləʤi/ | |
| it won't go any further | /ɪt ˈwəʊnt ,gəʊ ,eni ˈfɜːðə(r)/ | |
| it's just hearsay | /,ɪts ,ʤʌst ˈhɪəseɪ/ | |

| | | |
|---|---|---|
| keep it under your hat | /,kiːp ɪt ,ʌndə ,jɔː ˈhæt/ | |
| let (employees) go | /,let (ɪm,plɔɪiːz) ˈgəʊ/ | |
| listen in on a message | /,lɪsn ,ɪn ɒn ə ˈmesɪʤ/ | |
| London-based (adj) | /ˈlʌndən ,beɪst/ | |
| make a claim | /,meɪk ə ˈkleɪm/ | |
| malware (n) | /ˈmælweə(r)/ | |
| market-led (adj) | /ˈmɑːkɪt ,led/ | |
| misinformation (n) | /,mɪsɪnfəˈmeɪʃn/ | |
| monolingual (adj) | /,mɒnəˈlɪŋgwəl/ | |
| monorail (n) | /ˈmɒnəʊreɪl/ | |
| motel (n) | /məʊˈtel/ | |
| my lips are sealed | /,maɪ ,lɪps ə ˈsiːld/ | |
| not breathe a word to anyone | /,nɒt ,briːð ə ,wɜːd tuː ˈeniwʌn/ | |
| not let on (to anyone) | /,nɒt ,let ,ɒn (tuː ˈeniwʌn)/ | |
| not quote me (on that) | /,nɒt ˈkwəʊt ,miː (ɒn ,ðæt)/ | |
| obtain inside information | /əb,teɪn ,ɪnsaɪd ,ɪnfəˈmeɪʃn/ | |
| overbook (v) | /,əʊvəˈbʊk/ | |
| overwrite (v) | /,əʊvəˈraɪt/ | |
| Oxbridge (n) | /ˈɒksbrɪʤ/ | |
| pay out damages | /,peɪ ,aʊt ˈdæmɪʤɪz/ | |
| play politics | /,pleɪ ˈpɒlətɪks/ | |
| plot (n/v) | /plɒt/ | |
| political correctness (n) | /pə,lɪtɪkl kəˈrektnəs/ | |
| political hot potato | /pə,lɪtɪkl ,hɒt pəˈteɪtəʊ/ | |
| praiseworthy (adj) | /ˈpreɪzwɜːði/ | |
| pre-owned (adj) | /,priː ˈəʊnd/ | |
| public outcry (n) | /,pʌblɪk ˈaʊtkraɪ/ | |
| put on a few extra pounds | /,pʊt ɒn ə ,fjuː ,ekstrə ˈpaʊndz/ | |
| reach the asking price | /,riːtʃ ði ˈɑːskɪŋ ,praɪs/ | |
| remain a mystery | /rɪ,meɪn ə ˈmɪstri/ | |
| research an article | /rɪ,sɜːtʃ ən ˈɑːtɪkl/ | |
| rest room (US) (n) | /ˈrest ,ruːm/ | |
| restore somebody's fortunes | /rɪ,stɔː ,sʌmbədiz ˈfɔːtʃuːnz/ | |
| revelations emerge | /,revə,leɪʃnz iˈmɜːʤ/ | |
| roadworthy (adj) | /ˈrəʊdwɜːði/ | |
| rom-com (n) | /ˈrɒm ,kɒm/ | |
| rumour has it (that)... | /ˈruːmə ,hæz ɪt (ðət)/ | |
| safety-conscious (adj) | /ˈseɪfti ,kɒnʃəs/ | |
| secure a scoop | /sɪ,kjʊər ə ˈskuːp/ | |
| settle a lawsuit | /,setl ə ˈlɔːsuːt/ | |
| sitcom (n) | /ˈsɪtkɒm/ | |
| skort (n) | /skɔːt/ | |
| slander (n/v) | /ˈslɑːndə(r)/ | |
| smear campaign (n) | /ˈsmɪə kæm,peɪn/ | |
| smog (n) | /smɒg/ | |
| spin doctor (n) | /ˈspɪn ,dɒktə(r)/ | |
| spork (n) | /spɔːk/ | |
| staycation (n) | /,steɪˈkeɪʃn/ | |

| | | |
|---|---|---|
| student-led (adj) | /'stjuːdnt ˌled/ | _____ |
| technophile/phobe (n) | /'teknəʊfaɪl, -fəʊb/ | _____ |
| undercover (adj) | /ˌʌndəˌkʌvə(r)/ | _____ |
| underexpose (v) | /ˌʌndərɪk'spəʊz/ | _____ |
| update (v) | /ˌʌp'deɪt/ | _____ |
| upgrade (v) | /ˌʌp'greɪd/ | _____ |
| vlog (n) | /vlɒg/ | _____ |
| webinar (n) | /'webɪnɑː(r)/ | _____ |

## Unit 9

| | | |
|---|---|---|
| a bird in the hand is worth two in the bush | /ə ˌbɜːd ɪn ðə 'hænd ɪz ˌwɜːθ ˌtuː ɪn ðə 'bʊʃ/ | _____ |
| a stitch in time saves nine | /ə ˌstɪtʃ ɪn 'taɪm ˌseɪvz 'naɪn/ | _____ |
| alien invasion | /ˌeɪliən ɪn'veɪʒn/ | _____ |
| all work and no play makes Jack a dull boy | /ˌɔːl ˌwɜːk ən ˌnəʊ 'pleɪ ˌmeɪks ˌdʒæk ə ˌdʌl 'bɔɪ/ | _____ |
| asteroid impact | /'æstərɔɪd ˌɪmpækt/ | _____ |
| birds of a feather flock together | /ˌbɜːdz əv ə 'feðə ˌflɒk təˈgeðə(r)/ | _____ |
| born with a silver spoon in your mouth | /ˌbɔːn wɪð ə ˌsɪlvə 'spuːn ɪn jɔː ˌmaʊθ/ | _____ |
| break out (phr v) | /ˌbreɪk 'aʊt/ | _____ |
| bring up (phr v) | /ˌbrɪŋ 'ʌp/ | _____ |
| carry out (phr v) | /ˌkæri 'aʊt/ | _____ |
| caught up in (adj) | /'kɔːt ˌʌp ˌɪn/ | _____ |
| climate change (n) | /'klaɪmət ˌtʃeɪndʒ/ | _____ |
| combat a threat | /ˌkɒmbæt ə 'θret/ | _____ |
| come as a shock (to somebody) | /ˌkʌm əz ə 'ʃɒk (tə ˌsʌmbədi)/ | _____ |
| come out (phr v) | /ˌkʌm 'aʊt/ | _____ |
| come to an (untimely) end | /ˌkʌm tuː ən ʌnˌtaɪmli 'end/ | _____ |
| come to mind | /ˌkʌm tə 'maɪnd/ | _____ |
| come under fire | /ˌkʌm ˌʌndə 'faɪə(r)/ | _____ |
| come up with (phr v) | /ˌkʌm ˌʌp ˌwɪð/ | _____ |
| corruption (n) | /kə'rʌpʃn/ | _____ |
| crucial (adj) | /'kruːʃl/ | _____ |
| deal a deathblow | /ˌdiːl ə 'deθbləʊ/ | _____ |
| decisive (adj) | /dɪ'saɪsɪv/ | _____ |
| depose (v) | /dɪ'pəʊz/ | _____ |
| detonate (v) | /'detəneɪt/ | _____ |
| do harm | /ˌduː 'hɑːm/ | _____ |
| do the trick | /ˌduː ðə 'trɪk/ | _____ |
| do well | /ˌduː 'wel/ | _____ |
| do your utmost | /ˌduː jɔːr 'ʌtməʊst/ | _____ |
| don't count your chickens before they are hatched | /ˌdəʊnt ˌkaʊnt jɔː 'tʃɪkɪnz bɪˌfɔː ˌðeɪ ə 'hætʃt/ | _____ |
| die down (phr v) | /ˌdaɪ 'daʊn/ | _____ |
| economic collapse | /ˌiːkəˌnɒmɪk kə'læps/ | _____ |
| enjoy success | /ɪnˌdʒɔɪ sək'ses/ | _____ |
| essential (adj) | /ɪ'senʃl/ | _____ |
| exacerbate a problem | /ɪg'zæsəbeɪt ə ˌprɒbləm/ | _____ |
| face a nightmare | /ˌfeɪs ə 'naɪtmeə(r)/ | _____ |

| | | |
|---|---|---|
| fall into decline | /ˌfɔːl ˌɪntə dɪ'klaɪn/ | _____ |
| fight off (phr v) | /ˌfaɪt 'ɒf/ | _____ |
| finish off (phr v) | /ˌfɪnɪʃ 'ɒf/ | _____ |
| first come, first served | /ˌfɜːst ˌkʌm ˌfɜːst 'sɜːvd/ | _____ |
| foreign invasion (n) | /ˌfɒrən ɪn'veɪʒn/ | _____ |
| forewarned is forearmed | /ˌfɔːˌwɔːnd ɪz ˌfɔːr'ɑːmd/ | _____ |
| give (somebody) an indication of something | /ˌgɪv (ˌsʌmbədi) ən ˌɪndɪ'keɪʃn əv ˌsʌmθɪŋ/ | _____ |
| global pandemic | /ˌgləʊbl pæn'demɪk/ | _____ |
| go by | /'gəʊ ˌbaɪ/ | _____ |
| gobble up (v) | /ˌgɒbl 'ʌp/ | _____ |
| grind to a halt | /ˌgraɪnd tuː ə 'hɔːlt/ | _____ |
| hole up (phr v) | /ˌhəʊl 'ʌp/ | _____ |
| hurtle (v) | /'hɜːtl/ | _____ |
| ignorance is bliss | /ˌɪgnərəns ɪz 'blɪs/ | _____ |
| imperative (adj) | /ɪm'perətɪv/ | _____ |
| internal conflict | /ɪn,tɜːnl 'kɒnflɪkt/ | _____ |
| interplanetary collision | /ˌɪntəˌplænɪtri kə'lɪʒn/ | _____ |
| it takes all sorts to make a world | /ˌɪt ˌteɪks ˌɔːl ˌsɔːts tə ˌmeɪk ə 'wɜːld/ | _____ |
| look after (phr v) | /'lʊk ˌɑːftə(r)/ | _____ |
| nuclear holocaust | /ˌnjuːkliə 'hɒləkɔːst/ | _____ |
| only time will tell | /ˌəʊnli ˌtaɪm ˌwɪl 'tel/ | _____ |
| overpopulation (n) | /ˌəʊvəˌpɒpju'leɪʃn/ | _____ |
| overthrow (v) | /ˌəʊvə'θrəʊ/ | _____ |
| play a role (in something) | /ˌpleɪ ə 'rəʊl (ɪn ˌsʌmθɪŋ)/ | _____ |
| pole shift | /'pəʊl ˌʃɪft/ | _____ |
| pull out (phr v) | /ˌpʊl 'aʊt/ | _____ |
| put a stop to something | /ˌpʊt ə 'stɒp tə ˌsʌmθɪŋ/ | _____ |
| put one's foot in it | /ˌpʊt ˌwʌnz 'fʊt ɪn ˌɪt/ | _____ |
| put pressure on somebody / something | /ˌpʊt 'preʃər ɒn ˌsʌmbədi, ˌsʌmθɪŋ/ | _____ |
| put something into perspective | /ˌpʊt ˌsʌmθɪŋ ˌɪntə pə'spektɪv/ | _____ |
| put something into practice | /ˌpʊt ˌsʌmθɪŋ ˌɪntə 'præktɪs/ | _____ |
| robot ascension | /'rəʊbɒt əˌsenʃn/ | _____ |
| sack a city | /'sæk ə ˌsɪti/ | _____ |
| set up (phr v) | /ˌset 'ʌp/ | _____ |
| significant (adj) | /sɪg'nɪfɪkənt/ | _____ |
| slam into (v) | /'slæm ˌɪntə/ | _____ |
| spell disaster (v) | /ˌspel dɪ'zɑːstə(r)/ | _____ |
| spell the end of / for something | /ˌspel ði: 'end əv, fə ˌsʌmθɪŋ/ | _____ |
| stow away (phr v) | /'stəʊ əˌweɪ/ | _____ |
| supervolcanic eruption | /ˌsuːpəvɒlˌkænɪk ɪ'rʌpʃn/ | _____ |
| swell the ranks | /ˌswel ðə 'ræŋks/ | _____ |
| take charge | /ˌteɪk 'tʃɑːdʒ/ | _____ |
| take it for granted | /ˌteɪk ˌɪt fə 'grɑːntɪd/ | _____ |
| take no notice | /ˌteɪk ˌnəʊ 'nəʊtɪs/ | _____ |
| take pleasure (in something) | /ˌteɪk 'pleʒə(r) (ɪn ˌsʌmθɪŋ)/ | _____ |

| | | |
|---|---|---|
| the early bird catches the worm | /ðiː ˈɜːli ˌbɜːd ˌkætʃɪz ðə ˈwɜːm/ | _____ |
| the grass is always greener on the other side of the fence | /ðə ˌɡrɑːs ɪz ˌɔːlweɪz ˈɡriːnər ɒn ðiː ˌʌðə ˌsaɪd əv ðə ˈfens/ | _____ |
| there's no smoke without fire | /ˌðeəz ˈnəʊ ˌsməʊk wɪˌðaʊt ˈfaɪə(r)/ | _____ |
| too many cooks spoil the broth | /ˌtuː ˌmeni ˈkʊks ˌspɔɪl ðə ˈbrɒθ/ | _____ |
| track down (phr v) | /ˈtræk ˌdaʊn/ | _____ |
| trigger the demise (of something) | /ˌtrɪɡə ðə dɪˈmaɪz (əv ˌsʌmθɪŋ)/ | _____ |
| turn into (phr v) | /ˈtɜːn ˌɪntə/ | _____ |
| undermine a theory | /ˌʌndəˈmaɪn ə ˌθɪəri/ | _____ |
| unleash (v) | /ʌnˈliːʃ/ | _____ |
| vital (adj) | /ˈvaɪtl/ | _____ |
| where there's a will there's a way | /ˌweə ˌðeəz ə ˈwɪl ˌðeəz ə ˈweɪ/ | _____ |
| wipe out (phr v) | /ˌwaɪp ˈaʊt/ | _____ |
| wreak havoc | /ˌriːk ˈhævək/ | _____ |

# I Irregular verbs

| Base form | Past simple | Past participle |
|---|---|---|
| be | was / were | been |
| become | became | become |
| begin | began | begun |
| bend | bent | bent |
| bite | bit | bitten |
| blow | blew | blown |
| break | broke | broken |
| bring | brought | brought |
| build | built | built |
| burn | burned / burnt | burned / burnt |
| buy | bought | bought |

| | | |
|---|---|---|
| can | could | been able to |
| catch | caught | caught |
| choose | chose | chosen |
| come | came | come |
| cost | cost | cost |
| cut | cut | cut |

| | | |
|---|---|---|
| do | did | done |
| draw | drew | drawn |
| drink | drank | drunk |
| drive | drove | driven |

| | | |
|---|---|---|
| eat | ate | eaten |

| | | |
|---|---|---|
| fall | fell | fallen |
| feel | felt | felt |
| fight | fought | fought |
| find | found | found |
| fly | flew | flown |
| forget | forgot | forgotten |

| | | |
|---|---|---|
| get | got | got |
| give | gave | given |
| go | went | gone |
| grow | grew | grown |

| | | |
|---|---|---|
| hang | hung | hung |
| have | had | had |
| hear | heard | heard |
| hide | hid | hidden |
| hit | hit | hit |

| | | |
|---|---|---|
| keep | kept | kept |
| know | knew | known |

| | | |
|---|---|---|
| lay | laid | laid |
| lead | led | led |
| learn | learned / learnt | learned / learnt |
| leave | left | left |

| Base form | Past simple | Past participle |
|---|---|---|
| lend | lent | lent |
| lose | lost | lost |

| | | |
|---|---|---|
| make | made | made |
| mean | meant | meant |
| meet | met | met |

| | | |
|---|---|---|
| overcome | overcame | overcome |

| | | |
|---|---|---|
| pay | paid | paid |
| put | put | put |

| | | |
|---|---|---|
| read | read | read |
| ride | rode | ridden |
| ring | rang | rung |
| run | ran | run |

| | | |
|---|---|---|
| say | said | said |
| see | saw | seen |
| sell | sold | sold |
| send | sent | sent |
| set | set | set |
| shake | shook | shaken |
| shine | shone | shone |
| shoot | shot | shot |
| show | showed | shown/-ed |
| shut | shut | shut |
| sing | sang | sung |
| sink | sank | sunk |
| sit | sat | sat |
| sleep | slept | slept |
| smell | smelled / smelt | smelled / smelt |
| speak | spoke | spoken |
| spell | spelled / spelt | spelled / spelt |
| spend | spent | spent |
| spill | spilled / spilt | spilled / spilt |
| stand | stood | stood |
| steal | stole | stolen |
| swim | swam | swum |

| | | |
|---|---|---|
| take | took | taken |
| teach | taught | taught |
| tell | told | told |
| think | thought | thought |
| throw | threw | thrown |

| | | |
|---|---|---|
| understand | understood | understood |

| | | |
|---|---|---|
| wake | woke | woken |
| wear | wore | worn |
| win | won | won |
| write | wrote | written |